A Leader's Guide to

The Adding Assets Series for Kids

A Leader's Guide to The Adding Assets Series for Kids

Activities and Strategies for Positive Youth Development

by Ann Redpath, Ed.D., Pamela Espeland, and Elizabeth Verdick

free spirit
PUBLiSHiNG®

Helping kids
help themselves™
since 1983

ISBN-10 1-57542-210-7
ISBN-13 978-1-57542-210-7

At the time of this book's publication, all facts and figures cited are the most current available. All telephone numbers, addresses, and Web site URLs are accurate and active; all publications, organizations, Web sites, and other resources exist as described in this book; and all have been verified as of July 2006. The authors and Free Spirit Publishing make no warranty or guarantee concerning the information and materials given out by organizations or content found at Web sites, and we are not responsible for any changes that occur after this book's publication. If you find an error or believe that a resource listed here is not as described, please contact Free Spirit Publishing. Parents, teachers, and other adults: We strongly urge you to monitor children's use of the Internet.

Search Institute® and Developmental Assets® are registered trademarks of Search Institute.

The 40 Developmental Assets information contained in this publication is used with permission and is based on Search Institute's copyrighted and trademarked intellectual property. Copyright © 1997, 2006 Search Institute. No other use is permitted without prior permission from Search Institute, 615 First Avenue NE, Minneapolis, MN 55413; 800-888-7828; www.search-institute.org. All rights reserved.

We were grateful for the *Ideas for Parents* newsletters © 1997, 2003 by Search Institute, which were invaluable resources as we developed the "Adding Assets at Home" parent handouts.

Illustrated by Chris Sharp
Cover and interior design by Tasha Kenyon

10 9 8 7 6 5 4 3 2 1
Printed in the United States of America

Free Spirit Publishing Inc.
217 Fifth Avenue North, Suite 200
Minneapolis, MN 55401-1299
(612) 338-2068
help4kids@freespirit.com
www.freespirit.com

As a member of the Green Press Initiative, Free Spirit Publishing is committed to the three Rs: Reduce, Reuse, Recycle. Whenever possible, we print our books on recycled paper containing a minimum of 30% post-consumer waste. At Free Spirit it's our goal to nurture not only children, but nature too!

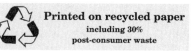

Printed on recycled paper
including 30%
post-consumer waste

Contents

The Sessions

List of Reproducible Pages

The Student Tracker pages are on the CD-ROM that accompanies this Leader's Guide.

Introduction

"If you knew ways to make your life better, right now and for the future, would you try them?"

Each book in the **Adding Assets Series for Kids** begins with this question. Even young children have the power to improve their own lives. They can learn to make reasoned choices, to think before they act, to get along better with others, and to seek out places that are safe and supportive. They even can look ahead toward the future, as far away as that might seem when you're eight years old, or ten, or twelve.

The Adding Assets Series invites and empowers kids to build their own **Developmental Assets**—in relationship with caring adults, including you. By *assets,* we don't mean property or resources. A simple definition of Developmental Assets is "good things you need in your life and in yourself." These include a supportive family, a caring neighborhood, integrity, self-esteem, resistance skills, conflict resolution skills, constructive activities, and a sense of purpose—concrete, positive experiences and qualities that create successful, contributing human beings.

Search Institute, a nonprofit research organization in Minneapolis, Minnesota, is a leading innovator in discovering what children and adolescents need to become caring, healthy, and responsible adults. Search Institute researchers have surveyed more than a million students in thousands of communities in the United States. The surveys consistently show that the *more* assets children and teens have, the *less* likely they are to engage in high-risk behaviors including alcohol use, illicit drug use, sexual activity, violence, school problems, and depression/suicide. The *more* assets they have, the *more* likely they are to engage in positive behaviors including staying healthy, helping others, valuing diversity, succeeding in school, and delaying gratification—being patient and planning ahead. It goes without saying that the sooner kids start building assets, the better. The Adding Assets Series for Kids recognizes that even children as young as eight can do this.

There are 40 Developmental Assets in all. They are divided into two main types:

★ **External Assets** are positive experiences kids receive from the world around them.

★ **Internal Assets** are values, skills, and self-perceptions kids develop internally, with help from caring adults.

The two main types are divided into eight categories:

★ The **Support Assets** are about surrounding kids with people who love them, care for them, appreciate them, and accept them. These people include family members, neighbors, and many others, as well as organizations and institutions with positive, supportive environments.

★ The **Empowerment Assets** are about helping kids feel valued and valuable, safe and respected. This happens when children have opportunities to contribute and serve, make a difference, and get noticed for their efforts.

★ The **Boundaries and Expectations Assets** are about providing kids with clear rules, consistent consequences for breaking rules, and encouragement to do their best. Kids learn which activities and behaviors are "in bounds" and "out of bounds."

★ The **Constructive Use of Time Assets** are about making sure kids have opportunities outside of school to learn and develop new skills and interests with other kids and adults. These opportunities include creative activities, youth programs, and quality time at home.

★ The **Commitment to Learning Assets** are about helping kids develop a sense of how important learning is and a belief in their own ability to learn, achieve, and grow—now and in the future. These assets build lifelong learners.

★ The **Positive Values Assets** are about guiding kids to develop strong values that enable them to make healthy life choices. Values inform decisions, shape priorities, and determine words and actions. Other words for *values* are *morals* and *conscience*.

★ The **Social Competencies Assets** are about helping kids develop the skills they need to interact effectively with others, to make difficult decisions, and to cope with new situations. They're about making plans, making friends, and getting along with all kinds of people while avoiding risky situations and resolving conflicts nonviolently.

★ The **Positive Identity Assets** are about encouraging kids to form a strong sense of their own power, purpose, worth, and promise. Kids need to believe they matter in the world—and to feel they have some control over the things that happen to them.

A complete list of all 40 assets, with definitions, is found on page 10. It is included here as a reproducible so you can display it in your classroom (or your home), tuck it into the front of this book for easy reference, and send copies home to students' parents and caregivers. This list also is included at the back of each student book as part of "A Note to Grown-ups."

Another list of all 40 assets, with definitions written in the second person and in "kid-friendly" language, is found on pages 18–19. These are the definitions used in the student books.

Assets are powerful, and they're not rocket science. They're easy to understand and anyone can build them—for oneself and for others. You're about to start building assets for the children in your classroom or group. It may be one of the most important things you ever do.

Six Tips for Building Assets

Here are six key points to keep in mind as you begin (and continue) to build assets with your students and other children in your life:*

1. **Everyone can build assets.** All adults, youth, and children can play a role. Building assets requires consistent messages across a community.

2. **All young people need assets.** While it's crucial to pay special attention to those youth who have the least (economically or emotionally), all young people can benefit from more assets than they have.

3. **Relationships are critical.** Strong relationships between adults and young people, young people and their peers, and teenagers and children are central to asset building.

4. **Asset building is an ongoing process.** It starts when a child is born and continues through high school and beyond.

5. **Consistent messages are important.** Young people need to receive consistent messages from their families, schools, communities, the media, and other sources about what's important and what's expected.

6. **Intentional redundancy is important.** Assets must be continually reinforced across the years and in all areas of a young person's life.

*Source: *What Kids Need to Succeed: Proven, Practical Ways to Raise Good Kids* by Peter L. Benson, Ph.D., Judy Galbraith, M.A., and Pamela Espeland. Minneapolis, MN: Free Spirit Publishing, 1998, pages 16–17.

About This Book

A Leader's Guide to The Adding Assets Series for Kids is written for any teacher or group leader who wants to help students in grades 3–6 add Developmental Assets to their lives. Prior knowledge of the assets or of Search Institute's research is not necessary. Anyone who is interested in helping children grow up to succeed in life, in work, as future parents, and as community members can jump right in and start using these sessions.

The Adding Assets Series for Kids includes one book for each asset category:

★ *People Who Care About You* (Support)

★ *Helping Out and Staying Safe* (Empowerment)

★ *Doing and Being Your Best*
(Boundaries and Expectations)

★ *Smart Ways to Spend Your Time*
(Constructive Use of Time)

★ *Loving to Learn* (Commitment to Learning)

★ *Knowing and Doing What's Right*
(Positive Values)

★ *Making Choices and Making Friends* (Social
Competencies)

★ *Proud to Be You* (Positive Identity)

The 42 sessions in this Leader's Guide include one for each asset, plus introductory and concluding sessions. The sessions are based on the student books and require that both you and your students be familiar with them. Ideally, each student will have his or her own copy of each student book. If that isn't possible, try to have several copies of each book available on a reading table for students to share.

The main focus of each session is a story in the student book. The story presents a particular asset in a true-to-life situation that students can identify with or at least understand. The story is always in two parts. The first part sets up a dilemma, and the second part offers a resolution—which isn't always a tidy, happy ending, because that's not how life works. The situations are realistic and the resolutions are plausible. The point of each story is to help children see an asset at work and understand that assets are real behaviors, choices, and circumstances, not just words.

Between the two parts of each story are suggestions for building the asset at home, at school, in the neighborhood, in the faith community, and with friends—the environments with which most children are familiar. Some activities are quick and easy; some take time. Some can be done independently; some require the presence and participation of friends, family members, and caring adults. We want kids to understand that *anyone* can build assets, and that even the smallest, simplest thought or action—a word or two written in a journal, a brief conversation with a parent or teacher, the decision to turn in one's homework on time—counts as authentic asset building.

This Leader's Guide follows the student books in order of the asset categories. *This doesn't mean that you have to teach the assets in order.* You'll notice that the student books are not numbered; neither are the individual assets within the student books. It doesn't matter which asset category you start with. You may want to choose one you think will be most interesting to your students—or one you think will benefit them most to work on first.

Time constraints may prevent you from teaching all of the sessions, and you may need to make a selection. Because all assets are important, and because their effects are cumulative—meaning that the more assets a child has, the better—we will leave that selection up to you. However, we encourage you to at least touch on all 40 assets with your students. You may decide to teach complete sessions for some of the assets and just read the stories for the others—and perhaps describe an asset-building activity or two? *Children need all of the assets.* Try your best not to skip any entirely.

Each asset session includes the following parts:

★ **Asset name and definition.**

★ **Backdrop:** Directive to write the name of the asset and its definition on the board, or to write the optional appropriate quotation on the board.

★ **Outcomes:** The purposes of the session, which always include helping students add that particular asset to their lives.

★ **Preparation and Materials:** A description of anything you need to do before the session, and a list of all the materials you and your students will need.

★ **Standards/Objectives Highlights box:** A highlight of standards that correlate to the session's asset. The charts on pages 255–268 show all the correlated standards.

★ **Getting Started:** A few moments during which students greet each other, reflect on what they have done to build the asset from the previous session (and write or draw on a handout called a *tracker page;* see pages 4–5 for information about the tracker pages), talk briefly with a partner about this session's asset, and learn what they will do during this session.

★ **The Asset Question:** A preliminary discussion of the session's asset or a topic related to it.

★ **Before the Story:** An activity or discussion to introduce the story or the asset.

★ **The Story:** Reading and questions for discussion.

★ **Asset-Building Activities At-a-Glance:** An overview of the activities suggested for building the session's asset.

★ **Session Activity:** A group or individual activity with a handout. Activities range from drawing maps to role-playing to writing-and-thinking activities.

★ **Closing Question:** A question that encourages students to start adding the session's asset to their lives.

★ **Preparation for Next Session:** Anything you need to do in advance.

Each session also includes an "Adding Assets at Home" handout for students to bring home to their parents or caregivers. Several sessions include optional activities that go deeper or build specific skills.

Because it's likely that you'll teach this course more than once, and you'll want to improve each time you teach it, we have included two evaluations: one for students (page 250) and one for parents and caregivers (page 251). Students also have the opportunity to do a self-evaluation at the start of the course. During the introductory session, they are asked to complete a checklist and identify the assets they already have. During the concluding session, they complete the same checklist again. Comparing the two checklists can be the start of self-reflection and positive action.

The Appendix includes a complete listing of standards correlating to the assets. We have used the latest available editions of the following standards:

★ *Character Education Quality Standards* (2003 revision), based on the Character Education Partnership's *Eleven Principles of Effective Character Education* and *The Eleven Principles Survey* by Tom Lickona and Matthew Davidson. Available from the Character Education Partnership, *www.character.org;* (800) 988-8081.

★ *National Health Education Standards* performance indicators for grades 3–5 cited from "Pre-publication document of National

Health Education Standards, PreK–12," American Cancer Society (December 2005–August 2006). Available from American Alliance for Health, Physical Education, Recreation and Dance, *www.aahperd.org;* (800) 213-7193.

★ *Expectations of Excellence: Curriculum Standards for Social Studies* developed by the National Council for the Social Studies. Available from the National Council for the Social Studies, *www.socialstudies.org;* (800) 683-0812.

★ *Standards for the English Language Arts* by the National Council of Teachers of English. Available from the National Council of Teachers of English, *www.ncte.org;* (877) 369-6283.

★ *SEL (Social and Emotional Learning) Competencies* from Collaborative for Academic, Social, and Emotional Learning (CASEL), University of Illinois at Chicago, *www.casel.org;* (312) 413-1008.

The CD-ROM included with this Leader's Guide features all of the reproducible forms from this book and an additional 40 pages of student handouts (the tracker pages). The handouts are in PDF format, ready to print out and use.

About the Student Tracker

The Adding Assets Series for Kids and this Leader's Guide are both about helping children add as many assets as possible to their lives—the more the better. The Student Tracker gives students a way to record their own progress toward building each asset.

Included on the CD-ROM are 40 tracker pages—one for each asset. They are formatted so you can print them in color if you wish; this makes them more special for the children. You'll find a sample tracker page (not in color) on page 5.

If possible, provide each student with a three-ring binder in which to collect and store the completed tracker pages. You'll hand out one page during each asset session (and two in whichever session you end with—the one for that session, and the one for the preceding session). Students might also use their binders to store a list of the Developmental Assets, their completed checklists, and other handouts or notes they want to keep.

(*Tip:* You may want to three-hole-punch all of the student handouts to make it easy for students to keep the ones they want.) A binder with ½" rings holds 100 pages; that should be big enough. Binders with clear overlays (front pockets) allow children to create their own cover and spine art.

Each tracker page invites kids to write or draw a way they are building each asset—or someone else is helping to build it with them. Please allow students to choose their preferred way to record this information: in words or in pictures, sketches, or comic book form. You may want to make colored markers available for students who want to use them. Never grade the tracker pages.

At the end of the course, all of your students will have concrete proof of their efforts to add assets to their lives. Each Student Tracker becomes a journal, a keepsake, and a reminder to students to keep building assets—now and for the future. Trackers-in-progress also make great displays for parent nights and school open houses.

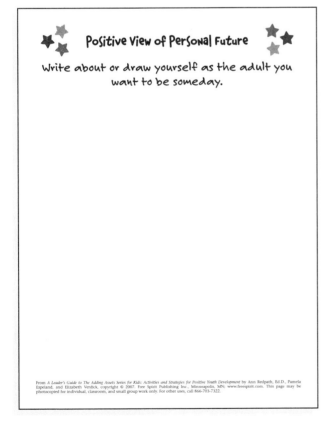

Sample Student Tracker from CD-ROM.

General Guidelines

★ Familiarize yourself with all eight student books and this Leader's Guide. Read this introduction first, followed by the student book you plan to start with. Then read the sessions for that student book.

★ Take time to read ahead and plan for each session. Study the outcomes and decide if you want to add or subtract anything. Make sure you have all the materials you and your students will need. Think about the asset and what it means. Read the story and the discussion questions. Familiarize yourself with the activity so you can explain it clearly and concisely. Consider ways to enhance the session or customize it for your group.

★ Approach each session with a positive attitude. Let students know you look forward to reading the stories with them, to hearing their thoughts and ideas, and to helping them add assets to their lives.

★ Add, subtract, and adapt activities and discussion questions to fit the needs of your students and the realities of your circumstances. Extend activities and discussions when things are going well and students are engaged. Shorten those that don't go over as well.

★ Take notes during each session on what works and what doesn't work. These will help you next time you teach the course.

★ Although the sessions include many reading and writing elements, they should not be too "schoolish." Use a lighter touch. If you must assign grades, be generous and grade primarily on participation, not performance.

★ Keep parents and caregivers informed about what you're doing with each session. Make use of the "Adding Assets at Home" handouts. Add notes that help parents get a sense of how you are handling these topics. Invite their comments and suggestions.

★ Although the Adding Assets Series for Kids empowers children to start building their own Developmental Assets, *building assets for and with young people is primarily an adult responsibility.* Never forget this.

★ Maintain an attitude of respect toward your students. Remind them often that you care about them and are proud of their efforts to add assets to their lives.

★ When appropriate, share your own life experiences with students. Tell them about adults who were important to you when you were growing up; about ways you helped others when you were their age; about how you formed your values—and what you did when your values were tested. Share ways in which you're still building assets for yourself and for other young people you know.

★ Keep in mind you're performing three roles: teacher, discussion leader, and role model. As a teacher, you're providing structure and implementing an organized curriculum. As a discussion leader, you're navigating your students' feelings and experiences, making sure everyone has a chance to contribute, and keeping the discussion on track. As a role model, you're an example—someone to look up to and emulate. All children need positive adult role models in their lives.

★ Be willing to listen, and try not to talk too much. Let students do most of the talking. Sometimes you'll need to move on before a student has completely finished a thought or an anecdote. Try saying, "I'll come back to you later if there's time."

★ Try not to judge what students say. When appropriate, you might point out choices they have, but never tell them which choice they should make, what they should think, or how they should feel.

★ Try to identify different leaders for different discussions and activities. Notice the range of skills and talents among your students. Give everyone a chance to shine.

Group Discussion Guidelines

You may already have guidelines in place for class or group discussions. If so, review them with your students ahead of time and make sure everyone understands them. For the purposes of this course, we suggest your guidelines include the following:

1. We want everyone in our group to add assets to their lives.

2. We want everyone in our group to feel valued and accepted.

3. We are polite and respectful to each other. We don't use hurtful words or put-downs.

4. We listen to each other. When someone is talking, we look at the person and pay attention. We try not to focus just on what we're going to say when it's our turn.

5. Everyone is welcome to share his or her thoughts and feelings. But no one has to share. It's okay to say "I pass" when you don't want to share.

6. What is said in the group stays in the group.*

*See "Child Protection Laws" below for an exception to this guideline.

Child Protection Laws

Confidentiality is important to the success of this course. What is said in the group should stay in the group, and if a child comes to talk with you one-on-one, he or she needs to know this is a safe thing to do. However, there are certain things you may hear or observe that you must report for the protection of the child and any others involved.

Before beginning the course, be absolutely clear you know what you're legally required to report and what the guidelines for reporting are. These reporting requirements usually fall under the category of child protection legislation.

Most school districts and youth organizations have developed guidelines to conform to child protection laws. Learn what those guidelines are and to whom you should report if the need arises.

Getting Ready

Planning the Course

Every course requires planning and preparation. You might use "Planning the Course" on pages 11–12 to focus in on your particular group of students, their needs, and the facilities and resources available to you.

Scheduling the Sessions

★ There are many possible ways in which to teach this course—as a class period during the school day, as part of an after-school program, on Saturdays, in religion class, as a summer program, and so on. Of course, where and when you teach it will influence your session times.

★ Try to allow 45–55 minutes for each session. If you don't have that much time, look over a few of the sessions and make preliminary adjustments.

★ As you teach the course for the first time, keep track of how long each session takes. This will help you plan and prepare when you teach the course again.

Involving Parents and Caregivers

★ As you look over the student books and this Leader's Guide, be thinking about any parents or caregivers you know who may be in a position to serve as mentors, experts, or helpers.

★ Depending on the size of your group, you may want to call your students' parents and caregivers ahead of time, briefly describe the course you're about to start teaching, and let them know you'll be sending home handouts for them to read. Start with the letter on page 13. You may use it as is or adapt it as appropriate.

★ Especially if your group includes students you're meeting for the first time, ask parents and caregivers if there is anything they would like you to know about their children before the class begins.

★ Encourage parents to follow along with the course by reading the student books. Figure out a borrowing method.

★ Invite parents to call you with questions or comments. Give them a phone number where they can reach you, and let them know the best times to call.

★ Add notes to the "Adding Assets at Home" handouts on how the course is proceeding.

★ Consider having a family night or an open house midway through the course. Display handouts related to the sessions, completed activities, and Student Trackers for parents and caregivers to see.

Professional Tips

Notes on Role Playing

Role playing is a big part of elementary-age students' learning. It invites creativity and a sense of make-believe. It enables children to experience what it might be like to walk in someone else's shoes. It gives them opportunities to try out different approaches to life's situations in a safe and protective environment. It challenges them to clarify what they think, feel, and believe.

Role playing is a way to practice solving problems, predicting consequences, arranging situations, and reacting to unplanned situations.

Your role as leader is simply to observe. Interrupt only when problems arise. Even then, avoid controlling the role play or taking on a role.

★ Start simply. Build students' confidence with straightforward situations—playing with a friend, sharing a game, arguing with a friend, feeling scared of something, or being left out.

★ Have students new to role playing try it in small groups first. Coach kids and offer cues.

★ Have students take turns playing different people in a situation so each child gets the chance to experience it from varying perspectives.

★ Give students time to think. Don't embarrass them by urging them to move things along.

★ Afterward, point out how each player showed confidence in his or her situation.

★ Discuss the role play as a group. Invite positive feedback.

Here's a game to start:

1. Choose someone to be the narrator and someone to be an actor. Have the actor choose another person to play a role.

2. Talk briefly and separately with the narrator about the situation to be role-played. Will it be a story from one of the student books or a made-up story? Either is fine. Agree with the narrator on how the story will progress.

3. Have the narrator begin by setting up the scene in the second person. *Example:* "You've just arrived at school. It's a beautiful day. You see a good friend at the lockers." Give the actors a moment or two to act out the scene. The narrator can make suggestions: "You talk about what you did over the weekend," or "You make plans to get together after school."

4. Now the narrator adds a surprise or two to the plot. *Example:* "You're walking down the hall with your friend when a bigger older kid bumps into you." The actors must react to the surprise—in character.

5. The story continues until the narrator says "Stop." Then the first actor becomes the narrator, and the second actor chooses another actor to play a role. The new narrator picks up the story and adds twists until the leader (you) says "Stop."

Notes on Readers' Theater

Everyone loves a play. Readers' Theater is a type of play in which everyone reads directly from scripts. No costumes or sets are necessary.

You might take one or more of the asset stories and perform it as Readers' Theater. If this works well for your group, you may want to do this with all of the stories instead of you reading them aloud. Make practice time part of your preparation for each session.

1. Skim the story to identify how many readers are needed—a narrator and any character with a speaking role.

2. Ask for volunteers or assign readers.

3. Give the cast members time to read the story on their own and to practice reading it as a group. Observe their practice. Guide them to communicate the feelings of the characters with their voices and also with body language.

4. When the cast is ready to perform, join the audience. Cheer wildly.

Notes on Art and Writing

Elementary-age students love to express themselves through art projects. Many also enjoy writing—when they are free to write without worrying about grammar, spelling, or handwriting skills.

This course includes many art and writing activities. Your role is to make sure that students understand the activities, provide them with the necessary materials, give them enough time to work—and then stand clear.

★ Respect each student's abilities and efforts.

★ Refrain from judgment and comparison.

★ Ask students to tell you more about their work.

★ Avoid assigning grades.

★ Value each student's work—and display it whenever possible.

★ Save completed projects to share with parents and caregivers at family nights and open houses.

Notes on Critical Thinking and Problem Solving

Promote students' natural curiosity by talking about problems and issues with an open mind to many different solutions. Follow a simple procedure, but allow your students to determine how deeply they can examine a problem.

1. Ask volunteers to identify the problem and put it into words.

2. Make sure everyone agrees on what the problem is.

3. Encourage students to come up with more than one solution. Brainstorm.

4. Help the group discern real possibilities by asking, "Which solutions will work for this problem? Which one will work best?"

5. Ask students to choose a solution and test it if possible.

Brainstorming Rules

1. Everyone tries to come up with as many ideas as they can.

2. All ideas are okay.

3. It is not okay to judge, criticize, or make fun of anyone else's ideas.

Before the Opening Session

★ A few days or a week before the course begins, tell students they will be starting something new very soon. They'll be learning ways to make their lives better, right now and for the future. They'll be hearing stories and doing fun activities.

★ If you are not able to provide three-ring binders for the Student Trackers, ask students to bring a three-ring binder to the first session.

★ Send home the "Dear Parents and Caregivers" letter (page 13), along with a copy of "The 40 Developmental Assets for Middle Childhood" (adult version; page 10).

★ Make copies of "The 40 Developmental Assets" (children's version; pages 18–19) and "Check It Out" (pages 16–17) for each student. Gather and prepare any other materials you will need for the first asset session you will be teaching.

Before the Closing Session

★ Ask students to bring a hat to the next session. Tell them they will be decorating their hats.

★ Have extra hats (like baseball-style caps) available for students who forget to bring their own.

★ Gather art materials for decorating the hats.

★ Make copies of the tracker page for the preceding session's asset (from the CD-ROM; this might be the "Positive View of Personal Future" page for Session 40, or it might be a different tracker page, depending on which session you chose to end with).

★ Make copies of "Add Up Your Assets," "Adding Assets: Student's Course Evaluation," "Adding Assets: Parent/ Caregiver's Course Evaluation," and "My Asset Promise to Myself."

★ If you can have a parade at the end of the closing session, arrange to have an audience. Perhaps your students can parade through another classroom or two, down the hall, across a playground during recess—or up the aisle at your place of worship.

Note: If you feel the asset hats activity in the closing session might seem too childish to your students, feel free to replace it with another activity of your choosing. Students might decorate T-shirts with fabric paints, for example, or make posters to share with younger kids. You might even ask your students how they would like to end this course. What ideas do they have for celebrating the assets and their own success at adding assets to their lives?

An Invitation

We'd love to know how the Adding Assets for Kids course works for you. Send us your success stories—and your suggestions for improving this course. Send us your ideas for building assets for and with young children. Building assets happens in community. We're all in this together!

Contact us by email:
help4kids@freespirit.com

Contact us through the Free Spirit Web site: *www.freespirit.com* (click on "contact us" at the bottom of any page)

Or send us a letter:
c/o Free Spirit Publishing
217 Fifth Avenue North, Suite 200
Minneapolis, MN 55401-1299

We hope to hear from you—and we wish you the very best as you work to build assets for and with the young people in your care.

Ann Redpath, Ed.D.
Pamela Espeland
Elizabeth Verdick

The 40 Developmental Assets for Middle Childhood

External Assets

Support

1. **Family support**—Family life provides high levels of love and support.
2. **Positive family communication**—Parent(s) and child communicate positively. Child feels comfortable seeking advice and counsel from parent(s).
3. **Other adult relationships**—Child receives support from adults other than her or his parent(s).
4. **Caring neighborhood**—Child experiences caring neighbors.
5. **Caring school climate**—Relationships with teachers and peers provide a caring, encouraging school environment.
6. **Parent involvement in schooling**—Parent(s) are actively involved in helping the child succeed in school.

Empowerment

7. **Community values children**—Child feels valued and appreciated by adults in the community.
8. **Children as resources**—Child is included in decisions at home and in the community.
9. **Service to others**—Child has opportunities to help others in the community.
10. **Safety**—Child feels safe at home, at school, and in her or his neighborhood.

Boundaries and Expectations

11. **Family boundaries**—Family has clear and consistent rules and consequences and monitors the child's whereabouts.
12. **School boundaries**—School provides clear rules and consequences.
13. **Neighborhood boundaries**—Neighbors take responsibility for monitoring the child's behavior.
14. **Adult role models**—Parent(s) and other adults in the child's family, as well as nonfamily adults, model positive, responsible behavior.
15. **Positive peer influence**—Child's closest friends model positive, responsible behavior.
16. **High expectations**—Parent(s) and teachers expect the child to do her or his best at school and in other activities.

Constructive Use of Time

17. **Creative activities**—Child participates in music, art, drama, or creative writing two or more times per week.
18. **Child programs**—Child participates two or more times per week in cocurricular school activities or structured community programs for children.
19. **Religious community**—Child attends religious programs or services one or more times per week.
20. **Time at home**—Child spends some time most days both in high-quality interaction with parent(s) and doing things at home other than watching TV or playing video games.

Internal Assets

Commitment to Learning

21. **Achievement motivation**—Child is motivated and strives to do well in school.
22. **Learning engagement**—Child is responsive, attentive, and actively engaged in learning at school and enjoys participating in learning activities outside of school.
23. **Homework**—Child usually hands in homework on time.
24. **Bonding to adults at school**—Child cares about teachers and other adults at school.
25. **Reading for pleasure**—Child enjoys and engages in reading for fun most days of the week.

Positive Values

26. **Caring**—Parent(s) tell the child it is important to help other people.
27. **Equality and social justice**—Parent(s) tell the child it is important to speak up for equal rights for all people.
28. **Integrity**—Parent(s) tell the child it is important to stand up for one's beliefs.
29. **Honesty**—Parent(s) tell the child it is important to tell the truth.
30. **Responsibility**—Parent(s) tell the child it is important to accept personal responsibility for behavior.
31. **Healthy lifestyle**—Parent(s) tell the child it is important to have good health habits and an understanding of healthy sexuality.

Social Competencies

32. **Planning and decision making**—Child thinks about decisions and is usually happy with the results of her or his decisions.
33. **Interpersonal competence**—Child cares about and is affected by other people's feelings, enjoys making friends, and, when frustrated or angry, tries to calm herself or himself.
34. **Cultural competence**—Child knows and is comfortable with people of different racial, ethnic, and cultural backgrounds and with her or his own cultural identity.
35. **Resistance skills**—Child can stay away from people who are likely to get her or him in trouble and is able to say no to doing wrong or dangerous things.
36. **Peaceful conflict resolution**—Child attempts to resolve conflict nonviolently.

Positive Identity

37. **Personal power**—Child feels she or he has some influence over things that happen in her or his life.
38. **Self-esteem**—Child likes and is proud to be the person she or he is.
39. **Sense of purpose**—Child sometimes thinks about what life means and whether there is a purpose for her or his life.
40. **Positive view of personal future**—Child is optimistic about her or his personal future.

PLANNING THE COURSE

1. Who will my students be?

What do I know about my students from other teachers and adult leaders, parents and caregivers, student portfolios, and other records?

_____

_____

What learning styles seem most appropriate for my students?

_____

_____

Does my group include students with special needs? What are those needs, and how will I address them?

_____

_____

Does my group include students who are not proficient in English? How will I address their needs?

_____

_____

2. How will I plan each session?

Which assets/skills do I prefer to teach?

_____

_____

Which assets/skills will be most beneficial for my students to learn about first? Next? After that?

_____

_____

What can I bring to this course from my own experience? Stories, activities, poems, humor, lessons learned?

_____

_____

How can I effectively combine writing and reading skills with asset building? Can I collaborate with other teachers and adult leaders? If so, how?

_____

_____

3. How will I set up our classroom/meeting space?

In rows of desks?

_____

In paired seating arrangements?

_____

In cooperative learning groups?

_____

With tables and chairs?

_____

4. What technology tools will I use?

What tools will I have available? (Copier, printer, computer?)

_____

_____

How will I use them?

_____

_____

5. What connections can I make outside the classroom?

What connections can I make with other groups outside the school or space?

_____

_____

What connections can I make with students' parents and caregivers?

_____

_____

What connections can I make with my colleagues and peers?

_____

_____

What connections can I make with the community?

_____

_____

More notes and thoughts to help me plan:

_____

_____

_____

Dear Parents and Caregivers,

I'm excited to tell you about a new course we'll be starting soon. It's called **Adding Assets**, and it's about helping children add **Developmental Assets** to their lives.

You might be thinking assets are about houses, cars, property, and other things worth money. The Developmental Assets aren't those kinds of assets. They include things like a loving, supportive family, a caring neighborhood, self-esteem, helping other people, telling the truth—even handing in homework on time. Along with this letter, I'm including a list of the 40 Developmental Assets. Read it over and you'll know what the assets are all about.

Developmental Assets are good for kids. This is something we know for a fact. Research by Search Institute, a nonprofit organization based in Minneapolis, Minnesota, has shown that the assets make a powerful difference in the lives of children and teens. The *more* assets kids have, the *less* likely they are to get into trouble and lose their way. And the *more* likely they are to grow up to be caring, healthy, contributing members of their community.

At the end of each session, I'll send home a handout about that day's asset, with ideas you may want to try at home. (Because kids tend to "lose" things in their desks or backpacks, you may want to ask your child about the handouts until he or she gets in the habit of bringing them to you.)

Your child will be reading and listening to stories from a series of books called the **Adding Assets Series for Kids.** If you're interested, I'd love for you to read them, too. The stories are short—and in between are ideas for your child to try at home, at school, in your neighborhood, in your faith community, and with his or her friends. Let me know if you want to see the books and we'll work something out.

This course can be a wonderful growing experience for your child—and maybe for you, too. I know it will be for me. Please take a moment now and then to talk with your child about the assets and how the course is going for him or her. And please feel free to contact me with questions or comments at any time along the way.

Yours sincerely,

_____

Telephone: _____

Best times to call:_____

Email: _____

Opening Session: Starting Out Right

Outcomes

★ to introduce students to the Developmental Assets

★ to start building assets immediately

Note: See "Before the Opening Session" on page 9 for preparation information.

Materials

★ the Adding Assets Series for Kids books on display

★ copies of "Check It Out," "The 40 Developmental Assets" (children's version), and "My Adding Assets Tracker" handouts

★ a three-ring binder for each student, with a few sheets of lined loose-leaf paper in each one. This binder will be used for the Student Tracker. The paper is for notes students want to write during the sessions

The Session

1. Ask students: **If you knew ways to make your life better, right now and for the future, would you try them?** Tell them to think about the question for a moment, then ask them to write down two things they would like to do to make their lives better. They don't have to share this page with anyone, but they should keep it, because they will look at it again at a later date.

2. Call students' attention to the Adding Assets Series for Kids books on display. Depending on the size of your group, invite them to go look at the books, or let them pass around copies as you proceed.

3. Read aloud or paraphrase the following as an introduction to the Developmental Assets and this course:

Over the next several weeks, you're going to learn about ways to make your life better. You're going to add assets to your life. The assets I'm talking about aren't the kind you might have heard about—money, houses, or cars. You'll be adding things called Developmental Assets. These are good things you need in your life and yourself. Things like a close, loving family. A neighborhood where you feel safe. Adults you look up to and respect. And even doing your homework.

There are 40 assets in all. That may sound like a lot, but don't worry. You won't be adding them all at once. No one is going to test you on how well you do. You're going to keep track of your own progress and successes.

We know the assets are good for you because researchers have studied them The researchers surveyed hundreds of thousands of kids and teens from all across the United States. They learned that some kids have a fairly easy time growing up, while others don't. Some kids get involved in harmful behaviors or dangerous activities, while others don't. What makes the difference? Developmental Assets do. Kids who have them are more likely to do well. Kids who don't have them are less likely to do well. And the more assets you have, the better. That's why we're going to try to add as many of them to your life as we can.

Even though you're young (some people might say you're "just a kid") you have the power to make choices in your life. Your choices can help you or hurt you. The choice to add assets to your life can help you. And you don't have to do it all by yourself. I'm going to help you. Other grown-ups will help you, too—like your parents or caregivers, your grandparents, and other adults you know.

We're going to add one asset at a time. We'll read stories about the assets and talk about the stories. We'll read and talk about ideas for adding assets. We'll come up with our own ideas. We'll write and draw and do fun activities. We'll laugh and joke around and get serious, too. We'll all add assets together.

Pretty soon, you won't be a child anymore. You'll be a teenager. Because you have assets, you'll feel and be a lot more sure of yourself. You'll make better decisions. You'll have a head start on being a successful person.

4. Hand out the binders and copies of "My Adding Assets Tracker," the cover/title page for the Student Tracker. Tell students they will use these binders during the course. If they have their own desks, they should keep them in their desks. Otherwise, you should collect them at the end of each session and hand them out at the start of the next session.

5. Hand out copies of "Check It Out." Allow a few moments for students to complete the checklist. Have them put their completed checklists in their binders.

6. Hand out copies of "The 40 Developmental Assets" (children's version). Tell students these are the assets they will add to their lives. Suggest they put the lists in their binders. Have extra copies available for students who want to bring one home to share with their parents or caregivers.

7. If time allows, move immediately into Session 1, or whichever session you choose to start with. This course is all about adding assets—the sooner, the better. Start now if you can.

Note: During one of the early sessions, try to build in time for students to decorate their "My Student Tracker" page. Provide colored pencils, colored markers, stickers, or any other art materials you think your students might enjoy using.

Check It Out

Put a checkmark next to each statement that seems true for you.

☐ **1.** I feel loved and supported in my family.

☐ **2.** I can talk to my parent(s). I feel comfortable asking them for advice.

☐ **3.** There are other adults besides my parent(s) who give me support and encouragement.

☐ **4.** I have neighbors who know me and care about me.

☐ **5.** I get along well with teachers and other kids at my school. I feel that school is a caring, encouraging place to be.

☐ **6.** My parent(s) are actively involved in helping me succeed in school.

☐ **7.** I feel that adults in my community value and appreciate me.

☐ **8.** I am included in decisions at home and in my community.

☐ **9.** I have chances to help others in my community.

☐ **10.** I feel safe at home, at school, and in my neighborhood.

☐ **11.** My family has clear and consistent rules and consequences for my behavior. They keep track of me and know where I am all or most of the time.

☐ **12.** My school has clear rules and consequences for behavior.

☐ **13.** My neighbors keep an eye on kids in the neighborhood.

☐ **14.** The adults in my family behave in positive, responsible ways. They set good examples for me to follow. So do other adults I know.

☐ **15.** My best friends behave in positive, responsible ways. They are a good influence on me.

☐ **16.** My parent(s) and teachers expect me to do my best at school and in other activities.

☐ **17.** I do something with music, art, drama, or creative writing two or more times a week.

☐ **18.** I go to an organized after-school activity or community program for kids two or more times a week.

☐ **19.** I go to a religious program or service once a week or more.

☐ **20.** On most days, I spend some time with my parent(s). I spend some time doing things at home besides watching TV or playing video games.

☐ **21.** I want to do well in school, and I try my best.

☐ **22.** I like to learn new things in and out of school.

☐ **23.** I usually hand in my homework on time.

☐ **24.** I care about and feel connected to the teachers and other adults at my school.

☐ **25.** I like to read, and I read for fun on most days of the week.

☐ **26.** My parent(s) tell me it's important to help other people.

☐ **27.** My parent(s) tell me it's important to speak up for equal rights for all people.

☐ **28.** My parent(s) tell me it's important to stand up for my beliefs.

☐ **29.** My parent(s) tell me it's important to be truthful.

☐ **30.** My parent(s) tell me it's important to be responsible for my own behavior.

☐ **31.** My parent(s) tell me it's important to have good health habits and an understanding of healthy sexuality.

☐ **32.** I think about the choices I make, and I'm usually happy with my decisions. I know how to plan ahead.

☐ **33.** I care about other people and their feelings. I enjoy making friends. When I feel angry or frustrated, I try to calm myself down.

☐ **34.** I know and am comfortable with people of different races, ethnic backgrounds, and cultures. I'm also comfortable with my own cultural identity.

☐ **35.** I stay away from people who could get me into trouble. I can say no to doing things that are dangerous or wrong.

☐ **36.** I try to resolve conflicts in a peaceful way, without using harsh words or violent actions.

☐ **37.** I feel that I have some control over things that happen in my life.

☐ **38.** I like myself, and I'm proud to be the person I am.

☐ **39.** I sometimes think about what life means and whether my life has a purpose.

☐ **40.** I feel hopeful about my own future.

Opening Session

THE 40 DEVELOPMENTAL ASSETS

20 External Assets: Good things you get from the world around you

The Support Assets: People Who Care About You

Family Support—You feel loved and supported in your family.

Positive Family Communication—You and your parent(s) can talk to each other. You feel comfortable asking your parent(s) for advice.

Other Adult Relationships—Other adults besides your parent(s) give you support and encouragement.

Caring Neighborhood—You have neighbors who know you and care about you.

Caring School Climate—You get along well with teachers and other kids at your school. You feel that school is a caring, encouraging place to be.

Parent Involvement in Schooling—Your parent(s) are actively involved in helping you succeed in school.

The Empowerment Assets: Helping Out and Staying Safe

Community Values Children—You feel that adults in your community value you and appreciate you.

Children as Resources—You are included in decisions at home and in your community.

Service to Others—You have chances to help others in your community.

Safety—You feel safe at home, at school, and in your neighborhood.

The Boundaries and Expectations Assets: Doing and Being Your Best

Family Boundaries—Your family has clear and consistent rules and consequences for your behavior. They keep track of you and know where you are all or most of the time.

School Boundaries—Your school has clear rules and consequences for behavior.

Neighborhood Boundaries—Your neighbors keep an eye on kids in the neighborhood.

Adult Role Models—The adults in your family behave in positive, responsible ways. They set good examples for you to follow. So do other adults you know.

Positive Peer Influence—Your best friends behave in positive, responsible ways. They are a good influence on you.

High Expectations—Your parent(s) and teachers expect you to do your best at school and in other activities.

The Constructive Use of Time Assets: Smart Ways to Spend Your Time

Creative Activities—You do something with music, art, drama, or creative writing two or more times a week.

Child Programs—You go to an organized after-school activity or community program for kids two or more times a week.

Religious Community—You go to a religious program or service once a week or more.

Time at Home—On most days, you spend some time with your parent(s). You spend some time doing things at home besides watching TV or playing video games.

The *40 Developmental Assets for Middle Childhood* list is adapted with permission. Copyright © 1997, 2006 Search Institute, 615 First Avenue NE, Minneapolis, MN 55413; 800-888-7828; www.search-institute.org. All rights reserved.

From *A Leader's Guide to The Adding Assets Series for Kids: Activities and Strategies for Positive Youth Development* by Ann Redpath, Ed.D., Pamela Espeland, and Elizabeth Verdick, copyright © 2007. Free Spirit Publishing Inc., Minneapolis, MN; www.freespirit.com. This page may be photocopied for individual, classroom, and small group work only. For other uses, call 866-703-7322.

THE 40 DEVELOPMENTAL ASSETS
20 Internal Assets: Good things you get from inside yourself

The Commitment to Learning Assets: Loving to Learn

Achievement Motivation—You want to do well in school, and you try your best.

Learning Engagement—You like to learn new things in and out of school.

Homework—You usually hand in your homework on time.

Bonding to Adults at School—You care about and feel connected to the teachers and other adults at your school.

Reading for Pleasure—You like to read, and you read for fun on most days of the week.

The Positive Values Assets: Knowing and Doing What's Right

Caring—Your parent(s) tell you it's important to help other people.

Equality and Social Justice—Your parent(s) tell you it's important to speak up for equal rights for all people.

Integrity—Your parent(s) tell you it's important to stand up for your beliefs.

Honesty—Your parent(s) tell you it's important to be truthful.

Responsibility—Your parent(s) tell you it's important to be responsible for your own behavior.

Healthy Lifestyle—Your parent(s) tell you it's important to have good health habits and an understanding of healthy sexuality.

The Social Competencies Assets: Making Choices and Making Friends

Planning and Decision Making—You think about the choices you make, and you're usually happy with your decisions. You know how to plan ahead.

Interpersonal Competence—You care about other people and their feelings. You enjoy making friends. When you feel angry or frustrated, you try to calm yourself down.

Cultural Competence—You know and are comfortable with people of different races, ethnic backgrounds, and cultures. You're also comfortable with your own cultural identity.

Resistance Skills—You stay away from people who could get you into trouble. You can say no to doing things that are dangerous or wrong.

Peaceful Conflict Resolution—You try to resolve conflicts in a peaceful way, without using harsh words or violent actions.

The Positive Identity Assets: Proud to Be You

Personal Power—You feel that you have some control over things that happen in your life.

Self-Esteem—You like yourself, and you're proud to be the person you are.

Sense of Purpose—You sometimes think about what life means and whether your life has a purpose.

Positive View of Personal Future—You feel hopeful about your own future.

My Adding Assets Tracker

My Name: _____

My Teacher's Name: _____

People Who Care About You: The Support Assets

★ The **Support Assets** are **External Assets.**

★ **External Assets** are positive experiences kids receive from the world around them.

★ The **Support Assets** are about surrounding kids with people who love them, care for them, appreciate them, and accept them. These people include family members, neighbors, and many others, as well as organizations and institutions with positive, supportive environments.

The Support Assets are:

1. **Family support**—Family life provides high levels of love and support.
2. **Positive family communication**—Parent(s) and child communicate positively. Child feels comfortable seeking advice and counsel from parent(s).
3. **Other adult relationships**—Child receives support from adults other than her or his parent(s).
4. **Caring neighborhood**—Child experiences caring neighbors.
5. **Caring school climate**—Relationships with teachers and peers provide a caring, encouraging school environment.
6. **Parent involvement in schooling**—Parent(s) are actively involved in helping the child succeed in school.

Session 1: Family Support

What this asset means to the child: You feel loved and supported in your family.

Backdrop

Write the name of the asset and its definition on the board.

> **Optional.** Write this quotation on the board: "Smile for each other, make time for each other in your family."—Mother Teresa

Note: Write the session backdrop quotation on the board when it is appropriate for your students. Always write the name of the asset and its definition on the board.

Outcomes

★ to help students add the Family Support asset to their lives

★ to discuss with students new ways for showing love and support within their families

★ to identify and gain appreciation for how students already benefit from family support

Preparation

A day or so before you begin this session, ask students to get permission to bring in one or two photographs of their families. If possible, have the photographs displayed when you begin the session.

Materials

★ copies of the book *People Who Care About You*

★ copies of the "Family Support" tracker page (from the CD-ROM)

★ copies of the "How Do You Spell SUPPORT?" and "Adding Assets at Home" handouts

1. Getting Started

Greeting. Have students say hello to someone near them in a new way. *Example:* "Hey, it's good to see you. I'm glad you're here."

Take 5. Hand out copies of the "Family Support" tracker page. Tell students you will give them a tracker page for each session. Explain that these pages will be their way to keep track of each asset as they learn about it and start building it in their lives. Offer an example from your own efforts with the current asset. Tell how you are making a real decision to build the asset in your life. Make sure students know it's always appropriate to share feelings or an experience related to this asset or any other one.

Note: Students won't be using the tracker page this session; this is just for them to look at. You can collect the copies during this session for use next time, or hand out new copies then—whatever you prefer.

Two-Minute Partners. Have students form partners. Using the asset definition or the quotation on the board as a springboard, ask the partners to each spend a minute describing their families to each other. Tell them they can move to where their family photos are displayed.

Preview. Tell students what they will do in this session. Make sure they have all necessary materials.

2. The Asset Question

Ask students: **What does it mean to be *supported?*** You may need to give a little background on the word *support*. Read aloud a definition of *support* to students. Show how a bookend gives *support* and keeps a stack of books from falling.

Note: You may want to reread "A message for you" on page 13 of *People Who Care About You* to see if you need to address the topic of family with your student group or privately with any student.

3. Before the Story

Tell students they are going to be hearing (or hearing and reading) stories about kids who are trying to build assets in their own lives. The stories will enable them to "see" the assets at work in true-to-life situations. The stories will help them understand why assets are needed, how they might work, and why they are helpful.

Note: Allow the story to be the central focus of each session.

4. The Story

Read It. Read aloud and discuss Sam's story on pages 6–7 and 17–18 of the student book. You may want to stop reading at the bottom of page 7 to talk about the comment that Sam doesn't feel he deserves his family's support.

Get-in-the-Mood Activity. Role-play a scene that addresses this question: **Why won't Sam accept his family's support?** (See "Notes on Role Playing" on pages 7–8.) Ask for volunteers to take each family member's role. Suggest that students ad lib, making up their own words for what they think Sam, Lindsey, and their parents might say. Remind them to stay focused on Sam feeling

like he's a loser and like he's not deserving of his family's support.

Story Questions for Discussion. Ask students:

★ **Why do you think Sam's younger sister knows exactly why Sam is upset?**

★ **How is Sam's mom supporting him by saying his team just isn't "winning right now"?**

★ **What words does Sam's dad use to show his support for Sam? What words make Sam laugh a little?**

★ **Have you ever felt like Sam: You know what you want but you don't know how to ask for it?** Ask a volunteer to tell about a real want he or she has, and ask the group to make suggestions for how to go about getting it.

5. Asset-Building Activities At-a-Glance

Read over the activities on pages 8–16 of the student book and decide which ones are most suitable for your students. *Suggestions:*

★ Discuss: **How do you send love messages? With words? Hugs? In what other ways do you let family members know you love them?**

Standards/Objectives Highlights

Character Education	Students engage families as partners; approach to behavior emphasizes values and consequences
Health	Students advocate for personal, family, and community health
Social Studies	Students describe ways family, gender, ethnicity, nationality, and institutional affiliations contribute to personal identity
Language Arts	Students use spoken and written language to accomplish their own purposes
SEL Competencies	Students identify and label feelings

★ How do you *give* support?

★ (Read aloud the "X-Treme example" on page 11.) **Have you ever had plans for something you really wanted to do, then changed your plans because someone needed your help? Tell us about it.**

★ You might ask student volunteers to check into neighborhood or community activities for families, then bring information to share with the group.

6. Session Activity

★ Hand out copies of "How Do You Spell SUPPORT?"

★ Tell students the first part is for them to describe how they would like to give support; the second part is to describe the support they'd like to receive.

Suggestions for students who have trouble getting started:

S (smiling, singing, being silly)

U (understanding, upholding, being united)

P (having patience, saying please)

P (being pleasant, playing)

O (feeling okay, being open)

R (being reasonable, reaching out)

T (being treated tenderly, saying thank you)

★ Hand out copies of "Adding Assets at Home."

Optional Activity: Vocabulary

Support Art. Have students draw a picture of what the word *support* means to their family. Make sure the word *support* is printed somewhere on the drawing. Hang the students' drawings throughout the room.

---

7. Closing Question

Ask students: **What will you do to start adding the Family Support asset to your life?** If there's time, encourage responses. Give an example of building this asset in your own life.

Preparation for Next Session

★ Make the book *People Who Care About You* available to students if you would like them to read ahead the story and/or activity ideas for the Positive Family Communication asset (Session 2).

★ Ask students to think about this question: **With all the ways we have to communicate, do you ever feel like it's still sometimes hard to say some things to the people in your own family? Think about what you and your family could do about that.**

How Do You Spell SUPPORT?

S
U
P
P
O
R
T

I want to *be* a support to my family by:

_____

_____

_____

_____

_____

_____

_____

S
U
P
P
O
R
T

I want to *feel* supported by my family in these ways:

_____

_____

_____

_____

_____

_____

_____

Family Support

Today your child was introduced to the **Support** assets. These assets are about having people in your life who love you, care for you, appreciate you, and accept you. They're also about having places to be and go where you feel safe, supported, and welcome. The first of these assets, **Family Support**, was the topic of today's session. For your child, this asset means: *You feel loved and supported in your family.*

The students did an activity with the word *support* and how it's like a safety net holding you up in different ways. The ideas of support are a little like a blanket toss activity, where a group of people hold a blanket to toss a person in the air and catch the person before he or she falls to the ground. We all know that kids need lots of people to support them and to keep them from falling too far and getting hurt.

Your love and support for your child are critical. So is receiving support from others—grandparents, other family members, friends, and neighbors. These other people around you help to hold the "support blanket" for your child.

Ideas and Activities to Try at Home

QT. One area all families can improve on is quality time (QT). Here are three ways to be supportive of your child and have some quality time together:

★ Get up 20 minutes earlier and eat breakfast together.

★ Let everyone help plan a weekly family fun night.

★ Make a snack together and talk about your day. Or go for a walk together around the neighborhood.

Not-So-Secret Messages. Try conversations that start with everyone writing down their ideas about a particular problem or issue. Write first and then talk. (If you write first, often you'll find everyone is more honest. And that's a good opener to conversation.) For example, ask your child to write ideas for the following questions:

★ What's your most favorite thing about our family? What's your least favorite?

★ When have you felt most supported by our family? Least supported?

★ How can our family support each other more?

Session 2: Positive Family Communication

> **What this asset means to the child:** You and your parent(s) can talk to each other. You feel comfortable asking your parent(s) for advice.

Backdrop

Write the name of the asset and its definition on the board.

> **Optional.** Write this quotation on the board: "Heirlooms we don't have in our family. But stories we've got."—Rose Chernin

Outcomes

★ to help students add the Positive Family Communication asset to their lives

★ to help students find ways to initiate and respond to positive family communication

★ to help students begin to practice positive family communication in other supportive environments

Preparation

At the end of the last session, you asked students to think about this question: **With all the ways we have to communicate, do you ever feel like it's still sometimes hard to say some things to the people in your own family? Think about what you and your family could do about that.** Remind students of the question and tell them you'll want to hear their ideas later in the session.

Materials

★ copies of the book *People Who Care About You*

★ copies of the "Family Support" tracker page (from the CD-ROM)

★ large paper bags, scissors, crayons or markers

★ copies of the "Talk Radio" and "Adding Assets at Home" handouts

1. Getting Started

Greeting. Have students say hello to someone near them.

Take 5. Hand out copies of the "Family Support" tracker page and allow a few moments for students to complete them.

Note: Make sure students know it's always appropriate to share feelings or an experience related to this asset or any other one. Sometimes, share your own examples as well.

Two-Minute Partners. Have students form partners. Using the asset definition or the quotation on the board, ask the partners to each spend a minute describing what the words mean to him or her.

Preview. Tell students what they will do in this session. Make sure they have all necessary materials.

2. The Asset Question

Ask students: **Why is it sometimes hard to talk to the people closest to us?** Begin a discussion of what the students think about this question.

3. Before the Story

Students can try the following activity when they're having difficulty finding the right words to start a conversation.

Step Aside Please. Sometimes starting a conversation about a different topic helps get the more important conversation going. Here's how:

★ Start a conversation over dinner or in the car or when you're out walking together with a parent or caregiver. Think up a big question such as, "If you had a million dollars to give away, who would you give it to and why?"

★ As you both answer and listen to each other's opinions, you'll find you're both enjoying the conversation because you're talking about an unfamiliar topic—not one that has the tiresome familiarity of an old conflict or issue.

★ This side-step conversation can be a lead-in to a more important conversation that you want to have with your parent or sibling.

Ask students who try an activity such as this to let the group know how it works for them. Ask students to share any other ways they thought of to talk about tough topics with their family.

4. The Story

Read It. Read aloud and discuss Jayde's story on pages 19–20 and 30–31 of the student book. You may want to stop reading at the bottom of page 20 and talk about Jayde being upset because she feels like she doesn't have the positive family communication asset.

Get-in-the-Mood Activity.* Follow these steps:

1. Hand out the paper bags, crayons or markers, and scissors. Have students make a friendly looking face mask on the front of the paper bag. Explain that they should make holes only for the ears (not for the eyes, nose, or mouth).

2. Ask students for examples of family conflicts, or suggest one. *Example:* One family member wants to keep the family cat's new litter of kittens, but another family member wants to give them away.

3. Start with two volunteers to act out a difficult conversation for a family. One student will be the listener and wear a mask while the other one talks. Then reverse roles.

4. After, ask students: **How did it feel to listen and make no comments? How did it feel to speak knowing there wouldn't be any interruptions?**

5. Have the rest of the class form pairs and act out other family conflict situations.

Story Questions for Discussion. Ask students:

★ **Why didn't Jayde like her mom's title for herself, "Queen of Multi-tasking"?**

Standards/Objectives Highlights

Character Education	School takes steps to help everyone appreciate core values
Health	Students describe the relationship between healthy behaviors and personal health
Social Studies	Students describe the influence of attitudes and values on personal identity and the influence of technological choices
Language Arts	Students adjust their spoken and written language to communicate effectively for different purposes
SEL Competencies	Students monitor and regulate feelings so they aid rather than impede the handling of situations

★ How did Tessa handle this problem for herself? How did she try to help Jayde?

★ Why would it "take some courage" for Jayde to talk to her mom about what's going on?

★ What was making Jayde's mom so busy? Why was Jayde's mom glad Jayde shared how she was feeling? What did her mom's words do to help Jayde understand her mother's point of view?

★ How did it happen that they both ended up admitting they were wrong and promising to do something specific about it?

★ What could you do to help out with all the tasks around your home?

Optional Activity: Reading Skill

Words in Context (Multi-tasking). Write the definition of multi-tasking on the board: *The ability to do more than one task at the same time.*

Have a discussion about what students think of multi-tasking. Make sure they give specific examples.

5. Asset-Building Activities At-a-Glance

Read over the activities on pages 21–29 of the student book and decide which ones are most suitable for your students. *Suggestions:*

★ Discuss: **It takes some imagination to have a good conversation. You have to be able to see, or visualize, what the other person is talking about.**

★ Ask students if they've asked their parents what life was like before having children.

★ Ask for a volunteer to tell how his or her conversation about a difficult topic went with a parent.

★ Copy onto the board the "4 Tips for Talking with Parents" (page 24) or make an abbreviated list of these tips for students to copy and keep in a notebook for when they're facing a difficult talk.

6. Session Activity

★ Hand out copies of "Talk Radio."

★ Read aloud the opening paragraph so all students understand the script starters. Encourage them to adapt their scripts to fit their own family's tastes and needs.

★ Circulate as students work on their DJ scripts. Help them express in words and song titles some of their fun and difficult family conversations. They can bring their handouts home and ask a family adult to complete the listener script.

★ Hand out copies of "Adding Assets at Home."

7. Closing Question

Ask students: **What will you do to start adding the Positive Family Communication asset to your life?** If there's time, encourage responses. Give an example of building this asset in your own life.

Preparation for Next Session

★ Make the book *People Who Care About You* available to students if you would like them to read ahead the story and/or activity ideas for the Other Adult Relationships asset (Session 3).

★ Arrange for a mentor to speak to your group. The mentor should be willing to tell students about what he or she does to support kids their age. Ideally, the mentor will be someone students know from school or an adult who has become important to one or more of your students.

 # Talk Radio

Imagine you're a DJ on a talk radio show. The focus of your show is on your own family as the audience. Use the first script card to list some song titles you'd like to play for your family, or make up titles such as "I Can Do It, I Know I Can," "Here Is the Love," and "My Sister Bugs Me, But I Love Her." You can ask a family member to fill in the second script card.

DJ Script Card

Welcome to WFAM, where we play songs that tell it like it is in this family. I'm your host, _____.

First, a word about songs that tell stories about my needs. The song titles are:

_____

_____.

I am playing these songs because_____

_____.

Now that I've told you all about what's going on in my head, I'd like to hear from you. Any requests from my listeners? Hey, I think I have a call on line one. What's on your mind, caller?

Radio Listener Script Card

Thanks, DJ! I liked hearing the song _____

that you just played. It made me feel _____.

I'm glad you played the song, because now I have a better idea of how you feel. But I

have a question about it: _____

_____.

I'd like to request a song of my own:_____.

I'm requesting this song because I'm crazy about you and I'd like to tell you so in this song. Thanks for the show. I want to listen in again.

Positive Family Communication

Today your child learned about the **Positive Family Communication** asset. For your child, this asset means: *You and your parent(s) can talk to each other. You feel comfortable asking your parent(s) for advice.*

Psychologist Lawrence Kutner said, "Communicating effectively with a child often requires that a parent combine the deductive skills of Sherlock Holmes with the boundless tact and patience of an ambassador."

If you're like most parents or other caregivers, you struggle with this balance on a daily basis. This asset helps your child realize that he or she wants to talk with you. It then gives your child some tools for communicating. Obviously, the asset works best when parents work toward the same goal, too.

Ideas and Activities to Try at Home

Doors. Communication has a lot to do with doors: open doors, closed doors, slammed doors. Arguments often end in slammed doors. Having an open door usually means having an open attitude and mind. It means taking time to listen and listening without giving advice or judging.

Tips for door-opening:

★ Listen to your child. Allow your child the opportunity to express concerns, grievances, excitement, wants, needs, and opinions.

★ After watching a television show or movie together, talk with your child about any reactions he or she has about the show.

★ Plan a family meeting (weekly or monthly) where everyone can discuss concerns, upcoming plans, celebrations, and other family issues.

★ Plan a surprise celebration and ask everyone to make a silly hat to wear. Lightheartedness not only opens doors—it helps keep them open.

Session 3: Other Adult Relationships

> **What this asset means to the child:** Other adults besides your parent(s) give you support and encouragement.

Backdrop

Write the name of the asset and its definition on the board.

> **Optional.** Write this quotation on the board: "All kids are our kids."—Peter Benson

Outcomes

★ to help students add the Other Adult Relationships asset to their lives

★ to provide ways for students to identify other adults to whom they could go for advice and support

★ to recognize other adult relationships already present in students' lives

Preparation

Arrange for a mentor to speak to your group. The mentor should be willing to tell students about what he or she does to support kids their age. Ideally, the mentor will be someone students know from school or an adult who has become important to one or more of your students.

Materials

★ copies of the book *People Who Care About You*

★ copies of "Positive Family Communication" tracker page (from the CD-ROM)

★ copies of the "Best Supporting Role Planning Sheet," "Best Supporting Role Award," and "Adding Assets at Home" handouts (have extra copies of "Best Supporting Role" available for students who want to complete more than one)

★ *optional:* disposable cameras (see Preparation for Next Session, page 35)

1. Getting Started

Greeting. Have students say hello to someone near them.

Take 5. Hand out copies of the "Positive Family Communication" tracker page and allow a few moments for students to complete them.

Two-Minute Partners. Have students form partners. Using the asset definition or the quotation on the board, ask the partners to each spend a minute describing what the words mean to him or her.

Preview. Tell students what they will do in this session. Make sure they have all necessary materials.

2. The Asset Question

Ask students: **What's a mentor?** (*Someone who serves as a trusted adviser or a guide.*) **Why are mentors important? Who are some people you know who have mentor roles?** (*Examples:* a tutor, a camp counselor, or a coach.)

3. Before the Story

Introduce the adult mentor you invited to speak to your group. Explain (or have the mentor explain) a little of what he or she does to help young people. Allow time for an informal give-and-take in which students can ask how the individual mentors students.

4. The Story

Read It. Read aloud and discuss Matt and Allie's story on pages 32–33 and 41–42 of the student book. Discuss it as a group.

Summarize It. One way to do this is by contrasting Matt and Allie's lives. Draw a chart on the board like the following. Ask students to describe Matt and Allie while you fill out the chart with their suggestions. Responses will vary and may include:

What Matt has	Similarities	What Allie has
Lots of relatives nearby	Both are willing to help each other; neither is afraid to ask for help	Lots of difficulties with her parents and no connection to supporting adults

Story Questions for Discussion. Ask students:

★ How did Matt show that he was a real friend to Allie?

★ What was causing Allie's situation at home?

★ Have you ever made a list like the one Paul asked Allie to make? If so, what did you do with it?

Optional Question and Activity: Reading Skill

Infer. When Paul asked Allie to write down the names of adults she trusts, why at first did Allie say there was no one? How did Paul's suggestions help get Allie thinking? Write a sentence that tells how Paul was a mentor to Allie.

---

5. Asset-Building Activities At-a-Glance

Read aloud some of the activities on pages 34–40 of the student book, or ask for volunteers to read them aloud. What activities appeal to the students—to do on their own or to do with a partner or in a small group? Ask volunteers to mention some of the activities they would like to try in the coming days. These may include:

★ Make address books of important people.

★ Make lists of people students want to know better.

★ Find mentors on the Web, at school, in the neighborhood, in one's faith community, among parents of friends.

Standards/Objectives Highlights	
Character Education	School fosters caring attachments among adults within school community
Health	Students see influence of culture and other factors on health
Social Studies	Students compare similarities and differences in ways groups meet human needs and concerns
Language Arts	Students participate as knowledgeable, reflective, creative members of various literacy communities
SEL Competencies	Students establish and work toward the achievement of short- and long-term pro-social goals

6. Session Activity

★ Have students work alone or in partners or groups to make lists of trusted adults, like the one Allie made. If some students have trouble coming up with names, talk with them privately to help them identify some possible people.

★ Hand out copies of "Best Supporting Role Planning Sheet" and "Best Supporting Role Award." Read aloud the first paragraph on the planning sheet. Go over the steps of the activity to make sure everyone understands the process. Decide if your students will best complete this activity on their own or with a partner. Or have students think through the planning sheet on their own, then work in pairs to complete the awards. Make extra copies of the award sheet for students who want to give them to more than one person.

★ Hand out copies of "Adding Assets at Home." Remind students that their parents or caregivers are the best resources for identifying other adults to support them.

Optional Activity: Vocabulary

Definition. The Points of Light Foundation (*www.pointsoflight.org*) came up with this definition of the word *mentor*: *A mentor is a caring adult who makes an active, positive contribution to the life of a child. By connecting with a young person, mentors help ensure he or she has a brighter future.*

Look up the origin of the word *mentor* in the dictionary or on the Internet. Write it on a sheet of paper and state one way in which the original meaning is similar to the definition from the Points of Light Foundation.

Note: The word history of *mentor* tells a good story. The word probably begins with Homer's *Odyssey* written 2,800 years ago about the journey of Odysseus. In Homer's story, Mentor was a trusted friend whom Odysseus left in charge of his household. Mentor was a good name for such a friend because the word meant "adviser" in Greek, and it came from the Indo-European root *men-*, meaning "to think."

7. Closing Question

Ask students: **What will you do to begin adding the Other Adult Relationships asset to your life?** If there's time, encourage responses. Give an example of building this asset in your own life.

Preparation for Next Session

★ Make the book *People Who Care About You* available to students if you would like them to read ahead the story and/or activity ideas for the Caring Neighborhood asset (Session 4).

★ Ask for two volunteers to use their cameras (or give them disposable cameras) to take random pictures of their neighborhood. If necessary, get the students' film developed—or if the students use digital cameras, arrange to have their pictures printed—before Session 4.

Best Supporting Role

Planning Sheet

In the movies, it's usually the main character who gets all the glory. Now it's your chance to change all that. Start by thinking about the people in your life who have been supportive of you. (Or you may want to ask someone to support you.) You're about to honor those people. Here's how:

1. Create a List of Nominees

List any person who has played an important supporting role in your life, or who has helped you solve a problem.

Name	What the person did for you

2. Decide How Many People to Honor

How many people deserve a Best Supporting Role award? You don't have to stop at just one.

3. Design and Name Your Award

★ Use the Best Supporting Role Award sheet to design and create your award. Draw a picture or attach a photograph of your nominee. Decorate your award.

★ Create a title that describes this person's "support" qualities. *Examples:* Best in Coaching, Best in Problem Solving, Best in Listening, Best in Making Me Laugh.

★ Fill out the award sheet. Use the blank lines at the bottom to add your own words of thanks.

4. And the Winner Is . . .

Post your award next to your classmates' awards. Invite others in the school to see your gallery of best supporting nominees.

Best Supporting Role Award

_____

is hereby honored with the

_____ Award

for playing an important supporting

role in helping _____

in this way: _____

_____

_____

_____

_____

_____

_____

Other Adult Relationships

Today your child read about and discussed the **Other Adult Relationships** asset. For your child, this asset means: *Other adults besides your parent(s) give you support and encouragement.*

The students made lists of other adults, besides their parents or caregivers, who make a difference in their lives. You may want to continue this discussion at home.

Ideas and Activities to Try at Home

Encourage Interaction. Find ways for your child to interact with other adults. After-school programs can provide opportunities for your child to get to know teachers, coaches, and parent volunteers. You may also want to look into weekend and summer activities, including:

- ★ camps
- ★ sports leagues or other physical activities
- ★ youth groups
- ★ tutoring
- ★ community theater
- ★ clubs
- ★ music lessons
- ★ neighborhood get-togethers

Talk About Adults Who Care. Let your child know that other grown-ups value him or her. Together, come up with examples of how they help your child learn new skills or solve problems. Ask your child why he or she enjoys spending time with certain adults. If you ever had a mentor or an adult who made a difference in your life, share this information (and photos, if you have them) with your child.

Get Your Child Thinking. Here are some conversation starters:

- ★ Are there adults outside our family you would like to get to know better (teachers, coaches, neighbors, friends' parents)? What qualities do you admire in each person?

- ★ If you had a problem you weren't sure how to handle and couldn't discuss it with me (us) at the time, who would you go to? (You may need to explain that it is not being disloyal to parents or caregivers to ask other adults for advice or support, especially when family grown-ups are unavailable at a given time.)

- ★ Can you think of creative ways to show appreciation for an adult you care about? (***Examples:*** handmade cards, letters of appreciation, home-baked treats.)

Session 4: Caring Neighborhood

What this asset means to the child: You have neighbors who know you and care about you.

Backdrop

Write the name of the asset and its definition on the board.

> **Optional.** Write this quotation on the board: "The world's children deserve to walk the earth in safety."—President Bill Clinton

Outcomes

★ to help students add the Caring Neighborhood asset to their lives

★ to help students discover practical ways for caring about their neighborhoods

★ to help students learn how to meet new people and new surroundings bravely

Preparation

★ Ask for two volunteers to use their cameras (or give them disposable cameras) to take random pictures of their neighborhood. If necessary, get the students' film developed—or if the students use digital cameras, arrange to have their pictures printed—before you begin this session.

★ Mount the neighborhood photos taken by the student volunteers on one or more large sheets of paper. Leave room for more photos to be added later.

★ Have on hand a few more disposable cameras.

Materials

★ copies of the book *People Who Care About You*

★ copies of the "Other Adult Relationships" tracker page (from the CD-ROM)

★ copies of the "Puzzle: Advice for Making a Move," "Map It!" and "Adding Assets at Home" handouts

★ crayons or markers

★ disposable cameras

1. Getting Started

Greeting. Have students say hello to someone near them.

Take 5. Hand out copies of the "Other Adult Relationships" tracker page and allow a few moments for students to complete them.

Two-Minute Partners. Have students form partners. Using the asset definition or the quotation on the board, ask the partners to each spend a minute describing what the words mean to him or her. Or ask students to name and describe one person or pet in his or her neighborhood.

Preview. Tell students what they will do in this session. Make sure they have all necessary materials.

2. The Asset Question

Ask students one or all of the following questions to start a brief discussion:

★ If you were asked to give a shape to your neighborhood, what would it be? Is it a tall neighborhood? Or a flat, rolling neighborhood? Or an up-and-down neighborhood?

★ If you had to pick any color for your neighborhood, what would it be? Why?

★ What's the best thing about your neighborhood?

3. Before the Story

★ Why do we look at each asset through a *story?* Because stories show us common experiences with unique details. Lucia's move to a new place is a situation that happens all the time. But her specific story gives readers a look at how one person deals with this challenge. Encourage students to read (or listen) to learn what Lucia does about her difficulties. You may call students' attention to how we don't have to experience exactly what the story's character does to understand the point.

★ Before reading the story, give students the handout, "Puzzle: Advice for Making a Move." As you read to the students (or as they read the story), have them keep track of all the ways Lucia discovers to survive a difficult move. Have students write each solution on a puzzle piece.

Alternate Activity

As an alternate to the handout, ask students to tell you the problems Lucia was having in the first half of the story. Write the list on the board.

4. The Story

Read It. Read aloud and discuss Lucia's story on pages 43–44 and 54–55 of the student book. You may want to stop reading at the bottom of page 44 to talk about Lucia being upset because she misses a caring neighborhood.

Story Questions for Discussion. Ask students:

★ Why does it seem like Lucia has lost her "safety net" by moving to a new neighborhood?

★ When Lucia brings up the issues she's having in the new neighborhood, how does talking about it help her parents, too?

★ Have you ever been in a situation like Lucia's? How did you deal with it?

Optional Activity: Writing Skill

Free-writing. Tell students that writing is a form of thinking. Brainstorming solutions to problems usually starts with writing lists. In pairs, have students decide on a problem they notice in their classrooms and make a list of possible solutions.

Standards/Objectives Highlights	
Character Education	School recognizes parents' role, extended families, and immediate community in the moral upbringing of children
Health	Students demonstrate the ability to advocate for personal, family, and community health
Social Studies	Students describe how people create places that reflect cultural values and ideals
Language Arts	Students employ strategies as they communicate with different audiences for a variety of purposes
SEL Competencies	Students accurately perceive situations in which a decision is to be made and assess factors that might influence a person's response

5. Asset-Building Activities At-a-Glance

Read over the activities on pages 45–53 of the student book and decide which ones are most suitable for your students. *Suggestion:*

★ Keeping the focus on Lucia's situation, draw a graphic organizer like the one pictured here to help students organize their thoughts on Lucia's problems and solutions. Suggest students make a graphic organizer of their own for ways they can improve their neighborhoods or feel more at home in them.

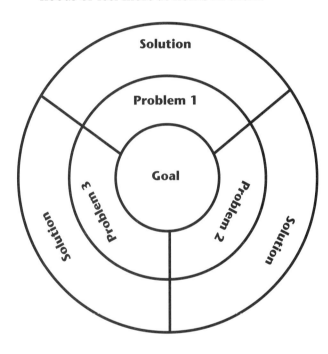

6. Session Activity

★ Hand out copies of "Map It!" Read aloud the introductory paragraph on the activity page and make sure everyone understands the "Map It!" activity. Display the completed maps in your classroom.

★ Draw students' attention to the sheet(s) of photos the student volunteers took of their neighborhood(s). Ask the volunteers to talk about how they went about taking the photographs and what the photos mean

to them. Tell students they will all have a chance to contribute photos of their own neighborhood(s).

★ Hand out copies of "Adding Assets at Home."

★ Over the next few weeks, have students take turns bringing home disposable cameras and taking photos of their neighborhoods. Have the pictures developed and add them to the sheet(s). Be sure to include a photo of your own neighborhood. When everyone has contributed a photo, have a "Neighborhood Festival" celebration. Take everyone in the group on a "virtual tour" of each other's neighborhoods, using the students' maps and photos. The festival is a good way for students to get to know their city or town.

7. Closing Question

Ask students: **What will you do to begin adding the Caring Neighborhood asset to your life?** If there's time, encourage responses. Give an example of using this asset in your own life. Suggest students share what they've learned about their own neighborhood and other neighborhoods in their city or town.

Preparation for Next Session

★ Make the book *People Who Care About You* available to students if you would like them to read ahead the story and/or activity ideas for the Caring School Climate asset (Session 5).

★ Be thinking about the idea or concept of "climate," or weather. In Session 5, you will be asking students to describe the climate *inside* a school or classroom. Keep track of the weather for a few days before the session to help you develop examples to offer students to provoke their thinking.

Puzzle

Advice for Making a Move

As you read or hear Lucia's story, keep track of all the ways Lucia discovers she can survive her difficult move. Write each solution on one of the puzzle pieces below.

Map It!

Draw the parts of your neighborhood that mean the most to you. Draw your route to school, to your friends' homes, to the store—wherever you go in a typical day. Then decide what part of your map you'd like to photograph. Use your own or the group camera to take this photograph.

library **park** **pizza** **movies** **school** **houses** **apartments**

Session 4

Caring Neighborhood

Today your child learned about the **Caring Neighborhood** asset. For your child, this asset means: *You have neighbors who know you and care about you.*

Your child heard a story about a girl moving to a new city. While the move was a difficult change for the story's character, your child saw that the girl in the story could miss her old neighborhood and, at the same time, look for ways to feel comfortable in her new surroundings.

Often it's the children in families who are the first to make acquaintances in new situations. Certainly, kids find other kids to play with on the same street, in the park, or at the corner store. Yet, kids also can notice a very elderly neighbor who sits in her window all day, or a friendly neighbor down the street who's always losing his cat, or the maintenance person who says a friendly hello. This asset builds on the natural openness in most children of this age.

Ideas and Activities to Try at Home

The Balancing Act. On the one hand, we want to encourage children to be friendly and helpful to neighbors. On the other hand, we need to teach children how to keep themselves safe. It's a balancing act we practice daily. Try these suggestions for making your neighborhood more caring for everyone.

★ Take a walking trip with your child around your neighborhood. Ask which places your child especially likes. Also ask your child to point out places that feel unsafe to him or her, and to tell you why he or she feels that way.

★ If possible, invite a different neighbor over for a meal once a month. The more people you know, the safer you'll all feel. Plus, neighbors who know your children are more likely to keep an eye out for them.

★ Model for your child ways to start conversations with neighbors. Try these "talk triggers" with a new neighbor or one you'd like to get to know better:

   ★ What do you like to do in your spare time?

   ★ What's your favorite thing about our neighborhood?

   ★ What things concern you most about the world today?

   ★ What would you like to do if you had more time?

★ Invite your child to come up with his or her own conversation starters.

Session 5: Caring School Climate

Backdrop

Write the name of the asset and its definition on the board.

> **Optional.** Write this quotation on the board: "Teachers open the door, but you must enter by yourself."—Chinese Proverb

Outcomes

★ to help students add the Caring School Climate asset to their lives

★ to help students identify ways in which teachers encourage them at school

★ to encourage students to have kind and supportive interactions with other students

Preparation

★ Be thinking about the idea or concept of "climate," or weather. In this session, you will be asking students to describe the climate *inside* a school or classroom. Keep track of the weather for a few days before the session to help you develop examples to offer students to provoke their thinking.

★ Make the thermometer for the "Checking the Temperature" activity (see page 46) to aid the discussion.

Materials

★ copies of the book *People Who Care About You*

★ copies of the "Caring Neighborhood" tracker page (from the CD-ROM)

★ copies of the "Power Role Model," "Adding Assets at Home," and "Family Grown-ups and School" handouts

1. Getting Started

Greeting. Have students say hello to someone near them.

Take 5. Hand out copies of the "Caring Neighborhood" tracker page and allow a few moments for students to complete them. Ask students if they feel any differently about their neighborhood(s) now that they know about the Caring Neighborhood asset.

Two-Minute Partners. Have students form partners. Using the asset definition or the quotation on the board, ask the partners to each spend a minute describing what the words mean to him or her.

Preview. Tell students what they will do in this session. Make sure they have all necessary materials.

2. The Asset Question

Ask students: **How do you figure out what the climate of your school is? Can you stick a thermometer in the front door to get a reading?** Ask a volunteer to read aloud the statement of what the asset means.

Have students name activities they are involved in at school—any in-class activities as well as after-school and Saturday activities. List the activities on the board.

3. Before the Story

Here's an activity for helping students think about what affects the "climate" within the school zone.

45

Checking the Temperature.

★ On the chalk board, white board, or large piece of paper, draw a large thermometer with either Fahrenheit or Celsius degree marks for freezing. Label the drawing "A Caring Thermometer." Create an exaggerated space between the above- and below-freezing markings. Label this space the "Help Zone."

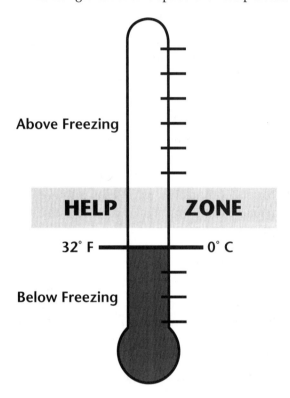

Above Freezing

HELP   ZONE

32° F ——— 0° C

Below Freezing

★ Ask students to name some positive experiences at school. Write their suggestions beside the thermometer's above-freezing zone. You can refer back to their list of school activities if they get stuck for ideas.

★ Next, ask students to volunteer some of the difficult experiences at school—such as being alone in the lunchroom or having trouble with schoolwork. Place these suggestions beside the thermometer's below-freezing zone.

★ Now discuss the kinds of help students need to get through difficult experiences and up into the above-freezing zone. List these ideas in the "Help Zone." Some suggestions may include friendliness from other students, peer and/or teacher help with homework, and becoming involved in a project with others in the group.

4. The Story

Read It. Read aloud and discuss Zach's story on pages 56–57 and 64–65 of the student book. You may want to stop reading at the bottom of page 57 to discuss what could be happening at Zach's school, or in his classroom, that would prompt the teacher to suggest a "welcome wagon." Keep the focus general since this story may not be

Standards/Objectives Highlights	
Character Education	School recognizes parents' role, extended families, and immediate community in the moral upbringing of children
Health	Students demonstrate the ability to advocate for personal, family, and community health
Social Studies	Students describe how people create places that reflect cultural values and ideals
Language Arts	Students employ strategies as they communicate with different audiences for a variety of purposes
SEL Competencies	Students understand that individual and group differences complement each other and make the world more interesting

signaling anything more than welcoming a new student. But the question may provoke students to begin thinking about their own school and class and how welcome each student feels. They may bring up examples of cliques or bullying. If they do, make time for this important discussion, or plan to discuss it at another time in the near future.

Story Questions for Discussion. Ask students:

★ Why do you think Zach was so well-liked at school?

★ Besides being friendly, what other skills does Zach have to be a good school guide to the new student?

★ What extra thing does Zach offer to do for Angie that shows he understands what it's like to be a new kid in school?

★ When Zach comes up with the Welcome Club idea for the whole school, what does he do that shows he'll probably be a good leader of this club?

★ Have you ever been the new kid at school? Or the tour guide? What was the experience like?

Optional Activity: Reading Skill

Activate Prior Knowledge. Explain to students that prior knowledge is what readers know about a topic from their own experience or reading. Ask if any students know how the "welcome wagon" idea started, or ask a small group to research it.

---

5. Asset-Building Activities At-a-Glance

Read over the activities on pages 58–63 of the student book and decide which ones are most suitable for your students. *Suggestions:*

★ Use the ideas in "Just Say Yes" (page 59) to talk about how joining school events helps kids feel more a part of the school. Try to elicit students' feelings about being shy or afraid of joining something and making mistakes.

★ Ask students how they would like to make their class and their school a more caring environment.

★ Ask students to give examples of how their parents help them with the extra activities they participate in at school.

★ Copy onto the board the "6 Ways to Be More Caring at School" (page 60). Ask students to give examples of how to put each "way" into action.

6. Session Activity

★ Hand out copies of "Power Role Model."

★ Read aloud the opening paragraph so all students understand what it means to be a role model.

★ Hand out copies of "Adding Assets at Home."

7. Closing Question

Ask students: **What will you do to begin adding the Other Adult Relationships asset to your life?** If there's time, encourage responses. Give an example of building this asset in your own life.

Preparation for Next Session

★ Make the book *People Who Care About You* available to students if you would like them to read ahead the story and/or activity ideas for the Parent Involvement in Schooling asset (Session 6).

★ Give students the "Family Grown-ups and School" handout. Students should complete the handout at home and bring it back for the next session. Call students' attention to the IMPORTANT note at the top of the handout. Make sure they understand that they are to complete it with a family grown-up.

Power Role Model

Did you know you are a powerhouse when it comes to influencing others at school? Being a good role model doesn't mean you have to be the best at everything or the smartest. It means being a leader by being a friend, or a person who calms people down, or someone who gets other kids laughing instead of fighting.

Role models influence others through their words and actions. Imagine yourself in these scenes at your school. How would you react? What would you say? How would you help people laugh or play together or solve a problem? Write about it here.

Scene 1: A student on the playground is bullying another student (with words). Before the scene turns into hitting or shouting, what can you do if no adults are around?

_____

_____

_____

Scene 2: A student drops a tray in the cafeteria. What can you do if you are sitting with a group of your friends and no one gets up to help?

_____

_____

_____

Scene 3: A substitute teacher can't remember anyone's name and doesn't know how to handle a small group of kids who are laughing and talking and not paying attention. What can you do?

_____

_____

_____

Scene 4: One student at the board in math class is taking a long time and can't seem to work out the problem. How can you help and not embarrass the student?

_____

_____

_____

_____

Caring School Climate

Today your child learned about the **Caring School Climate** asset. For your child, this asset means: *You get along well with teachers and other kids at school. You feel that school is a caring, encouraging place to be.*

The students discussed many ways to make their own school a more caring place. Parents and caregivers play an important role in helping children be practical about the ways they can help make school more caring. Start right at home—with ideas you and your child can put into action.

★ Talk about the adults your child notices at school who are especially caring. With your child, write a note of thanks to two or three of these friendly adults. Helping your child express gratitude can spread a sense of caring throughout a school.

★ Use opportunities to tell neighbors about the good things that happen at your child's school. Let your child hear you speak positively about the school. Help him or her learn to speak positively, too.

★ Nothing works better than setting a good example. When you can, try to get involved in parent-teacher organizations.

★ Learn about how your child's school works. (Sometimes you can learn about the politics and policies from other parents you know.) If your child experiences some difficulty at school, or if he or she is worried about how other kids play or behave, help your child by knowing who to talk with at school. Suggest that your child talk with that person, and offer to go along.

★ If your child likes to write, suggest writing an article for the school newsletter where he or she can express an opinion.

★ You may want to help your child, in fun and humorous ways, to raise or keep up a lively school spirit. Here are some suggestions to share with your child. In turn, your child might share them with a teacher or friends at school:

  ★ Decorate the hallways with school colors, pictures of the school mascot, and other school spirit inspiration.

  ★ Write a new school slogan, song, or cheer.

  ★ Design a school logo and put it on folders, posters, magnets, or T-shirts.

Remember, outside of your home, your child's school is the next most important environment.

Family Grown-ups and School

IMPORTANT: Do this worksheet with a family grown-up—a parent or other adult who cares for you in your home.

It's a good thing when parents and other caregivers are involved with the schools their kids go to. Maybe you already know this because one (or more) family grown-up is active in your school. Sit down together and talk about the ways your parent or caregiver is involved. Write them here:

_____

_____

_____

Many other family grown-ups often have lots to do and not enough time to get it all done. How can they fit in school stuff, too? First, you need to find out what keeps them busy. In the LEFT column, list the main things you think keep your parent/caregiver busy. Then ask this person to fill in the RIGHT column.

I think my parent/caregiver is busy with:	I am busy with:

Now think of ways you would like your parent/caregiver to be involved at your school. List them in the LEFT column. Then ask your parent/caregiver to respond in the RIGHT column.

I would like my parent/caregiver to:	I would like to:

Session 6: Parent Involvement in Schooling

> **What this asset means to the child:** Your parent(s) are actively involved in helping you succeed in school.

Backdrop

Write the name of the asset and its definition on the board.

> **Optional.** Write this quotation on the board: "When parents are involved in their children's education, kids do better in school."—National Education Association

Outcomes

★ to help students add the Parent Involvement in Schooling asset to their lives

★ to provide ways for students to invite their parents into the school setting

★ to find ways for parents to participate and to know what is happening at their child's school

Preparation

Remind students to bring the completed "Family Grown-ups and School" handout to this session. Check to see if they have read it over and jotted down ideas they had for their parents' involvement. See if they were able to have their parents or caregivers respond as well.

Materials

★ copies of the book *People Who Care About You*

★ copies of the "Caring School Climate" tracker page (from the CD-ROM)

★ students' completed "Family Grown-ups and School" handouts (see page 50)

★ extra copies of the "Family Grown-ups and School" handout for students who didn't complete theirs or remember to bring it back to the session

★ copies of the "Bringing School Home" and "Adding Assets at Home" handouts

★ homework folders (if students don't already have them, or extras for students who need them)

★ scissors, tape or glue

1. Getting Started

Greeting. Have students say hello to someone near them.

Take 5. Hand out copies of the "Caring School Climate" tracker page and allow a few moments for students to complete them.

Two-Minute Partners. Have students form partners. Using the asset definition or the quotation on the board, ask the partners to each spend a minute describing what the words mean to him or her.

Preview. Tell students what they will do in this session. Make sure they have all necessary materials.

2. The Asset Question

Ask students: **What are some ways your parents or caregivers are involved in school? Or, if they are very busy right now, what are ways you would like them to be involved?**

Begin a discussion of the "Family Grown-ups and School" handout and how students and their parents completed them. For students who didn't complete their handouts at home, or who didn't bring them back to the session, hand out extra copies and invite their comments and ideas.

51

3. Before the Story

Have a brief discussion-with-action. Ask volunteers to say and *show* what happens when they go home from school. Ask them to act out the scene. They may need some prompts such as: Do you ride the bus home? Do you get picked up after school or an after-school program, or do you go home by yourself? What does your parent say when you get home? What's your response? Do you talk first or go right to your room? What's the usual snack?

4. The Story

Read It. Read aloud and discuss Aisha and Grace's story on pages 66–67 and 77–79 of the student book.

Watching Others. At the bottom of page 67, stop and ask students what Grace is learning from Aisha. Talk about how Aisha talks to her mother and about the kinds of questions Aisha's mom asks both Aisha and Grace. Ask if anyone has learned something from their friends about how to talk with parents in ways that work. Ask them to share what they've learned.

Story Questions for Discussion. Ask students:

★ Why do you think it was important to Grace that she recognized Aisha's mother from school?

★ When Aisha's mom asked about the test on state capitals, Aisha put a lot of details in her answer. Why did the details matter?

★ Aisha's mom was good at organizing, so she offered to help Grace get organized. Is your parent particularly good at something you can use at school? What is it? Can you ask your parent to help you gain that skill?

5. Asset-Building Activities At-a-Glance

Read aloud some of the activities on pages 68–76 of the student book, or ask for volunteers to read them aloud. What activities appeal to the students? Some students may want to talk in small groups about how involved or not involved their parents are in school. Encourage students to talk together and share ideas about how to ask their parents to participate in school life. Caution students about being sensitive to one another's individual situations, especially with students whose

Standards/Objectives Highlights	
Character Education	School makes deliberate efforts to make values known throughout school and parent community
Health	Students demonstrate the ability to advocate for personal, family, and community health
Social Studies	Students describe ways family, gender, ethnicity, nationality, and institutional affiliations contribute to personal identity
Language Arts	Students use spoken and written language to accomplish their own purposes
SEL Competencies	Sudents use verbal and nonverbal skills to express themselves and promote positive and effective exchanges with others

parents can't be very available right now. Suggest students jot down in their notebooks some of the ideas and activities listed in these pages. Then they can check them off when they try them at home. These activities may include:

★ Bring home a copy of the class newspaper just for your parents.

★ Ask your parents to call or visit the teacher.

★ Find an activity or project that you really want your parents involved in, and show them you want them to participate.

★ Ask if you can hang the school calendar in a spot where everyone can see it.

★ Make a promise to yourself to bring home every school letter and also your work to show—even papers that didn't turn out so well.

6. Session Activity

★ Hand out copies of "Bringing School Home." Have students work alone or in partners or groups to make cover letters for their homework folders. Encourage them to share ideas for what to write in their letters.

Suggestions for students who have trouble getting started:

Dear [Mom, Dad, Mom & Dad, Grandma, or other family grown-up],

This folder contains VERY IMPORTANT PAPERS—my homework! Please look at them. I want you to know what I am doing in school. This is VERY IMPORTANT to me!

Thank you for taking the time to look at my homework.

Yours sincerely,
[your name here]

★ Hand out copies of "Adding Assets at Home." Remind students that their parents or caregivers want to know what is important to them—especially the events and issues that come up in school.

7. Closing Question

Ask students: **What will you do to begin adding the Parent Involvement in School asset to your life?** If there's time, encourage responses. Give an example of building this asset in your own life.

Preparation for Next Session

★ Make the book *Helping Out and Staying Safe* available to students if you would like them to read ahead the story and/or activity ideas for the Community Values Children asset (Session 7).

★ Visit the Web sites of national organizations that focus on mentoring, including Big Brothers Big Sisters of America *(www.bbbs.org)*, Boys & Girls Clubs of America *(www.bgca.org)*, Boy Scouts of America *(www.scouting.org)*, and Girl Scouts *(www.girlscouts.org)*. These organizations may be helpful to students who are looking for out-of-school activities or possible mentors.

★ Before the next session, see if any students are willing to talk to the group about an organization they belong to, what they do in it, and what they enjoy about it. Suggest students bring in items related to the organization, if possible (for example, brochures, badges, or special photos).

Bringing School Home

When adults send something to others they have written or read, they usually add something called a *cover letter*. A cover letter tells what the work is about and why the other person should look at the work.

Make a cover letter for your homework folder. Tell your parent or caregiver what's inside the folder (your homework!) and why he or she should look at it. You can use both words and pictures, if you like. When you're finished with your cover letter, cut it out and attach it to your homework folder with glue or tape.

Parent Involvement in Schooling

Today your child read and talked about the **Parent Involvement in Schooling** asset and how important you are to his or her life at school. For your child, this asset means: *Your parent(s) are actively involved in helping you succeed in school.* This is the last in a group of six assets called the **Support** assets.

It is fitting to end this support section with a session on parents' involvement, because this is what the support assets are all about—supporting children, giving them good examples, inspiring them, shielding them from harm. Parents are the first and foremost persons children count on—for support. In other words, building these assets in children is primarily an adult responsibility.

Here are some ways to stay connected to what your child is doing in school:

★ Join the parent-teacher organization at your child's school.

★ If possible, volunteer at your child's school—even if it's just in small ways.

★ Talk with your child about homework—ask specific questions about assignments and subjects to start and keep the dialogue going.

★ Post the school's calendar where everyone can see it. Use it to keep track of special events, and tests and assignments so you know what is going on at school.

Try one or more of the following suggestions for getting to know your child's teachers:

★ Speak with your child's teacher in person at least once a year.

★ Check in with the teacher by phone or email every other month.

★ Invite your child's teacher to dinner at your home.

★ Send occasional notes to your child's teacher, commenting on things you especially like about his or her teaching.

★ Try never to miss a parent-teacher conference. Reschedule if you miss one.

★ Try to attend events where your child's teacher is sure to be.

According to the National Education Association, "When parents are involved in their children's education, kids do better in school." Remember that anything you do—no matter how small it may seem—can make a big difference.

Helping Out and Staying Safe: The Empowerment Assets

★ The **Empowerment Assets** are **External Assets.**

★ **External Assets** are positive experiences kids receive from the world around them.

★ The **Empowerment Assets** are about helping kids feel valued and valuable, safe and respected. This happens when children have opportunities to contribute and serve, make a difference, and get noticed for their efforts.

The Empowerment Assets are:

7. Community values children—Child feels valued and appreciated by adults in the community.

8. Children as resources—Child is included in decisions at home and in the community.

9. Service to others—Child has opportunities to help others in the community.

10. Safety—Child feels safe at home, at school, and in her or his neighborhood.

Session 7: Community Values Children

> **What this asset means to the child:** You feel that adults in your community value you and appreciate you.

Backdrop

Write the name of the asset and its definition on the board.

> **Optional.** Write this quotation on the board: "Children are our most valuable natural resource." —Herbert Hoover

Note: Write the session backdrop quotation on the board when it is appropriate for your students. Always write the name of the asset and its definition on the board.

Outcomes

★ to help students add the Community Values Children asset to their lives

★ to help students realize they're valued by adults at home, at school, and in the community

★ to encourage students to treat each other more respectfully, and to acknowledge those who do this

Preparation

★ Visit the Web sites of national organizations that focus on mentoring, including Big Brothers Big Sisters of America *(www.bbbs.org)*, Boys & Girls Clubs of America *(www.bgca.org)*, Boy Scouts of America *(www.scouting.org)*, and Girl Scouts *(www.girlscouts.org)*. These organizations may be helpful to students who are looking for out-of-school activities or possible mentors.

★ A day or so before you begin this session, see if any students are willing to talk to the class about an organization they belong to, what they do in it, and what they enjoy about it. Suggest students bring in items related to the organization, if possible (for example, brochures, badges, or special photos).

Materials

★ copies of the book *Helping Out and Staying Safe*

★ copies of the "Parent Involvement in Schooling" tracker page (from the CD-ROM)

★ copies of the "And the Award Goes to . . . ," "A Good Reminder," and "Adding Assets at Home" handouts

1. Getting Started

Greeting. Have students say hello to someone near them in a way that shows appreciation. *Example:* "I'm glad I know you" or "You're a good friend."

Take 5. Hand out copies of the "Parent Involvement in Schooling" tracker page and allow a few moments for students to complete them.

Note: Make sure students know it's always appropriate to share feelings or an experience related to this asset or any other one. Sometimes, share your own examples as well.

Two-Minute Partners. Have students form partners. Using the asset definition or the quotation on the board, ask the partners to each spend a minute describing what the words mean to him or her.

Preview. Tell students what they will do in this session. Make sure they have all necessary materials.

2. The Asset Question

★ Ask students: **What happens when you get the feeling that an adult or older teen is disrespecting you or putting you down? How do you respond without causing conflict?**

★ Discuss how sometimes it can take a moment to realize someone has spoken rudely or disrespectfully to you. Even though the moment has passed, it's not too late to take action. Talk about what kids can do in such situations and how important it is to feel valued and respected. Talk honestly about how intimidating it can feel to approach adults or older teens and ask to be shown respect.

3. Before the Story

Talk more about something most kids can relate to: being disrespected, or "dissed." Have students role-play a situation in which someone older has disrespected them. Offer prompts such as: **Show with your body and face how this makes you feel. What do you say in return? What do you wish you *really* could say but are afraid to say? Are your words and actions different if the person is a parent, a teacher, or an older sibling?**

Note: Allow the story to be the central focus of each session.

4. The Story

Read It. Read aloud and discuss Jane's story on pages 6–7 and 17–18 of the student book. You may want to stop reading at the bottom of page 7, so you can talk about Jane's decision to pull back and avoid Angelica. Can students come up with ideas Jane could use right away that may lead to a real solution?

Story Questions for Discussion. Ask students:

★ Jane likes Angelica and looks up to her. Do you think this makes it easier or harder for Jane to talk about Curtis? Why?

★ Jane decides to stay away from Angelica's house because Curtis makes her uncomfortable. Have you ever done something like this? Did it help?

★ Sometimes people say something rude but then say, "I was just kidding" or pretend it was only a joke. Does this make their comments any less painful? Has someone done this to you?

★ When Jane finally tells Angelica about how Curtis has hurt her, Angelica doesn't take it very seriously. She says, "He's just being a guy." Is this fair or true? How does Jane help Angelica see what's really happening?

Standards/Objectives Highlights	
Character Education	School makes deliberate efforts to make values known throughout school and parent community
Health	Students describe how family influences personal health practices and behaviors
Social Studies	Students describe ways ethnic and national cultures influence daily lives
Language Arts	Students employ strategies as they write to communicate with different audiences for a variety of purposes
SEL Competencies	Students identify and understand the thoughts and feelings of others

★ What do you think of Angelica's idea for handling Curtis? Have you ever been in a situation where you're caught between two people you care about? What did you do?

5. Asset-Building Activities At-a-Glance

★ Choose a few of the activities on pages 8–15 of the student book or ask for volunteers to read them aloud. Talk about why it's important for adults to value children and vice versa. Students may want to share stories of people in their lives who appreciate and support them in a variety of ways.

★ Prompt students to think about the adults in their school, youth group, or faith community who are good advocates for them. Suggest that they list these people on paper. This may inspire them to to acknowledge these adult friendships.

★ Tell students that mentors are adults who value and appreciate kids. Mentors spend time with kids, guiding them and helping them. Share information about Big Brothers Big Sisters and other mentoring organizations. Invite students to talk about their mentors, whether these role models are family members or adults who are part of a mentoring organization. Allow a few moments for students to show and describe any materials they brought to class, such as brochures or photos.

A Note About Mentoring

Mentors have long been seen as an important resource for young people. MENTOR *(www.mentoring.org)* is a national advocate and resource for mentoring initiatives within the networks of state and local mentoring groups. According to MENTOR, "Although nearly 17.6 million young Americans need or want mentoring, only about 2.5 million are in formal, high-quality mentoring relationships." The goal of this nationwide organization is to close that gap and help kids who need mentoring most.

6. Session Activity

★ Hand out copies of "And the Award Goes to . . ." and "A Good Reminder."

★ Read aloud the opening paragraphs so all students understand the two handouts.

★ Hand out copies of "Adding Assets at Home."

7. Closing Question

Ask students: **What will you do to begin adding the Community Values Children asset to your life?** If there's time, encourage responses. Give an example of building this asset in your own life.

Preparation for Next Session

★ Make the book *Helping Out and Staying Safe* available to students if you would like them to read ahead the story and/or activity ideas for the Children as Resources asset (Session 8).

★ Ask students to come to the next session with a list of three ideas for a class party. Explain that you're going to plan a real party together, and you need their best ideas. These should be things that are possible to do in your classroom.

And the Award Goes to . . .

Many kids at school are recognized for their skills in sports, academics, or special activities. But other important qualities deserve recognition, too, like being willing to help others, being positive and friendly, and especially *not putting other people down*.

Do you know a student who's good at putting people UP? Someone who compliments other people and shows them respect? Finding someone who fits this description may be easy—or it may take a little detective work. To get started:

1. Think of someone in your class or grade who is often nice to others and seems to get along well with people.

2. Notice how this person acts and speaks. What does he or she do to help others feel good about themselves?

3. Jot down examples of how this student helps make your classroom or school a better place.

4. Make a list of the kind words (or "put-ups") you've heard this person use.

5. Fill in the award below or create one of your own to recognize this student. Give it to your teacher or group leader for a Student Recognition Award bulletin board.

Student Recognition Award

_____ is kind and respectful

to others.

For example: _____

_____

_____

★ **Thanks for helping others feel good!** ★

A Good Reminder

Have you ever heard of the Golden Rule? It means treating others the way *you* want to be treated. You probably like it when people smile at you, say hi, ask how you're doing, show you respect, and listen to what you have to say. And you probably *don't* like it when people ignore you, put you down, judge you, or act rude.

Every day, practice the Golden Rule. In the space below, write or draw a reminder for yourself that you can cut out and put where you can see it each day (such as your locker, bulletin board, mirror, or refrigerator).

Community Values Children

Today your child was introduced to the **Empowerment** assets. These assets are about feeling important and safe at home, in the neighborhood, at school, and within one's faith community. The first of these assets, **Community Values Children**, was the topic of today's session. For your child, this asset means: *You feel that adults in your community value you and appreciate you.*

The Community Values Children asset is about feeling valued and appreciated by adults such as parents, teachers, neighbors, coaches, and religious leaders—all of whom play a critical role in children's lives. Early on, children learn to appreciate those adults who are friendly and caring, and to distrust those who are not. As your child grows older, you'll need to continue to help him or her find supportive adults other than yourself, build relationships with them, and participate in community life.

Remember that you've been building this asset with your child for years, each and every time you've:

★ spent time talking with and listening to him or her

★ taken seriously what he or she has to say

★ exposed him or her to caring adults who truly value children

★ found neighborhood or community activities for your child to participate in

Ideas and Activities to Try at Home

Get Involved.

★ As a family, volunteer with a local charity or organization. Help in a soup kitchen, clean up a local park, or help take care of a neighborhood garden.

★ Attend a community event or fundraiser.

★ Organize a potluck or a picnic at a community park and invite other families from your neighborhood.

Set a Good Example.

★ Show that you value your child's friends by getting to know them better. Ask questions, listen, try not to judge.

★ Use positive language when you're talking about children and teenagers.

★ Volunteer in your child's classroom or special activities.

Session 8: Children as Resources

What this asset means to the child: You are included in decisions at home and in your community.

Backdrop

Write the name of the asset and its definition on the board.

> **Optional.** Write this quotation on the board: "The first step to getting the things you want out of life is this: Decide what you want."—Ben Stein

Outcomes

★ to help students add the Children as Resources asset to their lives

★ to give students opportunities to make decisions in the school or community environment

★ to encourage students to become more active decision-makers at home

Preparation

Ask students to bring a list of three ideas for a class party. Explain that you're going to plan a real party together, and you need their best ideas. These should be things that are possible to do in your classroom.

Materials

★ copies of the book *Helping Out and Staying Safe*

★ copies of the "Community Values Children" tracker page (from the CD-ROM)

★ copies of the "Decisions, Decisions!" "6 Tips for Terrific Family Meetings," and "Adding Assets at Home" handouts

1. Getting Started

Greeting. Have students say hello to someone near them.

Take 5. Hand out copies of the "Community Values Children" tracker page and allow a few moments for students to complete them.

Two-Minute Partners. Have students form partners. Using the asset definition or the quotation on the board, ask the partners to each spend a minute describing what the words mean to him or her.

Preview. Tell students what they will do in this session. Make sure they have all necessary materials.

2. The Asset Question

Ask students: **What have you enjoyed doing in this classroom or group that made it better?** This question will help students start thinking about how they are contributing to the success of the group. They can write their answer on paper and keep it to themselves.

3. Before the Story

Ask students to get out their lists of ideas for a class party. Have them work in small groups to decide which ideas to "pitch" to the rest of the class. Write the ideas on the board, then guide students to plan a party by choosing or voting on specific ideas and deciding who will do what. Have students form committees (decorating, refreshments, games, music, entertainment). Set a time and date for the party. Between now and then, check with students to see how their planning is coming along. Help out where needed. The party doesn't have to be a big deal, but it should be enjoyable for everyone.

4. The Story

Read It. Read aloud and discuss Kevin's story on pages 19–20 and 31–32 of the student book. You may want to stop reading at the bottom of page 20 to talk about the significance of Kevin realizing that adults planning the library renovation had overlooked a whole group of kids—the "in-between" kids like him (and the students in your classroom or group). Explain that Kevin can accept the way things are—or he can try to change them. What will he decide? Ask students: Has anyone ever had a good idea, but you decided to let it go because it seemed too hard to pursue?

Story Questions for Discussion. Ask students:

★ Why has the library grown so important to Kevin over the years?

★ What makes Kevin feel excluded? Can you relate to this feeling?

★ Why does Kevin's foster dad suggest that Kevin write down some of his ideas before going to the community meeting?

★ In addition to writing down his own ideas about the library, what else does Kevin do to gather resources?

★ It takes courage for Kevin to read his wish list at the community meeting. If you were in Kevin's place, how would you get up the nerve to speak in front of all those adults? How do you think you'd feel afterwards? Ask any students to share their own experiences with presenting ideas to adults.

Optional Activity: Brainstorming

Lists as a Way to Organize Thoughts. Discuss the ways in which Kevin's list helped him—to present clear ideas in front of a group, to write a letter to the editor of the newspaper, and to earn recognition from influential adults. Ask students to identify a problem at school, then brainstorm as a group some possible solutions. List them on the board, or have students list them. You might offer to share your students' ideas with the school principal.

5. Asset-Building Activities At-a-Glance

Read over the activities on pages 21–29 of the student book and decide which ones are most suitable for your students. *Suggestions:*

★ Ask students to talk about some of the ways they help out at home.

Standards/Objectives Highlights

Character Education	Students are involved in creating and maintaining a sense of community and in leadership efforts
Health	Students identify health-related situations that might require a thoughtful decision
Social Studies	Students identify examples of the rights and responsibilities of citizens
Language Arts	Students research issues and interests by generating ideas, questions, and posing problems; they communicate their discoveries
SEL Competencies	Students identify and cultivate strengths and positive qualities

★ Ask students if any have regular family meetings at home. Those who do can talk briefly about what happens during family meetings. Those who don't might discuss how they could go about starting family meetings.

★ Ask students if they want to change anything about their school or class. If so, form groups to discuss their ideas and come up with the steps to reach their goals.

★ If any students have events or programs they have helped organize in their neighborhood or faith community, ask them to describe how they worked together with the adults involved.

6. Session Activity

★ Hand out copies of "Decisions, Decisions!" Suggest students bring their handouts home to talk over with their parents. If they want, they can report back to the class about what happened.

★ Hand out "6 Tips for Terrific Family Meetings." Suggest students share this handout with their parents or other family adults.

★ Hand out copies of "Adding Assets at Home."

7. Closing Question

Ask students: **What will you do to start adding the Children as Resources asset to your life?** If there's time, encourage responses. Give an example of building this asset in your own life.

Preparation for Next Session

★ Make the book *Helping Out and Staying Safe* available to students if you would like them to read ahead the story and/or activity ideas for the Service to Others asset (Session 9).

★ Perhaps your students already participate in service clubs or projects at your school. If they don't, look around for appropriate opportunities. You might also ask your students for ideas.

★ Contact a high school in your area. Ask an administrator or teacher to recommend one or more students who are active in service clubs, as leaders or as participants. Arrange to have the student(s) visit your class.

Decisions, Decisions!

Who makes most of the decisions at home that affect you? It's probably your parents or other family grown-ups. As you get older, it's natural to want to make more decisions on your own. Maybe you're ready to start right now.

Make a list to organize your thinking. Then choose ONE decision you'd like to start making on your own. Talk with your parents and see what they say. Are you ready to show you're responsible enough to make that decision?

Decisions My Parents Make for Me

_____

_____

_____

_____

_____

ONE Decision I'd Like to Start Making for Myself

_____

_____

_____

_____

What I Will Do to Show I'm Responsible

_____

_____

_____

_____

6 Tips for Terrific Family Meetings

1. Set a starting time, ending time, and place for your meeting. ***Example:*** Every Thursday after dinner, from 7–7:30, at the kitchen table.

2. A few days before the meeting, put a piece of paper on the kitchen counter. Have family members write down things they want to talk about during the meeting. Bring the paper to the meeting. Use it as your *agenda*—your list of things to talk about and do.

3. Agree on a few simple ground rules in advance. ***Examples:*** Everyone gets a chance to talk. Everyone listens respectfully when someone else is talking. No whining or raised voices.

4. Decide on a leader for each meeting. Everyone should get a chance to lead—not just the grown-ups.

5. Take turns talking. You might pass around a "talking stick." The person holding the stick gets to talk without being interrupted. A talking stick can be almost anything—a chopstick, a ruler, a wooden spoon. Or your family might want to make a fancy decorated talking stick.

6. Try to end the meeting on time so it doesn't drag on and on.

Session 8

Children as Resources

Today your child learned about the **Children as Resources** asset. For your child, this asset means: *You are included in decisions at home and in your community.*

To better understand this asset, recall a time when, as a child, you were allowed to help plan a project or family event. How did you feel when the other planners listened to you, took you seriously, and helped bring your ideas to life? Most people feel energized and empowered after such an experience.

Our children may not yet be mature enough or have the skills to take on full leadership roles, but they can be part of decisions and plans—especially ones that affect them personally. This asset is not only about learning early leadership skills but also about giving young people *useful* roles. It asks us, as parents and caregivers, to put aside our usual desire to do things exactly our own—experienced—way. We can invite children to participate so they know we value *their* skills, interests, and opinions. This is not about "busy work"—it's about children feeling truly valued because they do *meaningful* work.

Children learn much of this at home, but as parents, you can help your child put these emerging skills to work at school, in the faith community, and in the larger community, too.

Ideas and Activities to Try at Home

★ Let your child teach you something—a new skill or hobby, a song, a shortcut or trick on the computer.

★ Use home projects to teach your child a skill. Build a birdhouse with a child who is interested in carpentry. Fix a bike with a child who likes to figure out mechanical things. Make clothes with a child interested in dolls or fashion.

★ Involve your child in the planning of a family reunion or party, a memorable birthday for an older relative, or a family vacation.

★ Instead of buying gifts for holidays and birthdays, ask your child to make something—or to create a gift certificate that can be exchanged for time or service such as mowing the lawn or two hours of baby-sitting. Let your child plan each step and take charge of the process.

Session 9: Service to Others

What this asset means to the child: You have chances to help others in your community.

Backdrop

Write the name of the asset and its definition on the board.

> **Optional.** Write this quotation on the board: "Service to others is the rent you pay for your room here on earth."—Muhammad Ali

Outcomes

★ to help students add the Service to Others asset to their lives

★ to inspire students to want to serve

★ to invite students to create a realistic plan for serving others

Preparation

★ Perhaps your students already participate in service clubs or projects at your school. If they don't, look around for appropriate opportunities. You might also ask your students for ideas. Have a list on the board for this session.

★ Contact a high school in your area. Ask an administrator or teacher to recommend one or more students who are active in service clubs, as leaders or as participants. Arrange to have the student(s) visit your class.

Materials

★ copies of the book *Helping Out and Staying Safe*

★ copies of the "Children as Resources" tracker page (from the CD-ROM)

★ copies of the "Paying My Rent" and "Adding Assets at Home" handouts

1. Getting Started

Greeting. Have students say hello to someone near them.

Take 5. Hand out copies of the "Children as Resources" tracker page and allow a few moments for students to complete them.

Two-Minute Partners. Have students form partners. Using the asset definition or the quotation on the board, ask the partners to each spend a minute describing what the words mean to him or her.

Preview. Tell students what they will do in this session. Make sure they have all necessary materials.

2. The Asset Question

Ask students: **What do you think Muhammad Ali meant when he said, "Service to others is the rent you pay for your room here on earth"? As human beings, why do we need to take care of others and our planet?**

3. Before the Story

Introduce the high school student(s) you invited to visit your class. Have them speak briefly about their service experiences—how they got started, what they do, and why they serve. Allow time for your students to ask questions.

4. The Story

Read It. Read aloud and discuss Kyoka's story on pages 33–34 and 44–45 of the student book. You may wish to stop at the bottom of page 34 to talk more about the specific sacrifices that might be required of Kyoka and her family if they choose to bring an Amity Scholar into their home.

Story Questions for Discussion. Ask students:

★ Why might Kyoka's family be a good candidate for hosting a student from another country?

★ What would it be like for you to bring someone new into your family—for a few months or an entire school year?

★ Mika wants to learn Spanish from the new student. In what other ways might Kyoka's family benefit or learn from the Amity Scholar?

★ Everyone laughed at the corny words Kyoka's father said. Why do you think it will help Kyoka's family to have a sense of humor when they bring the new student into their home?

Optional Question and Activity: Research and Reading Skills

Share Stories. There are all kinds of stories available about people—including children and teens—who are giving service to others. Perhaps you have resources in your classroom or school like *The Giraffe Heroes Program, It's Our World, Too!* by Philip Hoose, *Catch the Spirit: Teen Volunteers Tell How They Made a Difference* by Susan K. Perry, or *Build*

magazine, published by Do Something, Inc. (*www.dosomething.org*). Many stories are available on the Internet at the America's Promise Web site (*www.americaspromise. org*), the Points of Light Foundation Web site (*www.pointsoflight.org*), the Kids Care Web site (*www.kidscare.org*), and others. Have students locate stories they find inspiring— in books, magazines, or online. Have them share their stories with the group.

5. Asset-Building Activities At-a-Glance

Read aloud some of the activities on pages 35–43 of the student book or ask for volunteers to read them aloud. Which activities most appeal to students to try on their own, with a partner, or in a small group? *Suggestions:*

★ Make a list with their family about how their family can serve or volunteer.

★ Visit a volunteer center to learn what needs their community may have.

★ Start a service club if one isn't already available. (Do some of the investigative work by checking with administrators about the

Standards/Objectives Highlights	
Character Education	School sets expectations for moral action inside and outside of school
Health	Students describe how family influences personal health practices and behaviors
Social Studies	Students work independently and cooperatively to accomplish goals
Language Arts	Students develop a respect for diversity in language use across cultures
SEL Competencies	Students generate, implement, and evaluate positive and informed solutions to problems

steps required. Ask for reactions to the ideas offered on page 40 of the student book.)

★ Focus on one of the National Days of Service.

★ Visit the Web site for Kids Care *(www. kidscare.org)* and implement one of the suggested projects.

6. Session Activity

★ Hand out copies of "Paying My Rent." Read the first two paragraphs aloud and make sure everyone understands what to do. Refer students to the list of service opportunities you wrote on the board.

★ Hand out copies of "Adding Assets at Home."

7. Closing Question

Ask students: **What will you do to begin adding the Service to Others asset to your life?** If there's time, encourage responses. Give an example of building this asset in your own life.

Preparation for Next Session

★ Make the book *Helping Out and Staying Safe* available to students if you would like them to read ahead the story and/or activity ideas for the Safety asset (Session 10).

★ Gather materials on safety from various resources—your school office and media center, local police and fire departments, the public library, and wherever you have time to look. You can also find safety information on several Web sites including Safe Kids USA *(www.safekids.org)*, the Consumer Product Safety Commission's Kidd Safety site *(www. cpsc.gov/kids/kidsafety/)*, and FirstGov for Kids *(www.kids.gov/k_safety.htm)*.

Paying My Rent

Planning Sheet

"Service to others is the rent you pay for your room here on earth."—Muhammad Ali

Imagine that the great Muhammad Ali—boxer, champion, hero, humanitarian, winner of the Presidential Medal of Freedom, and one of the most famous people in the world—is speaking directly to you. He's standing in front of you, pointing his finger at you, and telling you to get out there and serve. You're totally inspired. You can't wait to start!

Make a plan to start paying your rent on our planet. This should be a *real* plan, not a fantastic or impossible one. Describe a service you would like to do right now. Be as specific as you can. If you want, you can invite a friend or two to join you—someone else who wants to serve. Then ask an adult for help—a parent, a teacher, a religious leader, a coach, or a mentor.

My Plan for Serving Others

_____

_____

_____

_____

_____

_____

_____

Service to Others

Today your child learned about the **Service to Others** asset. For your child, this asset means: *You have chances to help others in your community.*

Through its research, Search Institute has discovered that youth are more likely to grow up healthy when they serve others in the community one hour or more per week.

Children in elementary school are just beginning to broaden their sense of the world and are starting to see that not all families or neighborhoods are exactly like theirs. This is a good time to teach them the positive activity of reaching out and helping others. We know, and can introduce our children to knowing, how good it feels to help someone.

Ideas and Activities to Try at Home

Meet About It. Hold a family meeting to talk about the importance of helping others in the community. Think of ways the whole family—even the youngest members—can get involved. You might start by looking for ways to help in your child's school, in your neighborhood, or in your faith community. Doing one volunteer activity together may inspire you to try another, and another, until service to others becomes a regular part of family life.

Put It on the Calendar. You might choose one weekend day to help an elderly neighbor with errands, yard work, or household chores. Or set aside a couple hours during the week to gather items for a food shelf, pick up litter in the neighborhood, or walk dogs at an animal shelter. Make a point of putting these service activities on the calendar so you and your child can plan and look forward to them. Talk about your experiences afterward.

Remember Others in Small Ways. If you take your child to the park, invite a few neighboring children to join you. When you bake cookies, double the recipe so you can share them with neighbors. If you plan to run errands, offer to pick up classroom supplies for your child's teacher. Every little bit helps—and your child will see how helping others can become second nature.

Session 10: Safety

Backdrop

Write the name of the asset and its definition on the board.

> **Optional.** Write this quotation on the board: "Kids need to be safe."—Julie Nelson

Outcomes

★ to help students add the Safety asset to their lives

★ to help students recognize unsafe situations and seek adult help

★ to help students add the Safety asset for others

Preparation

Gather materials about safety from various resources—your school office and media center, local police and fire departments, the public library, and wherever you have time to look. You can also find safety information on several Web sites including Safe Kids USA *(www.safekids. org)*, the Consumer Product Safety Commission's Kidd Safety site *(www.cpsc.gov/kids/kidsafety/)*, and FirstGov for Kids *(www.kids.gov/k_safety.htm)*.

Materials

★ copies of the book *Helping Out and Staying Safe*

★ copies of the "Service to Others" tracker page (from the CD-ROM)

★ art materials for making posters—crayons, colored markers, magazines with pictures, tape, glue, poster board, scissors

★ copies of the "Poster Plan" and "Adding Assets at Home" handouts

1. Getting Started

Greeting. Have students say hello to someone near them.

Take 5. Hand out copies of the "Service to Others" tracker page and allow a few moments for students to complete them.

Two-Minute Partners. Have students form partners. Using the asset definition or the quotation on the board, ask the partners to each spend a minute telling how safe he or she feels in school and in the neighborhood. Give the safety a number on a scale from 1 to 10, with 1 being "very UNSAFE" and 10 being "very SAFE."

Preview. Tell students what they will do in this session. Make sure they have all necessary materials.

2. The Asset Question

Ask students: **Do you think kids need to be safe? Do you think kids *deserve* to be safe? Why?**

As students talk about the issue of safety, guide the discussion toward specific places or situations they consider to be unsafe.

3. Before the Story

Play a "What would you do if . . . ?" game. Ask questions like the following and discuss the answers. You might also invite students to ask "What would you do if . . . ?" questions for the rest of the group to answer.

★ **What would you do if a stranger called on the phone?**

★ **What would you do if you were home alone and someone knocked on the door?**

★ What would you do if you woke up in the middle of the night and smelled smoke?

★ What would you do if someone you were chatting with on the Internet asked you to meet him or her in person?

★ What would you do if you were walking home from school and a car pulled up next to you?

4. The Story

Read It. Read aloud and discuss Reggie's story on pages 46–47 and 59–60 of the student book. You may want to stop briefly at the bottom of page 47 and call attention to Reggie's belief that he *deserves* to be safe in his neighborhood.

Story Questions for Discussion. Ask students:

★ Reggie understands why his mom makes sure he stays in the house, so why does it bother him to stay inside where he's safe?

★ After Reggie talks with his mom about his fears and his safety, how does his mom deal with safety issues for Reggie?

★ A big asset for Reggie is having a parent who will help him in practical ways. What is Reggie learning from his mom?

★ What do you know about safety that you could tell Reggie?

5. Asset-Building Activities At-a-Glance

Read over the activities on pages 48–57 of the student book and decide which ones are most suitable for your students. If you suspect a child is excessively fearful, you may want to take the child aside and be the adult for that child to talk with, as suggested on page 52. *Suggestions:*

★ Ask the students if they discuss "What would you do if . . . ?" situations with their family. Are there additional situations the students know of and talk about?

★ Have volunteers demonstrate "Stop, Drop, and Roll."

★ Ask students: **How many of you think bullying is a problem at our school?** Ask for a show of hands. Have students write about what they mean. Say that you will not share their writing with other students. Explain the difference between *tattling* (telling on people to get them in trouble) and *reporting* (telling an adult about a problem that needs to be solved). Make sure they understand that it's right to report bullying problems to you.

Standards/Objectives Highlights

Character Education	School does not tolerate peer cruelty or violence
Health	Students identify how peers can influence healthy and unhealthy behaviors
Social Studies	Students apply knowledge of how to meet individual needs and promote the common good
Language Arts	Students use a variety of technological information resources to gather, synthesize, and communicate information
SEL Competencies	Students accurately perceive situations in which a decision is to be made and assess factors that might influence a person's response

6. Session Activity

★ Have students work in small groups to make safety posters for younger kids at your school. Hand out copies of "Our Poster Plan." Point students toward the materials on safety you gathered for this session. If your classroom has computers with Internet access, allow students to do some research on their own. Guide them to choose a topic appropriate for younger kids—school safety, playground safety, bike safety, sports safety, and so on. When the posters are completed, arrange to have your students present them to the younger kids. Remind your students that by making the posters, they are helping to add this asset for the younger kids.

★ Hand out copies of "Adding Assets at Home."

7. Closing Question

Ask students: **What will you do to begin adding the Safety asset to your life?** If there's time, encourage responses. Give an example of building this asset in your own life.

Preparation for Next Session

★ Make the book *Doing and Being Your Best* available to students if you would like them to read ahead the story and/or activity ideas for the Family Boundaries asset (Session 11).

★ Gather photos, illustrations, or other graphic images of everyday physical boundaries, such as fences, railings, seatbelts, and road signs. You will use them in the next session to show how useful physical boundaries are.

Poster Plan

The topic of our poster is: _____

_____

_____

_____

_____

_____

Safety tips to include on our poster: _____

_____

_____

_____

_____

_____

_____

_____

Art ideas for our poster: _____

_____

_____

_____

_____

_____

_____

_____

ADDING ASSETS AT HOME

Safety

Today your child learned about the **Safety** asset. For your child, this asset means: *You feel safe at home, at school, and in your neighborhood.* Even though the Safety asset is the last of the **Empowerment** assets, in many ways it is the foundation for all the others. Without safety, children can feel threatened and unable to protect themselves. This makes it difficult to feel valued, empowered, and important.

When our children feel safe, they're less likely to worry or act aggressive and more likely to get along with others. They feel more reassured and confident, which leads to an ability to take (safe) risks and dream big.

Ideas and Activities to Try at Home

Here are ways you can help your child feel safer at home, at school, in other people's homes, and in the community:

★ Let your child know it is your goal to keep him or her safe in every situation. Acknowledge your child's fears and worries, and discuss those feelings openly.

★ Help your child practice the safety skills needed in different situations (in the school hallways or restrooms, at the bus stop, in stores, in the neighborhood, and at friends' homes). Make sure your child knows basics such as the importance of wearing seatbelts and bike helmets, how to get adult help if being bullied at school, and why it is necessary to stay near you in parking lots, stores, and other community places.

★ Make sure every family member knows what to do in an emergency. Review "Stop, Drop, and Roll," for example, and have a plan of escape in case of a fire in your home. Teach your children how to dial 911 and what to say to the person who answers the call. The Safe Kids USA Web site has helpful home safety checklists. Visit the site together *(www.safekids.org)*.

Doing and Being Your Best: The Boundaries and Expectations Assets

★ The **Boundaries and Expectations** are **External Assets.**

★ **External Assets** are positive experiences kids receive from the world around them.

★ The **Boundaries and Expectations Assets** are about providing kids with clear rules, consistent consequences for breaking rules, and encouragement to do their best. Kids learn which activities and behaviors are "in bounds" and "out of bounds."

The Boundaries and Expectations Assets are:

11. Family boundaries—Family has clear and consistent rules and consequences and monitors the child's whereabouts.

12. School boundaries—School provides clear rules and consequences.

13. Neighborhood boundaries—Neighbors take responsibility for monitoring the child's behavior.

14. Adult role models—Parent(s) and other adults in the child's family, as well as nonfamily adults, model positive, responsible behavior.

15. Positive peer influence—Child's closest friends model positive, responsible behavior.

16. High expectations—Parent(s) and teachers expect the child to do her or his best at school and in other activities.

Session 11: Family Boundaries

What this asset means to the child: Your family has clear and consistent rules and consequences for your behavior. They keep track of you and know where you are all or most of the time.

Backdrop

Write the name of the asset and its definition on the board.

> **Optional.** Write this quotation on the board: "A child's conduct will reflect the ways of his or her parents."—Arnold Lobel

Note: Write the session backdrop quotation on the board when it is appropriate for your students. Always write the name of the asset and its definition on the board.

Outcomes

★ to help students add the Family Boundaries asset to their lives

★ to discuss with students the need for boundaries and expectations within their families

★ to identify and gain appreciation for how students benefit from clear and consistent family boundaries

Preparation

Gather photos, illustrations, or other graphic images of everyday physical boundaries, such as fences, railings, seatbelts, and road signs. Display them around your group's meeting area.

Materials

★ copies of the book *Doing and Being Your Best*

★ copies of the "Safety" tracker page (from the CD-ROM)

★ copies of the "A Silly Tale of a Child Who Would Not Follow Rules" and "Adding Assets at Home" handouts

★ paper and colored pencils, crayons, or markers

1. Getting Started

Greeting. Have students say hello to someone near them.

Take 5. Hand out copies of the "Safety" tracker page and allow a few moments for students to complete them.

Note: Make sure students know it's always appropriate to share feelings or an experience related to this asset or any other one. Sometimes, share your own examples as well.

Two-Minute Partners. Have students form partners. Using the asset definition or the quotation on the board, ask the partners to each spend a minute describing what the words mean to him or her. Or ask students to briefly describe one or two family rules they follow at home.

Preview. Tell students what they will do in this session. Make sure they have all necessary materials.

2. The Asset Question

Ask students: **Because families and home lives are all so different, how can we begin to talk about family boundaries? We may all have different rules about table manners, chores, homework, and behavior, for example. But even though the rules may differ, many of the reasons *behind* them are similar. Why do all families need rules? Who benefits? How? Try** to guide the discussion toward the *importance* of rules—how they keep us safe from harm or help us stay on our best behavior.

Note: You may want to reread "A message for you" on page 10 of *Doing and Being Your Best* to see if you need to address the topic of confusing rules—especially in families with divorced parents—with your student group or privately with any student.

3. Before the Story

Direct students' attention to the images of boundaries displayed around the room. Then have them work in small groups to brainstorm answers to these questions: **Why are boundaries important in life? What would happen if we *didn't* have boundaries?**

Remind students that brainstorming is about being creative, not about judging other people's ideas. Each group will need to appoint one student to (quickly) write down the ideas from the brainstorming. Afterward, display the notes the groups took during their brainstorming sessions.

Note: Allow the story to be the central focus of each session.

4. The Story

Read It. Read aloud and discuss Brandon's story on pages 6–7 and 17–18 of the student book. You may want to stop at the bottom of page 7 to talk about why Brandon feels like a "juggling ball."

Story Questions for Discussion. Ask students:

★ Why do you think Brandon's mom needs time away from him?

★ Do you think Brandon is better off being away from his mom for a while? Why or why not?

★ Why might it be hard for Brandon to deal with the rules at different relatives' homes? Do you think *adults* ever find it hard to make rules and stick to them?

★ When Brandon tells Aunt Tanya "nothing's wrong," she responds by saying, "Well, 'nothing' doesn't make this much noise. Let's talk about it." What do you think her tone is here? Why do her words help Brandon feel comfortable enough to talk? (If needed, try to help students see how Aunt Tanya's humor helps Brandon relax a little.)

★ What do you think would help Brandon believe Aunt Tanya when she says *many* relatives love him and his mom loves him, too?

Standards/Objectives Highlights

Character Education	School recognizes role of parents, extended families, and immediate community in the moral upbringing of children
Health	Students advocate for personal, family, and community health
Social Studies	Students describe ways family, gender, ethnicity, nationality, and institutional affiliations contribute to personal identity
Language Arts	Students apply knowledge of language conventions, media techniques, and figurative language to create and critique print and nonprint texts
SEL Competencies	Students achieve mutually satisfactory resolutions to conflict by addressing the needs of all concerned

5. Asset-Building Activities At-a-Glance

Read over the activities on pages 8–15 of the student book and decide which ones are most suitable for your students. *Suggestions:*

At home: Have you thought much about family rules?

★ Write about how *rules, privileges,* and *consequences* link together.

★ Would a "Family Rules Contract" help your family? Think about it, and then write some notes to yourself about how you might suggest it at home.

★ Start a list of rules you think your family needs to make your home run more smoothly.

At school and in the community: How do our family boundaries affect life *outside* the home?

★ Are there teachers or other adults at school whose opinions on family rules would be helpful? How about another grown-up you're close to?

★ On the school playground or in the neighborhood, do you sometimes act in ways you wouldn't want the adults in your family to see? What can you do to show that you *do* obey your family's rules, even when no family members are around? Write a "rules reminder" for yourself.

6. Session Activity

★ Hand out copies of "A Silly Tale of a Child Who Would Not Follow Rules."

★ Read aloud the instructions so all students understand what to do. Remind them of the brainstorming they did earlier about boundaries. Explain that it's sometimes easier to remember things if we do them in a silly way.

★ Circulate as students work, encouraging them to be as silly as possible.

★ Hand out copies of "Adding Assets at Home."

> **Optional Activity: Reading Comprehension**
>
> **Understanding Graphic Sources.** Students in grades 3–5 are beginning to understand complex graphic sources. They can see how pictures, charts, and maps are additional ways to understand what they're reading. Ask students to take another look at Brandon's story and focus on the illustrations—what do the pictures "say"? Have students write about how the illustrations add to or clarify the story.

7. Closing Question

Ask students: **What will you do to start adding the Family Boundaries asset to your life?** If there's time, encourage responses. Give an example of building this asset in your own life.

Preparation for Next Session

★ Make the book *Doing and Being Your Best* available to students if you would like them to read ahead the story and/or activity ideas for the School Boundaries asset (Session 12).

★ Gather rules that are used in your school or organization, such as rules written in a school handbook or displayed on posters.

A Silly Tale of a Child who Would Not Follow Rules

Your family may have a rule about cleaning your room. Imagine what might happen if you ignore the rule. Over time, your room fills up with trash, dirty clothes, and more until one day, the door is totally blocked and you can't even get out!

Or your family may have a rule about going to bed at a certain time on school nights. Imagine what might happen if you refuse to go to bed. You stay up all night. The next day, you fall asleep in school and snore so loudly that the people around you have to cover their ears.

Or your family may have a rule about how much TV you can watch. Imagine what might happen if you disobey the rule. You watch TV until you turn into a couch potato—a *real* potato.

Think of a few rules you have at home. Imagine the *worst* thing that can happen if you break them. Exaggerate. Be wild and crazy. Use the space to make notes and sketches—to brainstorm silly ideas. Then write a story about a character who goes to the extreme to break your house rules. Illustrate your story with silly pictures.

Family Boundaries

Today your child was introduced to the **Boundaries and Expectations** assets. These assets are about rules, consequences, and people who encourage children to do and be their best. The first of these assets, **Family Boundaries**, was the topic of today's session. For your child, this asset means: *Your family has clear and consistent rules and consequences for your behavior. They keep track of you and know where you are all or most of the time.*

In many ways, this asset boils down to the words of the popular expert on children and families, Dr. Benjamin Spock: "The main source of good discipline is growing up in a loving family, being loved, and learning to love in return." Love and good discipline can go hand in hand, especially when parents have clear expectations for their children.

Ideas and Activities to Try at Home

Set Boundaries/Have High Expectations.

★ Make your expectations *positive*. Say what you want, along with what you don't want. Whenever possible, start with a "do" instead of a "don't."

★ Be concise: State your family's rules in as few words as possible. Write them down; post them where your child can see them each day.

★ Be prepared to grow and change as your child does. You'll need to adjust the boundaries as your child gets older.

★ Follow the rules yourself. Be a role model. Admit mistakes.

When you notice the *good* things your kids do and praise them for it, positive behavior is reinforced. Soon your kids look for even more ways to please you, and life at home gets easier.

Have Family Meetings. When families meet on a regular basis to talk about rules and issues, everyone knows what's expected at home. This can lead to better communication and fewer arguments. During meetings, give each family member—the youngest ones included—a chance to talk. Keep it positive. You may want to end with a special cheer, handshake, motto, or prayer each time.

Session 12: School Boundaries

What this asset means to the child: Your school has clear rules and consequences for behavior.

Backdrop

Write the name of the asset and its definition on the board.

> **Optional.** Write this quotation on the board: "Students should be involved in the formation of classroom rules."—Edward Wynne and Kevin Ryan

Outcomes

★ to help students add the School Boundaries asset to their lives

★ to help students understand the reasons behind school rules and rights

★ to help students begin to be peer helpers and supporters of the rules

Preparation

Gather rules that are used in your school or organization, such as rules written in a school handbook or displayed on posters.

Materials

★ copies of the book *Doing and Being Your Best*

★ copies of the "Family Boundaries" tracker page (from the CD-ROM)

★ copies of the "Act It Out, Write It Out" and "Adding Assets at Home" handouts

1. Getting Started

Greeting. Suggest students say hello to someone near them.

Take 5. Hand out copies of the "Family Boundaries" tracker page and allow a few moments for students to complete them.

Two-Minute Partners. Have students form partners. Using the asset definition or the quotation on the board, ask the partners to each spend a minute describing what the words mean to him or her. Or ask students to describe which school or classroom rule seems most important to them.

Preview. Tell students what they will do in this session. Make sure they have all necessary materials.

2. The Asset Question

Ask students: **Who do you think should make the rules at school—teachers or students?** After students have offered their immediate responses, tell them they will have a short debate on that question.

3. Before the Story

Hold a Debate. Write on the board the two sides of the debate: *Side A:* Teachers have the authority, so they should set the school rules. *Side B:* Students have to *follow* rules, so they should be part of *setting* them.

1. Have students choose the side they'd like to represent (A or B). Make sure both sides have nearly equal numbers of students. You'll judge which team makes the strongest argument. If you'd like, choose one student to judge with you.

2. Give students about 10 minutes to figure out five good arguments that support their view.

3. Have each group select two students to represent their side. Hold the debate, allowing two minutes for each side to make their arguments. If there's time, allow rebuttals.

4. Leave time for the judges to evaluate the reasoning of each side.

4. The Story

Read It. Read aloud and discuss Lashondra's story on pages 19–20 and 29–31 of the student book. You may want to stop reading at the bottom of page 20 and ask students what they would do if they were in Lashondra's situation.

Story Questions for Discussion. Ask students:

★ What is an honor code? Does every school have one?

★ Why might two *good* students decide to cheat?

★ Why do you think it bothers Lashondra to see Amy and Brad cheating? How would you react if you saw other students cheating on a test or project?

★ What does Lashondra's stepdad say that helps her decide what to do?

★ Do you think Lashondra did the right thing? Why or why not?

★ Where have you found help when something doesn't go right at school?

5. Asset-Building Activities At-a-Glance

Read over the activities on pages 21–27 of the student book and decide which ones are most suitable for your students. *Suggestions:*

★ Ask students whose families have the school handbook at home (and know where it is) to check the rules or procedures.

★ If your school doesn't have a handbook, consider asking students to help you prepare a list or poster of the most important rules.

★ Suggest students make their own private "Trouble Tracker"—a journal just for themselves to track both trouble times and good times. Be available for students if they wish to speak with you; also suggest they may want to talk with their family about their journals.

★ Divide students into small groups to discuss rights, rules, and respect. Discussion starters may include: **Who has rights? How do rules help keep each person's rights secure? What does *respect* have to do with rights and rules?**

Standards/Objectives Highlights

Character Education	Students are involved in creating and maintaining a sense of community and in leadership
Health	Students practice good health behaviors and reduce risks
Social Studies	Students examine issues involving rights of individuals in relation to the general welfare
Language Arts	Students employ strategies as they write to communicate with different audiences for a variety of purposes
SEL Competencies	Students identify and understand the thoughts and feelings of others

★ Have students identify areas of the school where signs about rules might help: the lunchroom, the hallways, the gym? If time allows, students can make some signs.

Optional Activity: Research Skill

Peer Mediation. Ask students to find a definition of *peer mediation* (**example:** a process for resolving conflicts that uses persons of the same age). Besides solving problems, the process empowers students, helps the peer mediator earn the respect of others, and emphasizes the value of peaceful conflict resolution.

Have students report briefly on their findings, so that an understanding of peer mediation can underlie the session activity.

6. Session Activity

★ Hand out copies of "Act It Out, Write It Out."

★ Read aloud the steps so all students understand the role playing scenarios. Encourage them to adapt the situations to fit their own school settings.

★ Depending on the size of the group and the space you have, students can role-play and work in small groups. If the space is small, role-play as one group.

★ It's important that students write two responses to each role playing scenario—first, to jot down their immediate reactions to the scene; second, to write a more thoughtful response about their group's resolution to the conflict.

★ Hand out copies of "Adding Assets at Home."

7. Closing Question

Ask students: **What will you do to start adding the School Boundaries asset to your life?** If there's time, encourage responses. Give an example of building this asset in your own life.

Preparation for Next Session

★ Make the book *Doing and Being Your Best* available to students if you would like them to read ahead the story and/or activity ideas for the Neighborhood Boundaries asset (Session 13).

★ Read *The Three Little Pigs* and have on hand a copy of the story.

Act It Out, Write It Out

For each role playing scenario, follow these steps:

1. Read the scenario. Choose students to role-play the situation.

2. Watch and write. After students finish the role play, write your reaction to the conflict. What emotions do you feel? What rules do you think were broken?

3. Within your group, discuss the best ways to resolve, or handle, the conflict.

4. Write what you think about the resolution your group came up with.

5. If your group is on a "roll," create your own scenarios to act out! You can even make up situations that fit your particular school or group setting.

Role-Play This Scenario: Hilary overhears Kyle and his best friend Girard talking about how they copy each other's homework and never get in trouble for it because their teachers don't know. Hilary confronts them about what she heard, but the two boys deny they ever said such a thing.

(A) Write your reaction: _____

_____

_____

(B) Write what you think of your group's resolution: _____

_____

_____

Role-Play This Scenario: As Jamal writes a story at his desk, he looks up at the board for a minute. That's when Skye reaches over, grabs Jamal's paper, and tosses it to a friend, laughing. Jamal stands up and grabs Skye's arm. Just then, the teacher looks up and sees Jamal grab Skye. What should Jamal do?

(A) Write your reaction: _____

_____

_____

(B) Write what you think of your group's resolution: _____

_____

_____

Session 12

School Boundaries

Today your child learned about the **School Boundaries** asset. For your child, this asset means: *Your school has clear rules and consequences for behavior.*

Your child was introduced to the concept of a "Trouble Tracker"—a journal where students can list occasions when they get into trouble during class or at school, as well as times when things are going well. If your child chooses to continue using this sort of tracker, ask him or her to share it with you.

It's important that children learn respect for rules and good behavior. Such respect comes easier if children understand the *reason* for rules. As educator Alfie Kohn says: "To help students become ethical people, as opposed to people who merely do what they are told, we cannot merely tell them what to do. We have to help them figure out—for themselves and with each other—how one ought to act."

Ideas and Activities to Try at Home

Helpful Hints.

★ Get a copy of the school rules and go over them with your child.

★ Learn about your child's classroom rules and the teacher's expectations.

★ Get involved in a parent-teacher policy organization.

★ If your child has difficulty following the rules, stay calm and work toward peaceful solutions.

Arrange a School Visit. See for yourself what the boundaries are at school and how well they work. Here are some questions to ask yourself as you observe:

★ What's your overall opinion of how students behave?

★ How do teachers and students interact? What about school administrators and volunteers who help on the playground or in the lunchroom—how do they interact with students?

★ If you see a conflict, check out how it is resolved.

★ How do the school rules fit with the rules you have at home?

Session 13: Neighborhood Boundaries

> **What this asset means to the child:** Your neighbors keep an eye on kids in the neighborhood.

Backdrop

Write the name of the asset and its definition on the board.

> **Optional.** Write this quotation on the board: "There is no such thing as other people's children."—Hillary Rodham Clinton

Outcomes

★ to help students add the Neighborhood Boundaries asset to their lives

★ to invite students to identify those neighbors they can trust and count on

★ to help students recognize ways in which they can help keep their neighborhood safer and cleaner

Preparation

Read *The Three Little Pigs* and have on hand a copy of the story.

Materials

★ copies of the book *Doing and Being Your Best*

★ copies of the "School Boundaries" tracker page (from the CD-ROM)

★ copies of the "Neighborhood Notes," "Three Little Pigs," and "Adding Assets at Home" handouts

1. Getting Started

Greeting. Have students say hello to someone near them.

Take 5. Hand out copies of the "School Boundaries" tracker page and allow a few moments for students to complete them.

Two-Minute Partners. Have students form partners. Using the asset definition or the quotation on the board, ask the partners to each spend a minute describing what the words mean to him or her.

Preview. Tell students what they will do in this session. Make sure they have all necessary materials.

2. The Asset Question

Ask students: **What's your neighborhood like? Do you know your neighbors? Do they know you? What kinds of activities take place in your neighborhood?** Try to guide the discussion toward finding out what's similar and/or unique about each child's neighborhood.

3. Before the Story

Hand out "Neighborhood Notes" and ask students to fill in the questions. Let everyone know it's okay if they don't know much about what goes on in their neighborhoods. The purpose of this asset is to discover new ways of learning about our neighbors and communities. Have students keep their finished handouts. They may want to refer to them later in the session.

4. The Story

Read It. Read aloud and discuss Rostam's story on pages 32–33 and 42–43 of the student book. You may want to stop at the bottom of page 33 to ask students why Rostam has such mixed feelings about going to a neighborhood meeting, even though he generally likes his neighbors.

Story Questions for Discussion. Ask students:

★ It's not surprising Rostam would rather go skateboarding than to a neighborhood meeting, so why do you think his mom gives him "the look" and coaxes him to go to the meeting? Why isn't this meeting just for adults? Why is it important for Rostam, too?

★ Why does it bother Rostam that his neighbors look after him and ask him questions? Why do the neighbors act that way toward the kids they know?

★ Do you think rules and curfews should be discussed at neighborhood meetings? Why or why not?

★ What do you think the neighbors would tell Rostam if he asked them to give him more privacy?

★ Do you have a neighbor like Mr. Lee? In what way?

Optional Activity: Reading Skill

Drawing Conclusions. Drawing conclusions means thinking about facts and details in order to decide something about them. Ask students to draw a conclusion—by listing facts and details from Rostam's story—about how Rostam might act and participate in his neighborhood meeting.

5. Asset-Building Activities At-a-Glance

Read aloud some of the activities on pages 34–40 of the student book, or ask for volunteers to read them aloud. What activities seem like things students may already do or would like to try to do in their neighborhoods? Ask volunteers to mention some of the activities they would like to try. These may include:

★ Notice neighbors, greet them, and offer to lend a hand.

★ Watch the younger kids in the neighborhood more carefully to help them stay safe.

★ Ask family grown-ups to join a neighborhood watch program as a way to report suspicious incidents.

★ Copy the "4 Basic Neighborhood Boundaries" from page 39 and hang them up at home.

★ Respect the rules at other people's homes.

Standards/Objectives Highlights	
Character Education	School sets expectations for moral action inside and outside school
Health	Students describe how the school and community can support personal health practices and behaviors
Social Studies	Students use causality, change, conflict, and complexity to explain change and show connections
Language Arts	Students develop an understanding of and respect for diversity in language across cultures and ethnic groups
SEL Competencies	Students assume personal responsibility by recognizing their obligation to engage in ethical, safe, and legal behaviors

★ With a family member's help, fill in any unanswered sections on the "Neighborhood Notes" handout.

6. Session Activity

★ Read *The Three Little Pigs* story aloud to students.

★ Pass out copies of the "Three Little Pigs" handout.

★ Read aloud the instructions so all students understand they'll be writing about the three little pigs as if they were real residents of their neighborhoods.

★ Circulate as students work, encouraging them to see the pigs and their situations as if they were real neighbors.

★ Hand out copies of "Adding Assets at Home."

7. Closing Question

Ask students: **What will you do to begin adding the Neighborhood Boundaries asset to your life?** If there's time, encourage responses. Give an example of building this asset in your own life.

Preparation for Next Session

★ Make the book *Doing and Being Your Best* available to students if you would like them to read ahead the story and/or activity ideas for the Adult Role Models asset (Session 14).

★ Gather photographs and/or information about historical and contemporary heroes.

Neighborhood Notes

1. What's your neighborhood like? Describe it. Tell what you like and don't like about it.

_____

_____

2. Do people in your neighborhood know you? Name two or three people who would recognize you when you're out in your neighborhood.

_____

_____

3. Name two or three neighbors you can trust and count on—people you could go to if you needed help.

_____

_____

4. What activities go on in your neighborhood?

For fun: _____

_____

_____

For people who need help:_____

_____

For safety:_____

_____

5. Think of places in your neighborhood where there are fences, brick walls, or gates. Describe why those boundaries are there.

_____

_____

Three Little Pigs

in Your Neighborhood

Imagine that the three little pigs have just moved into your neighborhood. They're building houses. They're trying to fit in and get along. They don't know anything about your neighborhood. How will you help them?

You can see that the house of straw and the house of sticks won't be safe after they're built. Even if the wolf doesn't blow them down, either one could easily fall over in a strong wind. If it rains, both houses will leak. What can you do?

_____

_____

_____

_____

_____

You're watching the third little pig work hard to make his house as sturdy as can be. How might you lend a hand? How might the little pig feel if you offer to help?

_____

_____

_____

_____

If the wolf comes, it won't just be a problem for the pigs. It will also be a danger for everyone else in the neighborhood. What can you and your neighbors do to guard against the wolf?

_____

_____

_____

_____

_____

Session 13

Neighborhood Boundaries

Today your child was introduced to the **Neighborhood Boundaries** asset. For your child, this asset means: *Your neighbors keep an eye on kids in the neighborhood.* The students spent some time thinking about how important it is to have grown-ups in their neighborhood they can trust and who look out for their best interests. Do the adults in your neighborhood watch out for the kids? Do you and your child know your neighbors? Do neighbors work together to make the community safer and more fun?

Talk to your child about the people in your neighborhood who you know and trust. Ask your child which neighbors seem friendly and welcoming—and which ones don't. Remind your child about safety, as well as what it means for an adult to "look out for" him or her.

A caring community is a healthy community. You can do your part to make your neighborhood a more caring place simply by being friendly. Take interest in the people around you, and show your child what it means to be a good neighbor.

Ideas and Activities to Try at Home

Review the Rules.

★ Take a walk with your child to point out the safety issues in your neighborhood. Notice fences, signs, and other boundaries, and remind your child what each of them means.

★ Ask your local police department to help organize a neighborhood watch meeting to discuss neighborhood safety.

★ Suggest a parent get-together, with older kids supervising the younger ones. Talk about safety issues, rules, curfews, and neighborhood boundaries.

Relax with Your Neighbors.

★ Introduce your child to new neighbors. Invite them for a gathering at your home.

★ Spend time with your child at a local park or community center so you both can get to know more people.

★ Smile and wave when you see your neighbors. Help your child practice doing the same.

★ Have a block party. Invite your neighbors to an outdoor barbecue or a potluck dinner.

★ Organize a "dog day out." Invite all dog owners to walk their dogs together once a week.

Session 14: Adult Role Models

What this asset means to the child: The adults in your family behave in positive, responsible ways. They set good examples for you to follow. So do other adults you know.

Backdrop

Write the name of the asset and its definition on the board.

> **Optional.** Write this quotation on the board: "Really great people make you feel that you, too, can become great."—Mark Twain

Outcomes

★ to help students add the Adult Role Models asset to their lives

★ to help students learn to distinguish between real role models and celebrities

★ to help students recognize the adult role models they have in their lives (or how to seek out positive role models)

Preparation

Gather photographs and/or information about historical and contemporary heroes. Have them out and available for students to look at before the session begins and during the session activity.

Materials

★ copies of the book *Doing and Being Your Best*

★ copies of the "Neighborhood Boundaries" tracker page (from the CD-ROM)

★ copies of the "My World of Role Models" and "Adding Assets at Home" handouts

★ colored pencils, markers

1. Getting Started

Greeting. Have students say hello to someone near them.

Take 5. Hand out copies of the "Neighborhood Boundaries" tracker page and allow a few moments for students to complete them.

Two-Minute Partners. Have students form partners. Using the asset definition or the quotation on the board, ask the partners to each spend a minute describing what the words mean to him or her. Or ask students to describe one adult role model in their lives.

Preview. Tell students what they will do in this session. Make sure they have all necessary materials.

2. The Asset Question

Ask students: **Is an adult role model a kind of hero? Why or why not? What do you think are the differences (if any) between heroes, role models, and celebrities like sports stars, rock stars, rappers, and actors?**

3. Before the Story

★ As a group, talk about *real* heroes—what does *hero* mean? Do heroes have to save lives? Be famous? Or be adults? Help students draw conclusions by guiding the discussion toward "everyday" heroes who make a real and lasting difference in people's lives—without necessarily getting famous for it.

★ Next, make two columns on the board, giving one the heading "Heroes" and the other "Celebrities." Ask students to call out the names of some famous people—past and present—and tell you in which column to write the name. Let students pinpoint the differences in the lists; soon they'll see that heroes often give back to society in some way and many have had to overcome difficulties in their lives. Celebrities may not always fit that description (though some do).

4. The Story

Read It. Read aloud and discuss Tameka's story on pages 44–45 and 54–55 of the student book. You may want to stop reading at the bottom of page 45 to talk about why Tameka has doubts about herself when she looks at her mother.

Story Questions for Discussion. Ask students:

★ Why is it so special that Tameka's mom is graduating at the same time as Tameka?

★ Why do you think it's hard for Tameka to tell her mom about her fears?

★ Why do you think Tameka is a role model for her mother? How can a child be a role model to someone who's older and more experienced in life?

★ Describe all the role models in this story. Who does Tameka's mom call "a strong woman"? Even though the story doesn't say so directly, do you think Tameka's dad is a role model? Why?

5. Asset-Building Activities At-a-Glance

Read over the activities on pages 46–52 of the student book and decide which ones are most suitable for your students. Or choose one or several of the following activities for your students to try:

At home: Who do you look up to?

★ With a partner or with the group, discuss any qualities you admire in family members (parents, relatives, siblings, cousins).

★ Make a list of positive qualities you see in your family members. You can take the list home and share it with those family members to show your appreciation.

At school: Who's your role model? Are you one yourself?

★ Think about these questions: How does a person gain wisdom and the ability to make a difference in the world? Do any of the adults around you (at school or in the group setting) try to make a difference? If so, how?

★ Review "6 Ways to Be a Good Role Model" (page 48). Do any of your actions match the ones described?

Standards/Objectives Highlights	
Character Education	School provides opportunities for moral action in the larger community
Health	Students demonstrate the ability to use interpersonal communication skills to enhance health and avoid or reduce health risks
Social Studies	Students describe interactions of people with institutions
Language Arts	Students use a variety of information resources to gather and synthesize information
SEL Competencies	Students use verbal and nonverbal skills to express themselves and promote positive and effective exchanges with others

★ It's likely that many adult role models were once kid role models. Imagine yourself growing up to be a role model. What could you be doing *now* to get ready for this "role"?

6. Session Activity

★ Hand out copies of "My World of Role Models."

★ Read aloud the instructions so all students understand they'll be placing their personal role models onto their own illustrated globe, as well as creating a corresponding "legend" (or map key).

★ Circulate as students work, encouraging them to think of everyday heroes in their own lives as well as famous heroes.

★ Hand out copies of "Adding Assets at Home."

7. Closing Question

Ask students: **What will you do to start adding the Adult Role Models asset to your life?** If there's time, encourage responses. Give an example of building this asset in your own life.

Preparation for Next Session

★ Make the book *Doing and Being Your Best* available to students if you would like them to read ahead the story and/or activity ideas for the Positive Peer Influence asset (Session 15).

★ Collect cartoons and comic strips that show friends interacting (*examples:* "Peanuts," "Baldo," "Nancy"). Choose those that illustrate lessons of friendship, positive peer influence, and peer pressure.

My World of Role Models

Ask yourself two things: (1) What qualities are important for role models to have? (***Examples:*** kindness, humor, and bravery.) (2) Where are role models found? (***Examples:*** at home, at school, in the news, and in books.)

Below, "map" your role models. First create your map's "legend," or key, describing the qualities a role model should have. Next to each quality, create a symbol. For example, if you think a role model should be a peacemaker, put a peace symbol next to that word. If you think a role model should be funny, use a smiley face. If a role model should be caring, you could use a heart as your symbol.

Next, fill in your globe by showing *where* you might find those role models. You can show what country or region they come from, or draw a small image of your neighborhood or school, or illustrate book covers with titles. Anything goes! Label each location with the name of the role model who belongs there. Add one or more symbols beside each name to link the role models to your "legend." You can keep your world of role models for yourself or share it with your group or family.

Legend

My World

Adult Role Models

Today your child learned about the **Adult Role Models** asset. For your child, this assets means: *The adults in your family behave in positive, responsible ways. They set good examples for you to follow. So do other adults you know.* Most importantly, the grown-ups at home consistently show this quality. You are your child's most important role model. That makes you a hero in his or her life.

Ideas and Activities to Try at Home

Reminders for Parent Role Models.

★ You are your child's most important role model. Treat your child with love and respect.

★ It's important to spend time together often. Find ways to be involved in your child's life on a daily basis, even if you don't see each other every day.

★ When you make a mistake, admit it. Model appropriate behavior for your child, even during difficult times.

★ Share with your child who your role models were when you were growing up. Talk about who your role models are today and why you look up to them.

Most parents know they're very lucky if there's at least one other adult—a relative, a teacher, a friend of the family—who serves as a role model or mentor for their child. These adults become everyday heroes, improving the lives of the children they care about. If your child knows a grown-up like this, she's lucky. But then so is the grown-up, for in the words of the famous anthropologist Margaret Mead: "Adults need children in their lives to listen to and care for, to keep their imaginations fresh and their hearts young." Whether young or old, we all have much to learn and give.

Questions to Ask About Your Child's Heroes.

★ Of the adults in your life, who are your role models? Why?

★ What have you learned from these adults that has helped or inspired you?

★ Is there a grown-up you admire who you'd like to get to know better?

★ What famous people do you look up to? What qualities do they have that make them good role models?

Then, after asking the questions, remember that a hero really listens.

Session 15: Positive Peer Influence

> **What this asset means to the child:** Your best friends behave in positive, responsible ways. They are a good influence on you.

Backdrop

Write the name of the asset and its definition on the board.

> **Optional.** Write this quotation on the board: *"Aquellos son ricos que tienen amigos. When there are friends, there is wealth."*—Spanish proverb

Outcomes

★ to help students add the Positive Peer Influence asset to their lives

★ to give students practice in building skills needed to solve friendship problems

★ to encourage students to be a positive influence on their peers

Preparation

Collect cartoons and comic strips that show friends interacting (*examples:* "Peanuts," "Baldo," "Nancy"). Choose those that illustrate lessons of friendship, positive peer influence, and peer pressure. Display them around the room. These images can help spark discussion and ideas for the session activity.

Materials

★ copies of the book *Doing and Being Your Best*

★ copies of the "Adult Role Models" tracker page (from the CD-ROM)

★ copies of the "Funny Pages," "Cartoon Starters," and "Adding Assets at Home" handouts

★ colored pencils or markers, scissors, glue, large sheets of construction paper

1. Getting Started

Greeting. Suggest students say hello to someone near them.

Take 5. Hand out copies of the "Adult Role Models" tracker page and allow a few moments for students to complete them.

Two-Minute Partners. Have students form partners. Using the asset definition or the quotation on the board, ask the partners to each spend a minute describing what the words mean to him or her. If you wish, ask a volunteer to read both the Spanish and English versions of the proverb. You may want to ask students what the term "wealth" means in the context of the quote.

Preview. Tell students what they will do in this session. Make sure they have all necessary materials.

2. The Asset Question

Share with students the words of Ralph Waldo Emerson: "The only way to have a friend is to be one." Then ask: **When is it easy and when is it hard to be a friend to someone?** Allow a brief discussion.

3. Before the Story

"Friendship Trouble" Role Play. Choose two students to act out a scene in which two friends have just had an argument. They're both angry, and one says to the other: "Fine! Then you're not invited to my birthday party!" The other one responds with: "Well, if that's the way you want to be about it, then we're not friends anymore!" Encourage students to really get into their roles; their tone of voice and gestures (folded arms, clenched fists) should show anger.

Ask the group if they've ever been in a situation like this and what might be the best way to handle it. Lead them through the process of resolving the problem peacefully. *Example:*

1. First, the friends need to calm down. How might they do this? Suggest taking deep breaths or taking a brief timeout. Have them change their body language to reflect a calmer state.

2. Next, the friends could think about the *value* of their friendship. (Remind them of the "wealth" discussion you had earlier, if you'd like.) Is any argument worth the loss of a friendship?

3. Talk about what the friends could say to each other to resolve the conflict. Point out that, usually, someone has to be brave enough to make the first move. That person might say "I didn't mean what I just said" or "This argument is dumb, can we make up?"

4. Finally, both people involved in the conflict should apologize—and mean it. Have the role players say they're sorry to each other, and even smile and shake hands.

5. Talk about how some conflicts may require adult help. Have the students discuss who to go to for assistance.

4. The Story

Read It. Read aloud and discuss Alvero's story on pages 56–57 and 67–68 of the student book. You may want to stop reading at the bottom of page 57 to talk about the question on Alvero's mind: "How long is this going to keep up?" Ask students if they think Alvero will tell his friend Tanner that his behavior bothers him.

Story Questions for Discussion. Ask students:

★ Why doesn't Alvero help Bobby when Tanner trips him?

★ What does Tanner seem to get out of being mean to Bobby?

★ Why do you think Bobby doesn't say anything, even though Tanner teases him day after day?

★ How does Julia's comment affect Alvero? Why does her opinion matter so much to him? Do you think it plays a big part in what happens next?

★ What words have you used that have helped to settle a problem with a friend?

Standards/Objectives Highlights

Character Education	School tolerates no peer cruelty or violence
Health	Students encourage others to make positive health choices
Social Studies	Students describe the role of technology in communication as it helps resolve conflicts
Language Arts	Students apply strategies to interpret texts; they draw on prior experience and on their knowledge of word meaning and of context and graphics
SEL Competencies	Students believe that others deserve to be treated with kindness and compassion and feel motivated to contribute to the common good

5. Asset-Building Activities At-a-Glance

Read over the activities on pages 58–65 of the student book and decide which ones are most suitable for your students. *Suggestions:*

★ Have students write down names of friends they have in various communities — neighborhood, school, clubs and sports, faith community. If you wish, have them write a *positive* word or two to describe each friend. Suggest they keep this list private and they hold onto it, adding friends' names and descriptions as they think of them or meet new friends. Emphasize the benefits of friendship and the value these relationships bring to our lives.

★ Ask students to fill in the blank: **When my friends are around, I wish my parents would_____**. Follow this with: **When my friends are around, I wish my parents wouldn't_____**.
Ask for volunteers to read aloud what they wrote.

★ Talk about cliques. This might lead to a heated debate! Have students try to define cliques and talk about the pros and cons (or whether there are any "pros") of cliques. Are there differences between cliques and groups of friends? How do cliques influence their own members and the kids who aren't part of the clique?

6. Session Activity

★ Hand out copies of "Funny Pages" and "Cartoon Starters."

★ Divide students into small groups.

★ Read aloud the instructions so all students understand how each group will work together to create a comic strip about the ups and downs of friendship, or the pitfalls of peer pressure. Explain that students can use images from the "Cartoon Starters" handout or they can draw their own characters (but point out that the group has to *agree* on an art style to make the comic strip look like it fits together).

★ Suggest students look at the cartoons you posted earlier, for inspiration.

★ Circulate as students work, answering questions as needed.

★ Hand out copies of "Adding Assets at Home."

7. Closing Question

Ask students: **What will you do to start adding the Positive Peer Influence asset to your life?** If there's time, encourage responses. Give an example of building this asset in your own life.

Preparation for Next Session

★ Make the book *Doing and Being Your Best* available to students if you would like them to read ahead the story and/or activity ideas for the High Expectations asset (Session 16).

★ Think about some of the general expectations you have for the group.

Funny Pages

Friendship has its ups and downs. Peer pressure has its pitfalls. But guess what? Sometimes it helps to see the *humor* of the situation you're in. A little *laughter* can lighten things up.

Your group will work together to make a comic strip about friendship or peer pressure. You can show the "ups" of friendship or the "downs" when things go wrong. Try to show the characters in your comic strip learning life's lessons in a humorous way.

Use the square below for the cartoon you will add to the whole group's comic strip. It can look just like those in a newspaper's comics section. As a group, decide on a story you'll tell in pictures. You can use the faces on the "Cartoon Starters" handout for help; fill in the mouths, cut them out, and glue them onto the scenes you create. Or draw your own faces and characters. *Make sure your group agrees on an art style!* Each group member should complete a square. Then glue the scenes in sequence onto a large sheet of construction paper.

Session 15

Cartoon Starters

ADDING ASSETS AT HOME

Positive Peer Influence

Today your child learned about the **Positive Peer Influence** asset. For your child, this asset means: *Your best friends behave in positive, responsible ways. They are a good influence on you.*

You can model positive, healthy relationships for your child. Let your child see that you value your friendships, that you respect your friends and are there for them when they need you. Help your child understand that the best way to *have* a friend is to *be* one.

At this time in children's lives, peer relationships become more important than ever. Children begin to turn toward friends for information, support, and tips on how to behave. They watch how other kids talk and act, instead of always looking to adults for answers. This is why it's so important for every child to have friends who model positive, responsible behavior. These types of friendships help make your child stronger and more resistant to negative peer pressure. Put simply, they help bring out the best in your child.

Ideas and Activities to Try at Home

★ Find ways to get to know a new friend's family. Invite them for dinner, attend school events together, or spend extra time talking when you drop off your child for play dates.

★ Help your child arrange play dates at your home. Encourage your child to invite friends for a meal, for example, or to set up weekend plans in advance.

★ Express interest in your child's friends. Ask questions, listen, and observe how this child and your child act when spending time together.

★ Be honest with your child when you're concerned about a friendship. Gently bring up times when a friend hasn't treated him or her well.

★ Include your child's friends in family activities when possible. Get to know them in relaxed situations or invite them to more formal occasions if you feel comfortable doing so (for example, dinner in a restaurant, religious services, one of your child's performances).

★ When spending time with your friends, invite your children to join in when appropriate.

Session 16: High Expectations

What this asset means to the child: Your parent(s) and teachers expect you to do your best at school and in other activities.

Backdrop

Write the name of the asset and its definition on the board.

> **Optional.** Write this quotation on the board: "Shoot for the moon. Even if you miss it, you will land among the stars."—Les Brown

Outcomes

★ to help students add the High Expectations asset to their lives

★ to help students understand what expectations are and why they are important

★ to encourage students to talk to their families about expectations

Preparation

Make a list of some of the general expectations you have for the group. Write them on the board.

Materials

★ copies of the book *Doing and Being Your Best*

★ copies of the "Positive Peer Influence" tracker page (from the CD-ROM)

★ copies of the "The Power of Words" and "Adding Assets at Home" handouts

1. Getting Started

Greeting. Have students say hello to someone near them.

Take 5. Hand out copies of the "Positive Peer Influence" tracker page and allow a few moments for students to complete them.

Two-Minute Partners. Have students form partners. Using the asset definition or the quotation on the board, ask the partners to each spend a minute describing what the words mean to him or her. Or ask students to describe what "shoot for the moon" means to them.

Preview. Tell students what they will do in this session. Make sure they have all necessary materials.

2. The Asset Question

★ Discuss what expectations are and why it's important for adults to set them for children. High expectations give people something to reach for. It's been said "no one rises to low expectations." Talk to students about what this means.

★ Ask students: **Are you trying to do your best in school? Do the adults at home and at school expect you to work hard and succeed? Do you stretch to try to reach your academic goals?**

3. Before the Story

Use some creative movement to get students thinking about "stretching." In an open area of the room, have students stretch their arms toward the ceiling and stand on their toes to reach higher. As they reach, ask students to call out the names of things that stretch (rubber bands, gum, giraffe necks, taffy). Talk about how stretching feels good and is good *for* you.*

---

*Adapted with permission from *Powerful Teaching: Developmental Assets in Curriculum and Instruction.* Copyright © 2003 by Search Institute, Minneapolis, MN; 800-888-7828; www.search-institute.org. All rights reserved.

4. The Story

Read It. Read aloud and discuss Kira's story on pages 69–70 and 77–79 of the student book. You may want to stop at the bottom of page 70 and ask students if they can relate to Kira's feelings.

Story Questions for Discussion. Ask students:

★ What seems to be bothering Kira more—trouble with math or the possibility of letting down her parents? Why?

★ Kira misunderstood her parents' expectations for her. Why do you think this is?

★ When Kira's dad points out that there are lots of ways she could get help, she is surprised. What could she be doing differently when she feels pressured and stressed about her schoolwork?

★ Does this story help you think about your own approach to school, homework, and tests? In what way?

5. Asset-Building Activities At-a-Glance

★ Choose a few of the activities on pages 71–75 of the student book or ask for volunteers to read them aloud. Ask students to talk

about some of the expectations their parents have for them. Are there times when the expectations feel too high or too low?

★ Have students think about how their parents communicate their expectations. Do they talk about the expectations often? Are the expectations truly understood?

★ Talk about "stretching" to reach for something, such as a higher grade or a better performance. This kind of stretching often requires perseverance and positive risk-taking. Why is this difficult for some of us? What would make the stretching feel more comfortable?

★ Discuss that we all make mistakes. Admit some of your own mistakes and what you learned from them. Ask for volunteers to talk about mistakes that turned into learning opportunities.

6. Session Activity

★ Hand out copies of "The Power of Words." Read aloud the instructions so that students know what to do.

★ Hand out copies of "Adding Assets at Home."

Standards/Objectives Highlights

Character Education	School approaches behavior through emphasizing values and consequences
Health	Students use goal setting to enhance health
Social Studies	Students relate factors such as physical capabilities, learning, motivation, personality, and behavior to individual development
Language Arts	Students read a variety of works to build an understanding of texts, of themselves, and of the world's cultures; to respond to needs; and for personal fulfillment
SEL Competencies	Students achieve mutually satisfactory resolutions to conflict by addressing the needs of all concerned

7. Closing Question

Ask students: **What will you do to begin adding the High Expectations asset to your life?** If there's time, encourage responses. Give an example of building this asset in your own life.

Preparation for Next Session

★ Make the book *Smart Ways to Spend Your Time* available to students if you would like them to read ahead the story and/or activity ideas for the Creative Activities asset (Session 17).

★ Ask students to begin thinking about these questions: **What creative things do you like to do? How many times a week do you do something creative? How might you spend more time doing creative activities?** Tell students you will want to hear some of their ideas in the next session. Suggest that if there's something creative they have made and would like to share with the group, they can bring it to the next session. This might be a drawing, a poem, a model, a sculpture, a photograph, a rap or song, a knitted scarf, a collage—anything they choose.

The Power of words

Do you talk about school with the adults at home? What do you often hear? ***Examples:*** Some kids might hear things like, "What grade did you get on your spelling test?" or "Can't you do better in math?" Other kids might hear things like, "You're getting better at spelling. Good for you!" or "I'm proud of how you hand in your homework on time." Write some of the questions or comments you hear at home. Then circle how they make you feel.

words I Hear	How I feel		
	sad or angry	worried or pressured	happy or encouraged
	sad or angry	worried or pressured	happy or encouraged
	sad or angry	worried or pressured	happy or encouraged

Share this handout with the adults at home, so you can talk about your feelings. Here are some discussion-starters:

★ "How do you think I'm doing in school?"

★ "What do you expect of me when it comes to my schoolwork?"

★ "I wish we could talk more about my schoolwork. Do you have time right now?"

★ "I feel worried and pressured when you say I need to do better. Can we talk about it?"

★ "I feel good when you say that you know I'm doing my best."

ADDING ASSETS AT HOME

High Expectations

Today your child learned about the **High Expectations** asset. For your child, this asset means: *Your parent(s) and teachers expect you to do your best at school and in other activities.* Children need to know that their parents and teachers notice and care how they do. Although we can't expect them to *be* the best in every subject or activity, we can expect them to *do* their best, or at least to try—maybe not in everything, but certainly in some things. This asset is about putting forth effort, stretching, and reaching.

Expectations need to be set according to each child's abilities, strengths, and temperament. Some children know what is expected of them; others find it more difficult to understand these expectations and live up to them. You may want to continue this discussion at home by asking your child if he or she wishes to share today's activity sheet, "The Power of Words."

Ideas and Activities to Try at Home

Strike a Balance Between Your Expectations and Your Child's Abilities.

★ Learn about child development. Check out books from the public library, or ask your child's teachers or the media specialist at school for recommendations. What's realistic at each age and stage?

★ Every so often, stop and ask yourself: "What are my expectations for my child right now? Am I expecting too much? Not enough?"

★ Leave lots of room for your child to make mistakes. Never expect perfection. Mistakes are learning experiences, too.

Encourage Your Child to S-t-r-e-t-c-h . . . and Do Some Stretching of Your Own.

★ Remember that you are your child's most important teacher. Keep looking for ways to teach your child new things. Go on outings together. Read books. Try new activities. Play!

★ Look for and share inspiring stories of people who have overcome great difficulties in their lives or did amazing things.

★ Have high expectations of yourself. Be an example of someone who's willing to learn, grow, try new things—and sometimes make mistakes.

Smart Ways to Spend Your Time: The Constructive Use of Time Assets

★ The **Constructive Use of Time Assets** are **External Assets**.

★ **External Assets** are positive experiences kids receive from the world around them.

★ The **Constructive Use of Time Assets** are about making sure that kids have opportunities outside of school to learn and develop new skills and interests with other kids and adults. These opportunities include creative activities, youth programs, and quality time at home.

The Constructive Use of Time Assets are:

17. **Creative activities**—Child participates in music, art, drama, or creative writing two or more times per week.

18. **Child programs**—Child participates two or more times per week in cocurricular school activities or structured community programs for children.

19. **Religious community**—Child attends religious programs or services one or more times per week.

20. **Time at home**—Child spends some time most days both in high-quality interaction with parent(s) and doing things at home other than watching TV or playing video games.

Session 17: Creative Activities

> **What this asset means to the child:** You do something with music, art, drama, or creative writing two or more times a week.

Backdrop

Write the name of the asset and its definition on the board.

> **Optional.** Write this quotation on the board: "Every child is an artist. The problem is how to remain an artist once he grows up."
> —Pablo Picasso

Note: Write the session backdrop quotation on the board when it is appropriate for your students. Always write the name of the asset and its definition on the board.

Outcomes

★ to help students add the Creative Activities asset to their lives

★ to help students identify and appreciate their individual creativity

★ to encourage students to express their creativity

Preparation

★ At the end of the last session, you asked students to begin thinking about these questions: **What creative things do you like to do? How many times a week do you do something creative? How might you spend more time doing creative activities?** Remind students of the questions and tell them you'll want to hear from them during this session.

★ Write a short rhyme or draw a picture on the board to demonstrate personal creativity.

Materials

★ copies of the book *Smart Ways to Spend Your Time*

★ copies of the "High Expectations" tracker page (from the CD-ROM)

★ copies of the "Creative Juices" and "Adding Assets at Home" handouts

★ juice boxes (one for each student) to give out as treats during the "Creative Juices" activity

★ CDs and a CD player to give students some musical inspiration during the "Creative Juices" activity

1. Getting Started

Greeting. Have students say hello to someone near them.

Take 5. Hand out copies of the "High Expectations" tracker page and allow a few moments for students to complete them.

Note: Make sure students know it's always appropriate to share feelings or an experience related to this asset or any other one. Sometimes, share your own examples as well.

Two-Minute Partners. Have students form partners. Using the asset definition or the quotation on the board, ask the partners to each spend a minute describing what the words mean to him or her. Or ask students to describe their favorite creative activity, such as singing, writing stories, acting in plays, or drawing pictures.

Preview. Tell students what they will do in this session. Make sure they have all necessary materials.

2. The Asset Question

Ask students: **What does it mean to be** *creative?* **Why is creativity important to people of all ages?** You may want to inspire students by naming famous creative people: artists, dancers, actors, musicians.

3. Before the Story

Read aloud "A message for you" on page 12 of *Smart Ways to Spend Your Time.* Help students see that creative activities are not necessarily about impressing other people or performing in front of them. Creative activities can be a way for people to express and please *themselves.*

Explain that creativity can also be shared with others, and sharing isn't the same as showing off. Invite students who brought something creative—a drawing, a poem, a model, a sculpture, a photograph, a rap or song, a knitted scarf, a collage—to share it now. Depending on what students prefer, they can share with the whole group or within small groups.

Note: Allow the story to be the central focus of each session.

4. The Story

Read It. Read aloud and discuss Sanjay's story on pages 6–7 and 22–23 of the student book. You may want to stop reading at the bottom of page 7 and talk about Sanjay's wish to keep doing his favorite activity and his fear of letting down his friends.

Story Questions for Discussion. Ask students:

★ Why do you think Sanjay spends so much time creating music? How do you think he feels when he's involved in his music?

★ Have you ever been torn between doing the creative activities you love and spending time with your friends? How did you handle the situation?

★ Sanjay's friends quickly join him when he asks them to. Why do you think this is?

★ Do you think Kari sees Sanjay as creative? Why?

★ Why is Sanjay glad he has friends like Kari, Mike, Jamie, and Tyrell?

Standards/Objectives Highlights

Character Education	School strives to foster students' self-motivation; engages families and community members as partners in the character-building effort
Health	Students demonstrate the ability to use goal-setting skills to enhance health
Social Studies	Students explore factors that contribute to personal identity such as interests, capabilities, and perceptions
Language Arts	Students use spoken and written language to accomplish their own purposes
SEL Competencies	Students generate, implement, and evaluate positive and informed solutions to problems

5. Asset-Building Activities At-a-Glance

Read over the activities on pages 8–20 of the student book and decide which ones are most suitable for your students. Or choose one or several of the following activities.

★ Talk about ways to practice creativity, such as music lessons, dance classes, art, choir, or youth theater programs.

★ Have students name some of the creative activities (clubs, classes, after-school programs) sponsored by their school. Ask for volunteers involved in these activities to share their experiences.

★ Share your own talents, or share stories of the creative activities you were involved in as a child.

6. Session Activity

★ Hand out copies of "Creative Juices."

★ Explain to students that the handout is designed to help them "get their creative juices flowing." Students must identify two of their own creative interests and imagine incorporating them into their lives. Hand out the juice boxes and turn on some music to help inspire the students' creativity.

★ Hand out copies of "Adding Assets at Home."

7. Closing Question

Ask students: **What will you do to start adding the Creative Activities asset to your life?** If there's time, encourage responses. Give an example of building this asset in your own life.

Preparation for Next Session

★ Make the book *Smart Ways to Spend Your Time* available to students if you would like them to read ahead the story and/or activity ideas for the Child Programs asset (Session 18).

★ Gather information about organized activities and programs for children at your school and/or in your community.

★ Arrange for adults who supervise and/or kids who participate in organized after-school activities or community programs to speak to your group. You might check with your local YMCA or YWCA, Boys & Girls Clubs, scouting organizations, and other programs in your area, as well as those available at your school.

★ See if students in your group who participate in after-school activities or community programs would be willing to talk about their experiences.

Creative Juices

Questions to ask yourself before writing your answers:

★ **What is my creative interest?** What do I like to do? What have I seen others do that I may want to try?

★ **What will I need?** Lessons? Materials? Can I do this activity at home?

★ **When and where can I do the activity?** On my own? With a group? At school? At the community center?

★ **What might I learn from the activity?** What skills might I gain? How will this feel?

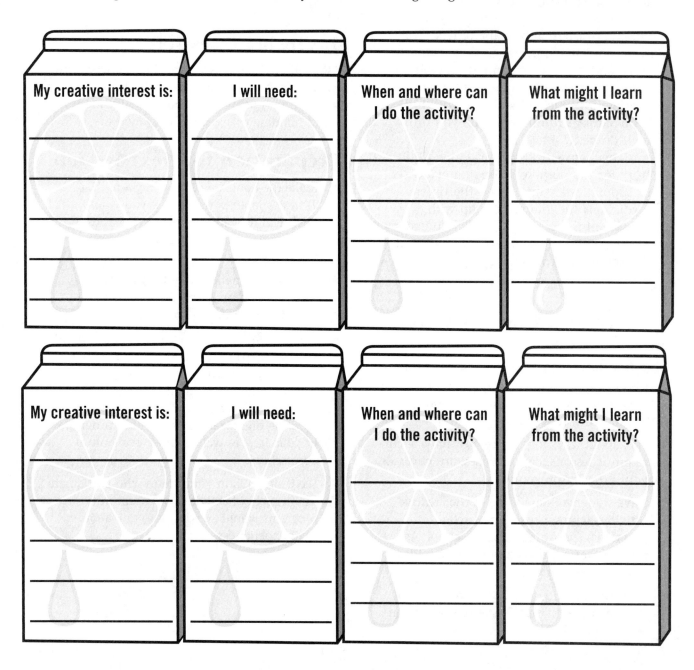

Creative Activities

Today your child was introduced to the **Constructive Use of Time** assets. These assets are about children spending time in positive, healthy ways. The first of these assets, **Creative Activities**, was the topic of today's session. For your child, this asset means: *You do something with music, art, drama, or creative writing two or more times a week.*

As part of today's session, your child identified two creative activities that he or she is interested in exploring. Perhaps you could help your child take the next step. Try to encourage your child's creative talents or urges whenever possible. Think about the resources that might be available at school, at your community center, in your neighborhood, or at your place of worship. It may be possible for your child to take lessons or join a club that focuses on creative activities. At home, continue to encourage drawing, singing, playing an instrument, writing stories, beading, or making works of art for friends and family members. Keep those creative juices flowing!

Ideas and Activities to Try at Home

Be an Artsy Family. Here are some ways to be creative while spending quality time together:

- ★ Work on a family project such as making home movies or photo collages.
- ★ Share music together. You could listen to recordings, play instruments, or sing karaoke.
- ★ Try reading plays or poems aloud. Start your own family book club.
- ★ Spread out some craft paper and draw or paint a mural together.

Support the Arts as a Family. Check out the Internet, local guides, and your Chamber of Commerce to learn about events and programs in your community. Here are more ways to support the arts:

- ★ Visit local museums and galleries together.
- ★ Attend free concerts and theater performances.
- ★ Attend school plays, concerts, and musicals, whether or not your child is performing.

Session 18: Child Programs

Backdrop

Write the name of the asset and its definition on the board.

> **Optional.** Write this quotation on the board: "Opportunities pop up everywhere—you just have to grab them."—Hannah Thomas

Outcomes

* to help students add the Child Programs asset to their lives
* to help students recognize how an organized activity can be a fun, healthy, and rewarding outlet
* to help students set personal goals for the programs they join

Preparation

* Gather information about organized activities and programs for children at your school and/or in your community.
* Arrange for adults who supervise and/or kids who participate in organized after-school activities or community programs to speak to your group. You might check with your local YMCA or YWCA, Boys & Girls Clubs, scouting organizations, and other programs in your area, as well as those available at your school.
* See if students in your group who participate in after-school activities or community programs would be willing to talk about their experiences.

Materials

* copies of the book *Smart Ways to Spend Your Time*
* copies of the "Creative Activities" tracker page (from the CD-ROM)
* copies of the "Touchdown!" and "Adding Assets at Home" handouts

1. Getting Started

Greeting. Have students say hello to someone near them.

Take 5. Hand out copies of the "Creative Activities" tracker page and allow a few moments for students to complete them.

Two-Minute Partners. Have students form partners. Using the asset definition or the quotation on the board, ask the partners to each spend a minute describing what the words mean to him or her.

Preview. Tell students what they will do in this session. Make sure they have all necessary materials.

2. The Asset Question

Ask students: **What is an *organized* after-school activity?** You may want to give one or two examples. Talk about how an organized child program is different from playing with friends after school.

3. Before the Story

Read aloud or ask a volunteer to read the "9 Fine Reasons to Join a Program for Kids" on page 32 of the student book. Talk about how organized programs provide a way for children to form strong friendships with others who share similar interests and goals.

Introduce the individuals you invited to speak to your group about organized after-school activities or community programs. Have them talk about what they do, what they like about their activities/programs, and what their activities/programs have to offer. Allow time for students to ask questions. If there are students in your group who participate in after-school activities or community programs, see if they're willing to talk about their experiences and answer questions.

If you gathered information about organized activities and programs for children at your school and/or in your community, make it available for students to look at during and after the session.

4. The Story

Read It. Read aloud and discuss Erika's story on pages 24–26 and 38–40 of the student book.

Story Questions for Discussion. Ask students:

★ In the story, it says that Erika, Abbie, Maria, and Jen are not a "clique." What does that mean? How is their friendship different from what might typically be found in a clique?

★ People grow and change, and so do their friendships. What is Erika learning about this?

★ Ms. Martinez says that being a troop means more than doing fun activities. What do you think she means by this?

★ Being part of a troop or team can be a bonding experience for members. Why might this be true?

5. Asset-Building Activities At-a-Glance

★ Read a few of the activities on pages 27–36 of the student book or ask for volunteers to read them aloud. Talk about why it's important to be a part of *something*—whether it's an organized program at school, in the community, or at a place of worship. Give students ideas for joining a group, team, or troop.

★ If students express an interest in starting a *new* organized activity at school, read aloud and discuss the paragraph on page 31 of the student book that begins, "If you're not excited by anything your school offers right now . . . ."

Standards/Objectives Highlights

Character Education	Students engage partners in character-building effort
Health	Students describe how school and community can support personal health practices
Social Studies	Students relate factors such as physical capabilities, learning, motivation, personality, and behavior to individual development
Language Arts	Students research issues and interests by generating ideas, questions, and posing problems
SEL Competencies	Students identify and cultivate strengths and positive qualities

6. Session Activity

★ Hand out copies of "Touchdown!"

★ Explain to students that by completing the handout's "football field," they will score a "touchdown"; that is, they will be on their way to finding a child program that interests them.

★ Hand out copies of "Adding Assets at Home."

7. Closing Question

Ask students: **What will you do to begin adding the Child Programs asset to your life?** If there's time, encourage responses. Give an example of building this asset in your own life.

Preparation for Next Session

★ Make the book *Smart Ways to Spend Your Time* available to students if you would like them to read ahead the story and/or activity ideas for the Religious Community asset (Session 19).

★ Consider how your own beliefs have guided your thinking and your life. If you teach in a public school, be ready to talk in a general way about why it's important to have beliefs. If you teach in a religious school, you can be more specific about your beliefs and how they relate to your faith.

Touchdown!

Why take part in an organized after-school activity? You might want to meet new friends, share common interests, or learn or do something new. Think about a program that interests you. Next, answer the questions on the "football field" below to score a "touchdown."

MY GOAL IN JOINING A PROGRAM IS:

_____

ONE PROGRAM THAT SOUNDS FUN IS:

_____

TO JOIN, I NEED TO:

_____

AN ADULT AT HOME WHO CAN HELP ME:

_____

I'LL TAKE THIS STEP TOWARD JOINING:

_____

Child Programs

Today your child learned about the **Child Programs** asset. For your child, this asset means: *You go to an organized after-school activity or community program for kids two or more times a week.* Such programs might include school or community sports, Scouts, or clubs. Maybe your child is already part of a program but is looking for new challenges or a change. Or your child might not yet be involved in a program and could use your support and guidance to find one that interests him or her.

In today's session, your child identified a program of interest but needs your help in following through.

Ideas and Activities to Try at Home

Talk About It. Ask your child about the program he or she expressed interest in, and then look into whether the program might be available through your school district, community, or place of worship. Find out about the schedule and requirements (such as age limits, transportation, or fees).

Be Supportive. If you and your child have chosen an activity or program, here are some suggestions for supporting your child in the endeavor:

- ★ Get to know the leader(s) of the activity or program. Make sure you're comfortable with the program first.

- ★ Determine whether your schedule allows for your child to regularly attend meetings and activities.

- ★ Talk with your child about his or her experiences with the program. Who are the other children involved, and what are they like? What are your child's thoughts about the group leader(s)? What's going well? What could go better?

- ★ Attend your child's meetings or activities when invited or when it is appropriate (for example, awards ceremonies or games). Get to know the other students and their parents or caregivers.

- ★ Volunteer your time for those activities or programs where the participation of caring adults is needed.

Review Choices. Check that an ongoing activity or program is right for your child by asking these questions:

- ★ Are the adults caring and thoughtful?
- ★ Does the program and its activities seem safe?
- ★ Is my child learning new skills or gaining knowledge?
- ★ Is my child forming friendships within the group?
- ★ Is my child excited to do the activities and to share time with the other children?

Session 19: Religious Community

What this asset means to the child: You go to a religious program or service once a week or more.

Backdrop

Write the name of the asset and its definition on the board.

> **Optional.** Write this quotation on the board: "Beliefs are like the foundation of a building, and they are the foundation to build your life upon."
> —Alfred A. Montapert

Outcomes

★ to help students add the Religious Community asset to their lives

★ to help students understand that religious community is an important source of the beliefs that guide their thinking and their lives

★ to encourage students to practice their own beliefs and respect the beliefs of others

Preparation

Consider how your own beliefs have guided your thinking and your life. If you teach in a public school, be ready to talk in a general way about why it's important to have beliefs. If you teach in a religious school, you can be more specific about your beliefs and how they relate to your faith.

Materials

★ copies of the book *Smart Ways to Spend Your Time*

★ copies of the "Child Programs" tracker page (from the CD-ROM)

★ copies of the "What I Believe" and "Adding Assets at Home" handouts

1. Getting Started

Greeting. Have students say hello to someone near them.

Take 5. Hand out copies of the "Child Programs" tracker page and allow a few moments for students to complete them.

Two-Minute Partners. Have students form partners. Using the asset definition or the quotation on the board, ask the partners to each spend a minute describing what the words mean to him or her.

Preview. Tell students what they will do in this session. Make sure they have all necessary materials.

2. The Asset Question

Ask students: **How can you tell the difference between the right thing to do and the wrong thing?** Encourage students to discuss where they get their ideas of what's right and what's wrong. Students probably will describe sources such as family, friends, and their faith communities. Suggest religion as a possible source if students don't bring it up themselves.

3. Before the Story

If you teach in a public school, talk in a general way about why it's important to have beliefs. For example, beliefs help you tell the difference between the right thing to do and the wrong thing—something you and the students just discussed in "The Asset Question" part of this session. They help you make decisions. They guide how you treat yourself and other people. You might invite students to briefly describe a belief that's important to them and how it affects their behavior.

If you teach in a religious school, you can be more specific about your beliefs and how they relate to your faith.

4. The Story

Read It. Read aloud and discuss Rob's story on pages 41–43 and 55–57 of the student book.

Know the Characters. Tell students that in Rob's story, two of the main characters, Rob and Tony, have a conflict. Explain that the more students understand about the two characters, the more they will understand the conflict and the better they will be able to predict how the characters might resolve it.

Draw the following character webs on the board. Have students give their suggestions on how to fill in each oval. Fill in the webs with their suggestions. (Possible suggestions are in brackets.)

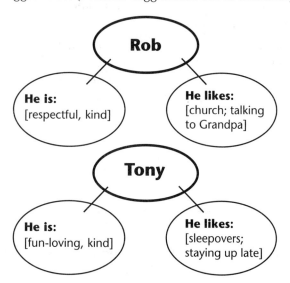

Rob

He is: [respectful, kind]

He likes: [church; talking to Grandpa]

Tony

He is: [fun-loving, kind]

He likes: [sleepovers; staying up late]

Story Questions for Discussion. Ask students:

★ Why do you think Tony thinks there is no problem with Rob skipping church "just this once"?

★ Why doesn't Rob want to miss church?

★ How would you describe Rob's relationship with Grandpa?

★ How does Grandpa help Rob solve his problem?

★ Why do you think Tony agrees to join Rob at his church on Sunday?

Point out to students that we don't really know how the story ends. Rob waits while Tony asks his dad if he can go to church with Rob, but we never learn what Tony's dad says. Have students predict what they think will happen. Ask:

★ What do you think Tony's dad will say— yes or no?

★ If Tony's dad says yes, what might happen?

★ If Tony's dad says no, what might happen? What choices will Tony and Rob have then?

★ If a friend of a different faith invited you to a religious service, would you want to go? Do you think your parents would let you go? Why or why not?

Standards/Objectives Highlights

Character Education	School takes steps to help students acquire understanding of core values in everyday behavior
Health	Students demonstrate refusal skills to avoid and reduce health risks
Social Studies	Students explain how people respond differently based on shared assumptions, values, and beliefs
Language Arts	Students use spoken and written language to accomplish their own purposes
SEL Competencies	Students recognize and understand their obligation to engage in ethical, safe, and legal behaviors

5. Asset-Building Activities At-a-Glance

Read over some of the activities from pages 44–53 of the student book and decide which ones are suitable for your students. *Suggestions:*

★ Share the big questions about life with family adults.

★ Practice religious beliefs by respecting others, helping around the house, and giving prayers of thanks for all the good things there are.

★ Join a faith community if the family does not have one. Encourage family members to join as well.

★ Discuss with parents how to resolve conflicts between school events and religious events.

★ Discuss with parents or religious leaders differences between one's own religious beliefs and other beliefs. Learn to be tolerant of the religious beliefs of others.

★ Participate in activities and programs that are offered in the faith community.

6. Session Activity

★ Hand out copies of "What I Believe." Read aloud the instructions so students know what to do. If you teach in a public school, tell students they can keep their handouts private. They don't have to show them to anyone unless they want to.

★ If you teach in a religious school, invite students to share what they wrote or drew. If some students aren't sure what they believe, you might take this opportunity to review the central beliefs of your school's faith tradition. You might also offer to be someone your students can talk to about their beliefs.

★ Hand out copies of "Adding Assets at Home."

7. Closing Question

Ask students: **What will you do to start adding the Religious Community asset to your life?** If there's time, encourage responses. Give an example of building this asset in your own life.

Preparation for Next Session

★ Make the book *Smart Ways to Spend Your Time* available to students if you would like them to read ahead the story and/or activity ideas for the Time at Home asset (Session 20).

★ Ask students to think about these questions: **How much time do you spend doing things with your family each week? Do you think it's enough? Why or why not?**

What I Believe

Do you believe in God or a Creator? Do you believe that when people pray, their prayers are answered? Where do you believe people go when they die? Think about your religious or spiritual beliefs. Write about them or draw them.

What if you're not sure what you believe? If you want, you can write about that. Or maybe you'll draw a big question mark! You might want to talk about beliefs with a grown-up you trust. If you belong to a faith community, you can talk with a religious leader or teacher. You can talk with a parent or other family adult.

Religious Community

Today your child read about and discussed the **Religious Community** asset. For your child, this asset means: *You go to a religious program or service once a week or more.* Research shows that children who belong to religious communities are less prone to risky behaviors than children who don't. Religious communities provide caring and support, nurturing and stability. They give children another place where they feel they belong.

Religious communities also teach values. Students talked about how they can tell the difference between the right thing to do and the wrong thing. They explored how ideas of what's right and wrong come from several places including family, friends, and faith communities. You might ask your child where his or her ideas of right and wrong come from. This might be a good time to review with your child what your family believes and/or what your faith tradition believes.

Ideas and Activities to Try at Home

★ If your family belongs to a religious community, have a family meeting to talk about your involvement. How does everyone feel about your religious community? What do you like about it? Is there anything you don't like about it? Why is belonging to a religious community important to your family? How has it shaped your beliefs? How does it affect your choices and behaviors?:

★ If your family doesn't belong to a religious community, you might consider finding one you like and getting involved. Visit various faith communities until you feel welcome and comfortable. Religious communities benefit children in so many ways that it may be worth exploring this possibility with your family.

Session 20: Time at Home

What this asset means to the child: On most days, you spend some time with your parent(s). You spend some time doing things at home besides watching TV or playing video games.

Backdrop

Write the name of the asset and its definition on the board.

> **Optional.** Write this quotation on the board: "Home is where the heart is."—American proverb

Outcomes

★ to help students add the Time at Home asset to their lives

★ to provide ways for students to identify how to spend more quality time with their families

★ to help students plan an activity for a regular family night at home

Preparation

In the last session, you asked students to think about these questions: **How much time do you spend doing things with your family each week? Do you think it's enough? Why or why not?** Remind students of the questions and tell them you'll want to hear their thoughts later in the session.

Materials

★ copies of the book *Smart Ways to Spend Your Time*

★ copies of the "Religious Community" tracker page (from the CD-ROM)

★ copies of the "Family Night Menu" and "Adding Assets at Home" handouts

1. Getting Started

Greeting. Have students say hello to someone near them.

Take 5. Hand out copies of the "Religious Community" tracker page and allow a few moments for students to complete them.

Two-Minute Partners. Have students form partners. Using the asset definition or the quotation on the board, ask the partners to each spend a minute describing what the words mean to him or her.

Preview. Tell students what they will do in this session. Make sure they have all necessary materials.

2. The Asset Question

Ask students: **What do you think the phrase *quality time* means? Do you spend quality time with your parents?** Prompt students by asking: **Is playing video games all day the way to spend quality time at home? How about watching TV during family dinner?** These prompts should lead to further discussion of the concept of quality time.

3. Before the Story

Have students discuss the things they like to do at home with their families. Ask: **About how much time do you spend with your family each day? Each week? Do you feel you spend too much time? Too little?** Encourage students to think about which activities help them to learn more about their family members. Ask: **How do you feel when family plans are interrupted or cancelled?**

4. The Story

Read It. Read aloud and discuss Ona's story on pages 58–60 and 76–77 of the student book.

Plot It. Explain to students that they can understand Ona's story better if they understand its *plot*. *Plot* is the order of events in a story.

To help students understand what happens first, next, and last in the story, list the following events on the board in the order shown:

★ The family has a group hug.

★ Carmen rings the doorbell.

★ Ona comes home.

★ Carmen joins the family for dinner.

★ Ona thanks Mom quietly.

Next, draw the following diagram on the board. Ask volunteers to fill in the sequence of events. (The answers are in brackets.)

First [Ona comes home.]
Next [The family has a group hug.]
Next [Carmen rings the doorbell.]
Next [Carmen joins the family for dinner.]
Last [Ona thanks Mom quietly.]

Story Questions for Discussion. Ask students:

★ Why is Ona excited at the beginning of the story?

★ Both Ona and her dad do not get angry at different points in the story, even though they have reason to. Why don't they get angry?

★ Why does the whole family put on their pajamas before dinner?

★ Why does Ona's mom react differently to Carmen's arrival than Ona does?

★ Why does Ona thank her mom at the end of the story?

5. Asset-Building Activities At-a-Glance

Read over the activities on pages 61–75 of the student book. Write some of the activities on the board. *Suggestions:*

★ Eat dinner together as a family.

★ Set aside a time for the whole family to do an activity together.

★ Play board games together. Choose a game that everyone in the family can play.

Standards/Objectives Highlights

Character Education	School communicates with parents and guardians on character education and general parenting skills
Health	Students describe how family influences personal health practices and behaviors
Social Studies	Students study interactions among individuals, groups, and institutions
Language Arts	Students participate as creative members of literacy communities
SEL Competencies	Students achieve mutually satisfactory resolutions to conflict by addressing the needs of all concerned

★ Watch old movies together to learn more about your parents' and grandparents' past.

★ Find other ways to spend time at home besides watching TV and playing video games.

★ Make a list of three things you like about each member of your family.

★ Have regular family meetings.

6. Session Activity

★ Hand out copies of "Family Night Menu."

★ Review "Eat Dinner Together as a Family" on pages 61–62 of the student book.

★ Suggest students plan a family night like the one in Ona's story. They should discuss their plans with, and get agreement from, every member of the family. To get the ball rolling, have students use the handout to create a menu to bring home.

★ Hand out copies of "Adding Assets at Home."

7. Closing Question

Ask students: **What will you do to start adding the Time at Home asset to your life?** If there's time, encourage responses. Give an example of building this asset in your own life.

Preparation for Next Session

★ Make the book *Loving to Learn* available to students if you would like them to read ahead the story and/or activity ideas for the Achievement Motivation asset (Session 21).

★ Plan a scavenger hunt in which you hide objects around the classroom and provide written clues for students to follow. For fun, write the clues as riddles or rhymes and have students work as partners or teams to solve them. Have small prizes available for the winning team (sticker packs, pencils, notepads). This is intended to be a quick, fun activity that motivates students, so keep the clues simple.

Family Night Menu

Come up with your "dream menu" for a family night dinner. Bring your menu home and share it with your family. Work together to plan a fun and tasty dinner. Talk with your family about fun things you might do before and after dinner.

Tonight's Menu

First Dish: _____

Chef: _____

Second Dish: _____

Chef: _____

Third Dish: _____

Chef: _____

Dessert: _____

Chef: _____

Beverage: _____

Chef: _____

Session 20

Time at Home

Today your child read about and discussed the **Time at Home** asset. For your child, this assets means: *On most days, you spend some time with your parent(s). You spend some time doing things at home besides watching TV or playing video games.* Students learned about the importance of spending quality time with their families.

For many families, quality time starts at the dinner table. Family dinners aren't just a good idea. They're good for kids. Studies have shown that children and teens who have frequent family meals are less likely to smoke cigarettes, drink alcohol, use illegal drugs, have suicidal thoughts, and develop eating disorders, and are more likely to get better grades in school, among other benefits. Family meals are the perfect time to get in touch and stay in touch with what our kids are thinking and doing, and to monitor their behavior. They also build closer family ties.*

During today's session, your child created a menu for a family meal. If your child brought it home, you and the rest of your family might want to give it a try. Or work together to create a menu, then set a date to enjoy it. Come up with fun things to do before and after dinner, or other ways to make that time even more special for everyone.

Ideas and Activities to Try at Home

Tips for a Successful Family Dinner. Here's how to help things go smoothly:

★ Make sure all family members know the date and time of the family night dinner.

★ Make sure all family members are available for family night. If conflicting schedules don't allow for this, have a weekend brunch instead.

★ Keep the dishes simple. This will leave time for other fun activities.

★ If some family members are too young to cook, they may be able to help set and clear the table. Try to give everyone a meaningful role.

★ Display the menu where everyone in the family can see it.

*Reported in "Benefits of the Dinner Table Ritual" by Laurie Tarkan, *New York Times,* May 3, 2005.

Loving to Learn: The Commitment to Learning Assets

★ The **Commitment to Learning Assets** are **Internal Assets.**

★ **Internal Assets** are values, skills, and self-perceptions that kids develop internally, with help from caring adults.

★ The **Commitment to Learning Assets** are about helping kids develop a sense of how important learning is and a belief in their own ability to learn, achieve, and grow—now and in the future. These assets build lifelong learners.

The Commitment to Learning Assets are:

21. **Achievement motivation**—Child is motivated and strives to do well in school.

22. **Learning engagement**—Child is responsive, attentive, and actively engaged in learning at school and enjoys participating in learning activities outside of school.

23. **Homework**—Child usually hands in homework on time.

24. **Bonding to adults at school**—Child cares about teachers and other adults at school.

25. **Reading for pleasure**—Child enjoys and engages in reading for fun most days of the week.

Session 21: Achievement Motivation

> **What this asset means to the child:** You want to do well in school, and you try your best.

Backdrop

Write the name of the asset and its definition on the board.

> **Optional.** Write this quotation on the board: "Education is our passport to the future, for tomorrow belongs to the people who prepare for it today."—Malcolm X

Note: Write the session backdrop quotation on the board when it is appropriate for your students. Always write the name of the asset and its definition on the board.

Outcomes

★ to help students add the Achievement Motivation asset to their lives

★ to help students recognize what it feels like to be motivated from the *inside*

★ to introduce students to new ways to get motivated

Preparation

Plan a scavenger hunt in which you hide objects around the classroom and provide written clues for students to follow. For fun, write the clues as riddles or rhymes and have students work as partners or teams to solve them. Offer a small prize for the winning team (sticker packs, pencils, notepads). This is intended to be a quick, fun activity that motivates students, so keep the clues simple.

Materials

★ copies of the book *Loving to Learn*

★ copies of the "Time at Home" tracker page (from the CD-ROM)

★ copies of the "Motivation Station" and "Adding Assets at Home" handouts

★ small prize for scavenger hunt winner

1. Getting Started

Greeting. Suggest students say hello to someone near them in a new way. *Example:* "Hey, it's good to see you. I'm glad you're here."

Take 5. Hand out copies of the "Time at Home" tracker page and allow a few moments for students to complete them.

Note: Make sure students know it's always appropriate to share feelings or an experience related to this asset or any other one. Sometimes, share your own examples as well.

Two-Minute Partners. Have students form partners. Using the asset definition or the quotation on the board, ask the partners to each spend a minute describing what the words mean to him or her. Other topics to consider are to ask students to discuss what their favorite school subject is and why, or to describe what "passport to the future" means to them.

Preview. Tell students what they will do in this session. Make sure they have all necessary materials.

2. The Asset Question

Ask students: **What does it mean to be *motivated?* Where does this feeling come from?** Invite students to respond.

3. Before the Story

Scavenger Hunt. Pass out clues for the hunt and have students form partners or teams. Let them know that the winners will receive a small prize. After the scavenger hunt, return to the discussion of motivation. Ask students: **What got you interested in following the clues and looking for the hidden items?** While many students may say they were motivated to win a prize, others will likely reply that they were excited to figure out the clues. Talk about how motivation is that "I want it!" or "I want to know it!" feeling that gives people energy and helps them rise to a challenge.

Note: Allow the story to be the central focus of each session.

4. The Story

Read It. Read aloud and discuss Mitchell and Tyler's story on pages 6–8 and 20–21 of the student book. You may want to stop reading at the bottom of page 8 and ask students to talk about the similarities and differences between Mitchell and Tyler.

Story Questions for Discussion. Ask students:

★ Although there is nothing wrong with being interested in baseball, Tyler's interest is a problem at the beginning of the story. Why do you think this is?

★ How does Mitchell feel when Tyler shows him the baseball cards during the dinosaur lesson?

★ Mitchell has mixed feelings when Ms. Kingston scolds Tyler. At first he feels glad, then kind of rotten. Why?

★ How does Mitchell get Tyler motivated to do the assignment? Why do you think this helped?

★ Have you ever helped another student get more motivated about a subject or assignment in school? Tell us about it.

5. Asset-Building Activities At-a-Glance

Read over the activities from pages 9–18 of the student book. Choose three or four you think may motivate your students. *Examples:*

★ Tell students that knowing where to find answers is as important as having questions. Ask if they know good places to find answers. Write their responses on the board. If students don't mention the resources listed on pages 12–13 of the student book, you may want to read all or parts of this section aloud.

Standards/Objectives Highlights	
Character Education	School provides a meaningful and challenging academic curriculum that respects all learners and helps students achieve success
Health	Students demonstrate the ability to use goal setting to enhance health
Social Studies	Students identify the influence of attitudes, values, and beliefs on personal identity
Language Arts	Students research issues by generating questions and posing problems; they communicate their discoveries
SEL Competencies	Students establish and work toward the achievement of short- and long-term pro-social goals

★ Invite students to share ways that teachers or other adults have helped them succeed with school subjects or assignments. For each example, ask: **How did this person help get you motivated?**

★ Have students write a response to this question: **Are you more motivated by grades and rewards, or does your "I want it" feeling come from *inside*?**

6. Session Activity

★ Hand out copies of "Motivation Station." Read aloud the opening paragraph so all students understand what to do. Have students work in groups to complete the activity. If time allows, have students share ideas they came up with in their groups.

★ Hand out copies of "Adding Assets at Home."

Optional Activity: Vocabulary

Web of Motivation. Write the word *motivated* in large letters in the center of the board. Have students look up synonyms for *motivated,* add them to the board, and draw lines between *motivated* and its synonyms. If time allows, they also can look up synonyms for the synonyms. The goal is to create a web of related words. *Examples:* motivated, driven, determined, stubborn.

---

7. Closing Question

Ask students: **What will you do to start adding the Achievement Motivation asset to your life?** If there's time, encourage responses. Give an example of building this asset in your own life.

Preparation for Next Session

★ Make the book *Loving to Learn* available to students if you would like them to read ahead the story and/or activity ideas for the Learning Engagement asset (Session 22).

★ If possible, bring in some fresh or dried fruits, fruit juices, or other healthful snacks for everyone in your group.

Motivation Station

Let's face it: Sometimes you have an assignment to do, homework to finish, or a test to study for and *you just don't feel like doing it.* How do you motivate yourself to do it anyway? Maybe you promise to reward yourself when you're through. Maybe you break it into small steps. Maybe you give yourself a pep talk. Maybe you imagine what might happen if you don't get it done. What works for you? In your group, share ideas. Write or draw new ideas you hear and want to try. Keep this page in your notebook so you can look at it the next time you need motivation.

Achievement Motivation

Today your child was introduced to the **Commitment to Learning** assets. These assets emphasize the importance of being serious about school and other learning opportunities. The first of these assets, **Achievement Motivation**, was the topic of today's session. For your child, this asset means: *You want to do well in school, and you try your best.*

Keeping children motivated in school takes effort, but a good way to start is to be aware of your child's interests so you can build on them. You may want to ask your child:

★ Which subjects are you excited to learn more about? Which ones aren't as exciting? Why?

★ Do you feel motivated or bored in school? What might help you get more interested?

★ What do you like to learn about outside of school? Why?

Ideas and Activities to Try at Home

Watch and Take Notice. Observe your child at play. What kinds of activities naturally grab his or her attention? Does your child seem to enjoy words, numbers, concepts, projects, or figuring out how things work? Think of ways to incorporate these special interests into other subjects that may be more challenging.

Tips to Help Your Child Become Motivated to Learn.

★ Tie your child's learning to real life—for instance, visit the state capitol or other landmarks when your child is studying state history. Ask about school. Be informed about your child's homework assignments, reports, and tests.

★ Help your child develop a homework routine that works. Set up a study area and schedule, with your child's help. Make sure the area has adequate lighting and a desk with supplies. Be available for homework questions and to check over your child's work.

★ Find learning opportunities every day. Read to your child, visit educational Web sites together, spend time at the local library, and talk to each other. Limit TV and video games.

Session 22: Learning Engagement

What this asset means to the child: You like to learn new things in and out of school.

Backdrop

Write the name of the asset and its definition on the board.

> **Optional.** Write this quotation on the board: "The cure for boredom is curiosity."—Ellen Parr

Outcomes

★ to help students add the Learning Engagement asset to their lives

★ to help students tune in and stay alert at school

★ to encourage students to develop curiosity and new interests

Preparation

If possible, bring in some fresh or dried fruits, fruit juices, or other healthful snacks for everyone in your group.

Materials

★ copies of the book *Loving to Learn*

★ copies of the "Achievement Motivation" tracker page (from the CD-ROM)

★ copies of the "Curious Cat" and "Adding Assets at Home" handouts

1. Getting Started

Greeting. Have students say hello to someone near them.

Take 5. Hand out copies of the "Achievement Motivation" tracker page and allow a few moments for students to complete them.

Two-Minute Partners. Have students form partners. Using the asset definition or the quotation on the board, ask the partners to each spend a minute describing what the words mean to him or her.

Preview. Tell students what they will do in this session. Make sure they have all necessary materials.

2. The Asset Question

Ask students: **Do you like to learn new things? What do you like to learn about? What interests you more than anything else in the whole world?** You might share an example of something that interests you—something you're excited about learning.

3. Before the Story

Ask students if they have heard of a man named Michelangelo. Some may identify him as an artist. You might explain a little about him—Michelangelo was a sculptor, painter, architect, and poet who lived about 500 years ago, and he created some of the most famous works of art in the world today: the Sistine Chapel ceiling, the statue of David, and many more. Tell students that when Michelangelo was in his eighties, he said, "I am still learning." Ask: **What do you think about that? What does it take to stay excited about learning for your whole life?**

4. The Story

Read It. Read aloud and discuss Wendy's story on pages 22–23 and 35–36 of the student book. You may want to stop reading at the bottom of page 23 and ask students if they have experienced what it is like to get lost in their thoughts or so engrossed in an activity that they lose track of time. Ask: **Are there ups and downs to this?**

Story Questions for Discussion. Ask students:

★ Wendy has lots of ideas and she acts on them. She's a "questioner" and a "doer."

What are some of the advantages of having qualities like these?

★ Does it seem like Wendy's mother supports her daughter's love of learning? How can you tell?

★ Wendy read an article that got her interested in caves. Where did her question about caves lead Wendy in her conversation with Mr. Chen? Can you see how curiosity can lead you in whole new directions?

★ Mr. Chen is a good teacher because he respects Wendy's questions, and he is a good resource because he takes Wendy's interest in caves and bats a step further. Are your teachers or parents good resources for you? In what way?

★ If you were Wendy, where would you go first to find out about *echolocation?*

5. Asset-Building Activities At-a-Glance

Read over the activities on pages 24–34 of the student book and decide which ones are most suitable for your students. *Suggestions:*

★ Hand out the snacks you brought to share with the group. Talk briefly about how a healthy diet helps us stay focused and pay attention while learning.

★ Turn the "8 Signs That You're Not Getting Enough Sleep" on page 28 into questions:

1. Do you yawn a lot?
2. Do you have a hard time listening at home and at school?
3. Do you forget what you learned in school?
4. Do you feel tired most of the time?
5. Are you often sad or grumpy?
6. Do you find that you don't have much energy for sports, games, or chores?
7. Do you have trouble making good choices?
8. Do you head for the couch (or your bed) the minute you get home?

Read the questions aloud and ask for a show of hands after each one. Talk with students about the importance of getting enough sleep.

★ Talk with students about how learning is *active,* not *passive.* You have to participate, not just sit there. Ask: **What are ways to be an active learner—to participate in class?**

★ Ask students to talk about their hobbies.

Standards/Objectives Highlights

Character Education	School infuses character education throughout the school day
Health	Students analyze the influence of culture, media, technology, and other factors on health
Social Studies	Students explain how information can be interpreted by people of diverse cultural perspectives
Language Arts	Students apply knowledge of language conventions to create and critique texts
SEL Competencies	Students generate, implement, and evaluate positive and informed solutions to problems

★ Have students outline a plan for learning something new. They should write down what they want to learn and who might help them—a teacher, a parent, a friend. Perhaps they can report back to the class at a later date on how it's going.

6. Session Activity

★ Hand out copies of "Curious Cat." Read aloud the opening paragraph so everyone understands what to do.

★ Hand out copies of "Adding Assets at Home."

7. Closing Question

Ask students: **What will you do to start adding the Learning Engagement asset to your life?** If there's time, encourage responses. Give an example of building this asset in your own life.

Preparation for Next Session

★ Make the book *Loving to Learn* available to students if you would like them to read ahead the story and/or activity ideas for the Homework asset (Session 23).

★ Get a copy of Jack Prelutsky's book *The New Kid on the Block* (Greenwillow Books, 1984) so you can read aloud his hilarious poem "Homework! Oh, Homework!" If you can't find Prelutsky's book, try to find another funny poem or two about homework—or write one of your own.

Curious Cat

Did you know that curiosity is one of the keys to getting ahead in school and in life? When you're curious, your mind opens up. You stay awake and alert—you ask questions and you learn. Fill in the spaces below to help awaken your own curiosity.

I'm curious about _____.

I could learn more about this by_____

_____.

If I could make an amazing discovery, it would be _____ because

_____.

If I could time travel, I would want to see _____ because

_____.

If I could visit anyplace in the world today, it would be _____ because

_____.

If I were an inventor, this is what I would invent _____.

A word I would like to know the meaning of is _____.
(Now look it up!)

When I learn something new, I feel _____.

Session 22

Learning Engagement

Today your child was introduced to the **Learning Engagement** asset. For your child, this asset means: *You like to learn new things in and out of school.*

Every day, whether we're aware of it or not, we teach our children. They see if we value education and our work. They absorb our values and attitudes, and in the process, develop ideas about whether learning is exciting and rewarding—or something to be done only when necessary. We can encourage children to take every opportunity to learn by showing how we, ourselves, are lifelong learners. It is never too early—or too late—to start.

Be a partner in learning with your child. Try to set up your home environment so it is as stimulating and engaging as the classroom. Make sure books, magazines, and educational toys are available. Go to the library to find books that teach new skills—anything from knitting, to magic tricks, to card games. Let your child explore the natural world as often as possible, whether this means spending time at a local park or in your own backyard. *Tip:* When kids are excited about learning at home, they're more excited about learning at school.

Ideas and Activities to Try at Home

Start with the Basics.

★ Make sure your child gets enough sleep, eats well, and has help dealing with academic or social and emotional challenges.

★ Let your child know that you expect him or her to make a good effort to learn at school.

★ Stay involved by knowing about your child's teachers, subjects, friendships, assignments, and homework.

★ Respond immediately to problems at school by talking with teachers.

Learn Every Day.

★ Together, start a new hobby and make time for it as often as you can.

★ Learn something new together—look up words in the dictionary, pose a question and seek the answer online, or read sections of the newspaper aloud.

★ Watch educational television programs to learn more about science, history, or travel. Expand on your learning by visiting the library.

★ Learn about the plants, trees, or insects you see while taking walks.

★ Research your own family history.

Session 23: Homework

Backdrop

Write the name of the asset and its definition on the board.

> **Optional.** Write this quotation on the board: "The brain is like a muscle. When it is in use, we feel very good. Understanding is joyous."
> —Carl Sagan

Outcomes

★ to help students add the Homework asset to their lives

★ to provide students with a new perspective on homework as a stimulating activity

★ to help students recognize ways to turn the "have to" part of homework into an efficient and satisfying activity

Preparation

Have on hand a copy of Jack Prelutsky's book *The New Kid on the Block* (Greenwillow Books, 1984) so you can read aloud his hilarious poem "Homework! Oh, Homework!" If you can't find Prelutsky's book, try to find another funny poem or two about homework—or write one of your own.

Materials

★ copies of the book *Loving to Learn*

★ copies of the "Learning Engagement" tracker page (from the CD-ROM)

★ copies of the "Mission: Possible!" and "Adding Assets at Home" handouts

1. Getting Started

Greeting. Have students say hello to someone near them.

Take 5. Hand out copies of the "Learning Engagement" tracker page and allow a few moments for students to complete them.

Two-Minute Partners. Have students form partners. Using the asset definition or the quotation on the board, ask the partners to each spend a minute describing what the words mean to him or her. Or ask students to say what *homework* means to them.

Preview. Tell students what they will do in this session. Make sure they have all necessary materials.

2. The Asset Question

Ask students: **Who loves homework? Who hates homework?** (Ask for a show of hands.) **Does homework exist just to make your life miserable? Do dogs really eat homework? What's the *worst* thing about homework?** This should be a lighthearted moment in the session.

3. Before the Story

Read aloud Jack Prelutsky's "Homework! Oh, Homework!" or another humorous short poem about homework. If you read the Prelutsky poem, ask: **What would happen if homework really *did* disappear?** Tell students that this time you want more serious answers. If they need help, read aloud "A message for you" on page 47 of the student book.

4. The Story

Read It. Read aloud and discuss Kenny and Nina's story on pages 37–38 and 50–52 of the student book.

Story Questions for Discussion. Ask students:

★ What plans do the twins come up with to finish their homework fast?

★ When Kenny and Nina take shortcuts with their homework, what happens? Who gets hurt?

★ Besides copying, what other bad homework habits do Kenny and Nina have?

★ When Kenny and Nina's parents say they are proud of them, why does this make the twins feel uncomfortable?

★ How does this family handle the homework issue? How do you handle it at your home?

★ What does this story teach you about trust?

5. Asset-Building Activities At-a-Glance

Read aloud some of the activities on pages 39–49 of the student book, or invite volunteers to read them aloud. Then ask questions like the following:

★ How do you keep your brain turned on after school so you can stay sharp for homework?

★ What are your homework habits? Tell us about the good ones—and the not-so-good ones. What's *one* horrid homework habit you'll try to change, starting today?

★ What is your homework space like? What's the best part about it? The worst part? Is there a way you can make your homework space better?

★ Is there someone at home or in your neighborhood who helps you with homework? If you don't have anyone now, can you think of someone who might be able to help you, if you ask for help?

Note: Because homework is so important to school success, take some time over the next few weeks to work with students (individually or in small groups) to improve homework habits. Do students know how to use assignment sheets? Do they use student planners? Do they know how to organize their backpacks? Remind students often that if they have homework problems, they should come talk to you.

6. Session Activity

★ Introduce the "Mission: Possible!"* activity. Tell students they are secret agents, and their assignment is to train themselves and their

Standards/Objectives Highlights	
Character Education	School sets expectations for moral action inside and outside school
Health	Students identify how peers can influence healthy and unhealthy behaviors
Social Studies	Students identify key concepts to show connections among patterns of change and continuity
Language Arts	Students employ strategies to communicate with different audiences for a variety of purposes
SEL Competencies	Students recognize and understand their obligation to engage in ethical, safe, and legal behaviors

*Adapted with permission from *Building Assets Is Elementary: Group Activities for Helping Kids Ages 8–12 Succeed* (Mission Possible). Copyright © 2004 by Search Institute, Minneapolis, MN, 800-888-7828; www.search-institute.org. All rights reserved.

friends to get homework done and have fun doing it. They will work in small groups to complete their missions.

* The *Language Specialists* will come up with positive-sounding names for homework. *Examples:* "Homework Storm," "Operation Homework." They also will make a list of sayings they can use to motivate themselves and each other.

* The *Headquarters Specialists* will draw a plan of "homework headquarters"—an ideal place to do homework.

* The *Equipment Specialists* will make a list of supplies and tools needed to do homework.

* The *Success Specialists* will think of ways to reward oneself for doing homework and celebrate getting homework done.

★ Hand out copies of "Mission: Possible!" and review it with students. Divide the class into four small groups. Circulate while students work to see how they're doing and offer advice. Allow time for each group to report back to the class. Write on the board anything you think students should remember and try. Congratulate students on completing their mission.

★ Hand out copies of "Adding Assets at Home."

7. Closing Question

Ask students: **What will you do to begin adding the Homework asset to your life?** If there's time, encourage responses. Give an example of building this asset in your own life.

Preparation for Next Session

★ Make the book *Loving to Learn* available to students if you would like them to read ahead the story and/or activity ideas for the Bonding to Adults at School asset (Session 24).

★ Obtain a list of all school personnel.

★ Ask students to say a friendly hello to at least one school staff person before the next session.

MISSION: POSSIBLE!

You are a secret agent. Your assignment is to train yourself and your friends to get homework done and have fun doing it.

The head of your agency (your teacher) has given your group one of four possible assignments. Circle your group's assignment:

Your mission: To come up with positive-sounding names for homework. ***Examples:*** "Homework Storm," "Operation Homework." You also will make a list of sayings you can use to motivate yourselves and each other.

Your mission: To draw a plan of "homework headquarters"—an ideal place to do homework.

Your mission: To make a list of supplies and tools needed to do homework well and efficiently.

Your mission: To think of ways to reward yourselves for doing homework and celebrate getting it done.

 Use this space for notes and ideas:

Homework

Today your child learned about the **Homework** asset. For your child, this asset means: *You usually hand in your homework on time.* In today's session activity, the students became "agents" on a mission to find better, more satisfying ways to handle homework. You may want to ask your child to tell you more about this activity.

Ideas and Activities to Try at Home

★ Let your child know homework is serious, you take it seriously, and you expect your child to take it seriously, too. You can agree with your child that homework isn't fun, that it can be hard, that it can be boring, and/or that it takes up time your child would rather spend doing other things. Those are all basic truths about homework. Still, homework must be done.

★ Work with your child to create a homework schedule. This can be difficult in families where adults work outside the home and/or where children have a lot of other scheduled activities. Even so, it's important to carve out some time each day (and, if possible, the *same* time each day) for homework. Right after school? Before dinner? After dinner? What works best in your family? Be flexible—but be firm. If there's truly no time for homework, maybe your child is overscheduled.

★ Make sure your child has a regular homework place. If your child has a room of his or her own, you can help your child set up a homework desk or corner with the supplies he or she needs. If your child shares a room with one or more siblings, you may need to help them negotiate who gets what space when. Lots of kids do homework at the kitchen table; that's fine, too.

★ Why not study together? While your child is doing homework, you can read or catch up on paperwork. This way, you're available to your child. You're also spending time together.

What if your child has big homework problems, or you think your child has too much homework? Please talk with your child's teachers (including me). Homework should not be a horrible burden on any child. It should not be the main focus of family life. Most teachers (including me) want to know when kids are having homework problems. That's part of what we're here for.

> **Tip:** Check your local library for a book called *How to Help Your Child with Homework* by Jeanne Shay Schumm, Ph.D. (Minneapolis: Free Spirit Publishing, 2005). This book has helped many parents end the "homework wars" and really help their children.

Session 24: Bonding to Adults at School

> **What this asset means to the child:** You care about and feel connected to the teachers and other adults at your school.

Backdrop

Write the name of the asset and its definition on the board.

Optional. Write this quotation on the board: "It's not what you know, but who you know."
—Anonymous

Outcomes

★ to help students add the Bonding to Adults at School asset to their lives

★ to encourage students to recognize and appreciate the adults at school who help and support them

★ to invite students to show their appreciation in a special letter

Preparation

Obtain a list of all school personnel.

Materials

★ copies of the book *Loving to Learn*

★ copies of the "Homework" tracker page (from the CD-ROM)

★ copies of the "Letter of Appreciation" and "Adding Assets at Home" handouts

★ art supplies (markers, colored pencils)

1. Getting Started

Greeting. Have students say hello to someone near them.

Take 5. Hand out copies of the "Homework" tracker page and allow a few moments for students to complete them.

Two-Minute Partners. Have students form partners. Using the asset definition or the quotation on the board, ask the partners to each spend a minute describing what the words mean to him or her. Ask students why they think the quote says the important thing is *who* you know." Or ask students to tell one thing about an adult at school they know.

Preview. Tell students what they will do in this session. Make sure they have all necessary materials.

2. The Asset Question

Ask students: **What does it mean to *bond* with someone?** *(To form a relationship; to feel connected to the person in some way.)* Talk with students about easy ways to connect with adults at school. *Example:* You can smile and wave to teachers, administrators, or lunchroom helpers when you see them in the hall. Ask: **How is being friendly different from being a "teacher's pet"?**

3. Before the Story

Have students describe or name as many adults as they can who work at their school. As they say the names, write them on the board, along with their positions: teacher, aide, principal, lunchroom helper, custodian, counselor, media specialist, parent volunteer, etc. Consult the list of school personnel for names, spellings, and titles.

Tell students to start thinking about *one* adult at school who is special to them—someone they feel thankful to know.

4. The Story

Read It. Read aloud and discuss T. J.'s story on pages 53–54 and 64–65 of the student book. You may want to stop reading at the bottom of page 54 and talk about how T. J. feels about his former teacher, Mrs. Levitz.

Story Questions for Discussion. Ask students:

★ Why is T. J.'s dad concerned about how things are going for T. J. in his new classroom?

★ What do you learn about T. J.'s new teacher, Mr. Hoffman, at the start of the story?

★ T. J. gets to see his former teacher, Mrs. Levitz, outside of school—during dinner at his own house! Have you ever had the chance to spend time with one of your teachers outside of school? Tell us about it.

★ T. J. learns that Mr. Hoffman has said nice things about him to Mrs. Levitz. Do you think this changes the way T. J. feels about Mr. Hoffman? In what way?

★ Why is it important for T. J. to feel connected to the adults at school? Why is it important for *any* student to have this feeling?

5. Asset-Building Activities At-a-Glance

Have some of the activities from pages 56–63 of the student book written on the board. *Examples:*

★ Tell your family about the adults at your school.

★ Invite your teacher to dinner.

★ Be friendly to the adults at your school.

★ Talk more with your teachers.

★ Make a pact with your friends to be friendly and respectful to adults at school.

Ask students if they have other ideas for building this asset. Add their ideas to the list on the board.

6. Session Activity

★ Hand out copies of "Letter of Appreciation."

★ Draw students' attention to the list of names and positions you wrote on the board earlier in the session. Remind them that you asked them to start thinking about *one* adult at school who is special to them—someone they feel thankful to know. Explain that they will use the handout to write a letter to

Standards/Objectives Highlights

Character Education	School fosters caring attachments among adults within the school community
Health	Students demonstrate how to ask for assistance to enhance personal health
Social Studies	Students demonstrate an understanding of such concepts as role and status in describing human interactions
Language Arts	Students use a variety of resources to gather information
SEL Competencies	Students establish and maintain healthy and rewarding connections with individuals and groups

that person. Say that they should come up with at least one specific example of something the person does that they appreciate.

Sample letter for students who have trouble getting started:

Dear Mr. Patterson,

Thank you for being such a great gym teacher. I appreciate the way you smile at me in the hallways and how you cheer me on when we play sports in gym. It sure is nice to have a teacher like you.

★ Invite students to decorate their letters with drawings.

★ Collect the letters to deliver in person (if you can) or place in the recipients' mail slots at school.

★ Hand out copies of "Adding Assets at Home."

7. Closing Question

Ask students: **What will you do to start adding the Bonding to Adults in School asset to your life?** If there's time, encourage responses. Give an example of building this asset in your own life.

Preparation for Next Session

★ Make the book *Loving to Learn* available to students if you would like them to read ahead the story and/or activity ideas for the Reading for Pleasure asset (Session 25).

★ Gather copies of some of your all-time favorite books. If possible, include books you loved when you were the age of students in your group. If you're lucky, you still have some of these in your personal library. If not, see if the media center specialist at your school or a librarian at your public library can help you find copies. When you share these books with your students, you'll be modeling an authentic love of reading— one that has endured for years. They will remember the warmth and enthusiasm with which you talk about these treasures from your past. You might also bring in a book or two you're reading now to demonstrate that you still read for pleasure.

★ You'll spend part of Session 25 pretending to be a visitor from another planet. If possible, bring in an alien mask (not too scary!), a head bopper (a headband with balls on springs), or something else silly and fun to wear.

Letter of Appreciation

Date:

To:

From:

Dear _____,

Sincerely,

_____

Session 24

Bonding to Adults at School

Your child was introduced to the **Bonding to Adults at School** asset today. For your child, this asset means: *You care about and feel connected to the teachers and other adults at school.*

In today's session, students named school personnel who are special to them, then chose one and wrote a letter of appreciation. You may wish to continue this discussion at home. Talk to your child about the adults you're familiar with at school. Find out if your child has a good relationship with his or her teacher and other adults at school. Suggest ways for your child to get to know these important people a little better.

Why Bonding Matters. Research shows that students are more likely to stay in school and stay motivated to learn if they feel connected to the people there. When students know that people at school care about them and notice when they're absent, they feel they are part of a community. School becomes more stimulating and challenging and feels like a good place to be.

Send Positive Messages Back to School.

★ Encourage your child to make homemade cards or gifts for special days: teachers' birthdays, holidays, or the last day of school.

★ Invite a teacher to meet you for breakfast or coffee on the weekend. Or invite a teacher to dinner at your home.

★ Stay in touch with your child's teacher with notes or emails. Write thank-you notes or leave voicemail messages when you're pleased about something at school.

Quick Tip: Tell your child about *one* adult at school who cared about you when you were young. How did this person make a difference in your life? Ask your child which adult at school he or she likes best and why.

Session 25: Reading for Pleasure

> **What this asset means to the child:** You like to read, and you read for fun on most days of the week.

Backdrop

Write the name of the asset and its definition on the board.

> **Optional.** Write this quotation on the board: "A good book is the best of friends."
> —Martin Tupper

Outcomes

* to help students add the Reading for Pleasure asset to their lives

* to communicate the love of reading

* to invite students to share information about their favorite books

Preparation

* Gather copies of some of your all-time favorite books. If possible, include books you loved when you were the age of students in your group. If you're lucky, you still have some of these in your personal library. If not, see if the media center specialist at your school or a librarian at your public library can help you find copies. You might also bring in a book or two you're reading now to demonstrate that you still read for pleasure.

* You'll spend part of this session pretending to be a visitor from another planet. If possible, bring in an alien mask (not too scary!), a head bopper (a headband with balls on springs), or something else silly and fun to wear.

Materials

* copies of the book *Loving to Learn*

* copies of the "Bonding to Adults at School" tracker page (from the CD-ROM)

* copies of the "Take Me to Your Reader Survey" and "Adding Assets at Home" handouts

1. Getting Started

Greeting. Have students say hello to someone near them.

Take 5. Hand out copies of the "Bonding to Adults at School" tracker page and allow a few moments for students to complete them.

Two-Minute Partners. Have students form partners. Using the asset definition or the quotation on the board, ask the partners to each spend a minute describing what the words mean to him or her. Or ask students to describe what reading means to them.

Preview. Tell students what they will do in this session. Make sure they have all necessary materials.

2. The Asset Question

Pick up on the "Two-Minute Partners" discussion by asking students: **What does reading mean to you? Do you view books as best friends, as strangers, or as things to be avoided?** In an age of computers, the Internet, high-definition TV, and text messaging, many students may view books as boring or hopelessly old-fashioned. Tell students that today you want everyone to get excited about books.

Ask students who enjoy reading to raise their hands. Call on as many as time allows. Ask them to name their all-time favorite book and briefly tell the group why they like it so much. Afterward, show and tell the group about some of your all-time favorite books. Pass them around the room to give students a close-up look at them.

3. Before the Story

Talk about the ways in which books can open up a whole new world for people. Through reading, we can travel the world, imagine life on other planets, find fascinating facts, learn new skills, and delve into the past.

Discuss how one of America's founding fathers, Benjamin Franklin, started the first library in the American colonies in 1731. Franklin once said, "The doors to wisdom are never shut," and he read every book he could get his hands on.

Remind students that libraries let people borrow books for free. Everyone who has access to a library has the opportunity to discover the world.

4. The Story

Read It. Read aloud and discuss The Rockin' Readers' story on pages 66–68 and 79–80 of the student book. You may want to stop reading at the bottom of page 68 and talk about why the comments from the different members of the club show that Katie's book choice was a good one.

Story Questions for Discussion. Ask students:

★ Why are the book club members all reading the same book? What's the point of doing that instead of reading whatever you want?

★ Do you read poetry, or have you ever read a story that was written mostly in poetry? Tell us about it.

★ Has anyone read *Love That Dog* by Sharon Creech? Tell us about it.

★ Author Walter Dean Myers has said that reading "saved" him. What did it save him from?

★ Would you be interested in starting your own book club? How might you get others to join?

5. Asset-Building Activities At-a-Glance

Read over the activities on pages 69–77 of the student book, or ask for volunteers to read them aloud. Ask students to name one or two activities they might like to try in the coming days and weeks. *Suggestions:*

★ Spend time at a library. Just explore.

★ Ask someone at home to read to you.

Standards/Objectives Highlights	
Character Education	School has a range of strategies to accommodate diverse cultures, skills, and interests
Health	Students identify resources to assist in achieving a personal health goal
Social Studies	Students describe how people create places that reflect cultural values and ideals
Language Arts	Students read from many genres to build understanding of the ethical and aesthetic aspects of human experience
SEL Competencies	Students understand that individual and group differences complement each other and make the world more interesting

★ Offer to read to someone at home.

★ Start a reading journal.

★ Join or start a reading club.

★ Visit a children's bookstore in your town or city.

★ Share a book with a friend.

★ Borrow a book from a friend.

6. Session Activity

Put on the alien mask, the head bopper, or whatever else you brought to wear. Introduce yourself as a visitor from another planet. Say that you've just arrived on Earth and you've seen a lot of people doing something they call *reading*. Tell the students you need more information about this strange *reading* thing so you can report back to the leaders on your planet.

★ Hand out copies of "Take Me to Your Reader Survey." Read aloud the "Dear Earthling" letter at the top to make sure everyone understands what to do. Tell students that it's okay to put several checkmarks by the same answer, or several answers in the same blank.

★ Divide students into small groups to discuss and answer the questions on the survey. Have one person in each group record the survey results and report back to the class.

★ Compile the survey results and write the totals on the board or chart paper. In your

alien guise, say something like, "Hmmmm, very interesting. This is what I'll report to the leaders on my planet: _____." Of course, what you say will depend on the survey results!

★ Hand out copies of "Adding Assets at Home."

7. Closing Question

Ask students: **What will you do to start adding the Reading for Pleasure asset to your life?** If there's time, encourage responses. Give an example of building this asset in your own life.

Preparation for Next Session

★ Make the book *Knowing and Doing What's Right* available to students if you would like them to read ahead the story and/or activity ideas for the Caring asset (Session 26).

★ Read over the suggestions in the next session for making a care package (page 168), and collect small items for students and put them in a box or basket.

★ Visit the Kids Care Clubs Web site *(www.kidscare.org)*. If it seems appropriate to start a Kids Care Club with your students, find out what steps you'll need to take. Be prepared to tell your group about the Kids Care Club during the next session and ask if this is something they would like to do.

Take Me to Your Reader Survey

Dear Earthling,

The leaders on my planet have asked me to find out about the Earth activity called *reading*. Please answer the questions on this survey. Ask other Earthlings to answer them, too. Help us understand why you do this strange thing.

Yours sincerely,

1. WHERE do you most like to read?
_____ In my bed
_____ In a library
_____ At school
_____ Under a shady tree
_____ On the couch in my living room
_____ Other: _____

2. WHAT do you most like to read?
_____ Books
_____ Magazines
_____ Comic books
_____ Zines
_____ Blogs
_____ Other: _____

3. What are your favorite kinds of books?
_____ Books with made-up stories (fiction)
_____ Books with true stories (nonfiction)
_____ Books of facts
_____ Books of poems
_____ Books that make me laugh
_____ Books that make me dream
_____ Books about: _____

4. What kind of FICTION do you most like to read?
_____ Action stories
_____ Sad stories
_____ Romantic stories
_____ Funny stories
_____ Mystery stories
_____ Science fiction or fantasy stories
_____ Other: _____

5. What kind of NONFICTION do you most like to read?
_____ Newspapers
_____ Current-events magazines
_____ Biographies
_____ How-to-books
_____ Science and nature books
_____ History books
_____ Other: _____

Reading for Pleasure

Today your child learned about the **Reading for Pleasure** asset. For your child, this asset means: *You like to read, and you read for fun on most days of the week.*

The best way to encourage our children to read is to be readers ourselves. Invite your child to sit next to you and read. You can read aloud from the same book or simply sit side-by-side as you each read something you enjoy. Read again before bed. These moments not only encourage a love of reading but also can bring you closer.

More Ways to Encourage Reading at Home

Make a Sign. Ask your child to make and decorate a sign that says "Read for fun every day." Display the sign in your home. Have all sorts of reading materials available: books, poems, comic books, newspaper cartoons, magazines.

Start the Reading Habit. Establish a weekly family reading time, complete with popcorn or other treats. Model how to discuss books and articles by talking with your child about what you're reading. Take weekly trips to the library. Make sure everyone in your family has a library card.

Take Good Care of Books. Encourage your child to treat books well and model how to do so. *Example:* Use bookmarks instead of folding down page corners. Remind your child about the importance of returning borrowed books on time and in good condition.

Make It Inviting. Make the spaces for reading at home comfortable and cozy. Make sure the lighting is good and provide lots of different choices for reading materials.

Knowing and Doing What's Right: The Positive Values Assets

★ The **Positive Values Assets** are **Internal Assets.**

★ **Internal Assets** are values, skills, and self-perceptions that kids develop internally, with help from caring adults.

★ The **Positive Values Assets** are about guiding kids to develop strong values that enable them to make healthy life choices. Values inform decisions, shape priorities, and determine words and actions. Other words for *values* are *morals* and *conscience.*

The Positive Values Assets are:

26. **Caring**—Parent(s) tell the child it is important to help other people.

27. **Equality and social justice**—Parent(s) tell the child it is important to speak up for equal rights for all people.

28. **Integrity**—Parent(s) tell the child it is important to stand up for one's beliefs.

29. **Honesty**—Parent(s) tell the child it is important to tell the truth.

30. **Responsibility**—Parent(s) tell the child it is important to accept personal responsibility for behavior.

31. **Healthy lifestyle**—Parent(s) tell the child it is important to have good health habits and an understanding of healthy sexuality.

Session 26: Caring

Backdrop

Write the name of the asset and its definition on the board.

> **Optional.** Write this quotation on the board: "When we perform acts of kindness, we get a wonderful feeling inside."—Rabbi Harold Kushner

Note: Write the session backdrop quotation on the board when it is appropriate for your students. Always write the name of the asset and its definition on the board.

Outcomes

★ to help students add the Caring asset to their lives

★ to discuss with students new and practical ways for showing care to people beyond the family

★ to identify ways children and their families can help others

Preparation

★ Read over the suggestions on page 168 for making a care package, and collect small items for students and put them in a box or basket.

★ Visit the Kids Care Clubs Web site (*www.kidscare.org*). If it seems appropriate to start a Kids Care Club in your group or organization, find out what steps you'll need to take. Be prepared to tell your group about the Kids Care Club and ask if this is something they would like to do.

Materials

★ copies of the book *Knowing and Doing What's Right*

★ copies of the "Reading for Pleasure" tracker page (from the CD-ROM)

★ copies of the "Tune In, Reach Out" and "Adding Assets at Home" handouts

1. Getting Started

Greeting. Suggest students say hello to someone near them in a new way. *Example:* "Hey, it's good to see you. I'm glad you're here."

Take 5. Hand out copies of the "Reading for Pleasure" tracker page and allow a few moments for students to complete them.

Note: Make sure students know it's always appropriate to share feelings or an experience related to this asset or any other one. Sometimes, share your own examples as well.

Two-Minute Partners. Have students form partners. Using the asset definition or the quotation on the board, ask the partners to each spend a minute describing what the words mean to him or her. Or ask students to describe one way their families try to help others.

Preview. Tell students what they will do in this session. Make sure they have all necessary materials.

2. The Asset Question

Tell students that we've all been cared for since we were infants. In the words of a Cree elder, "Now it's our time to care." Ask: **What does it mean to say "it's our time to care"?** Discuss with students examples of caring that are familiar to them.

3. Before the Story

Introduce students to the idea of care packages by having a basket or box of small items that students like—stickers, cookies, pencils. Have enough items to give each child one thing. Ask students to define *care package*. Tell them the features of a care package:*

★ It's a surprise

★ It usually has more than one item

★ Its contents can be inexpensive and homemade

★ The items can be fun or practical, and they always show the giver cares about the receiver

Give one item to each child and ask the group how it feels to receive an unexpected present. Suggest to students that surprising someone with an act of kindness is a little like giving a care package. Perhaps they can keep that in mind as you read Hanna and Tim's story.

If you looked into the Kids Care Clubs (*www. kidscare.org*) and decided to pursue this further, take some time now to tell students about the program and what the clubs do. Ask if they would like to start a Kids Care Club. If they are interested, follow through.

Note: Allow the story to be the central focus of each session.

4. The Story

Read It. Read aloud and discuss Hanna and Tim's story on pages 6–7 and 17–19 of the student book. You may want to stop reading at the bottom of page 7 and talk about whether Hanna is old enough or ready to accept Tim's challenge.

Story Questions for Discussion. Ask students:

★ **What are some examples of caring in the first two pages of the story?**

★ **What role do you think Fat Cat played in this story?**

★ **Have you ever felt afraid, as Hanna did, of old or sick or poor people? What do you do about that feeling?**

★ **Why is it a good sign that Hanna is curious about all that she sees when she first arrives at the senior center?**

★ **When Hanna meets Mrs. Brooks, she notices all the photos around the elderly woman. How do the photos become a way for Mrs. Brooks to make Hanna feel more comfortable?**

	Standards/Objectives Highlights
Character Education	School fosters caring attachments between adults and students and among students
Health	Students demonstrate communication skills to enhance health
Social Studies	Students describe personal connections to community, nation, and world
Language Arts	Students draw on prior experience and their interactions to interpret texts
SEL Competencies	Students believe others deserve to be treated with kindness

*Adapted with permission from *Building Assets Is Elementary: Group Activities for Helping Kids Ages 8–12 Succeed* (Care Package). Copyright © 2004 by Search Institute, Minneapolis, MN; 800-888-7828; www.search-institute.org. All rights reserved.

★ How is Mrs. Brooks' offer to share some comebacks with Hanna an example of caring?

★ What is the biggest thing Hanna does to show she cares about the people in the center?

- -

Optional Activity: Vocabulary

Original Comeback. Have students look up the origin of the word *comebacks*. Ask students how the word relates to the conversation between Hannah and Mrs. Brooks.

- -

5. Asset-Building Activities At-a-Glance

Read over the activities from pages 8–16 of the student book. Write some or all of the following statements on the board and discuss as many as you have time for:

★ Walk in Someone Else's Shoes. (Discussion questions: **What is *empathy?* Why is it important? Have you ever had *empathy* for another person? Tell us about it.**)

★ Show You Care Every Day. (Discussion questions: **What's one way you can show you care about your mom? Your dad? Another family member? What are some everyday chores you might do to help out around your home?**)

★ Go Further. (Discussion questions: **What's *one* way you and your family could help other people? Or maybe you already do. Tell us about it.**)

★ Be a Caring Neighbor. (Discussion questions: **What's *one* idea you have about how to do this? Can you think of a caring thing a neighbor has done for you or someone else you know?**)

★ Care for Your Friends. (Discussion questions: **What have you done lately to show that you care for your friends? What have your friends done for you?**)

6. Session Activity

★ Ask a student volunteer to read aloud the paragraph under "In Your Faith Community" on page 14 of the student book. Discuss what it means to *tune in* to what people are saying. Explain that *tuning in* is a good first step toward showing you care for other people. You have to *notice* a need before you can offer to help.

★ Hand out copies of "Tune In, Reach Out."

★ Read the introductory paragraphs to students. Make sure they understand the first part of the handout is for identifying people in need they know or have heard about. The second part is for describing how they will help one or two of the people on their list.

★ Hand out copies of "Adding Assets at Home."

7. Closing Question

Ask students: **What will you do to start adding the Caring asset to your life?** If there's time, encourage responses. Give an example of building this asset in your own life.

Preparation for Next Session

★ Make the book *Knowing and Doing What's Right* available to students if you would like them to read ahead the story and/or activity ideas for the Equality and Social Justice asset (Session 27).

★ Gather and create a list of statements that reflect values and beliefs. See the "Preparation" section of Session 27 on page 172 for examples.

Tune In, Reach Out

Helping somebody—by raking a yard, carrying groceries, or spending time with a lonely person—is a little like giving "care packages" of yourself. To help somebody, you first have to notice that he or she needs help. Think about people in need. They can be people you know or people you have heard about from others. Start your own People In Need (PIN) list:

My PIN List

_____

_____

_____

_____

_____

Now choose one or two people you will help or try to help. Write their names. Then write what you'll do for each person. What kind of "care package" will you give? Will you visit an elderly neighbor? Help make cookies for a new family in the neighborhood? Give up a Saturday afternoon to help an aunt with a chore? No act of caring is too small. Everything counts.

This week I will try to help:

Name   **What I'll Do**

_____   _____

_____   _____

_____   _____

Note to Myself: I will stay tuned in and add other names to my PIN list as I hear about more people who need help.

ADDING ASSETS AT HOME

Caring

Today your child was introduced to the **Positive Values** assets. These assets are about the beliefs that guide one's choices and behaviors. Some people might call these *morals*; others, *conscience*. The first of these assets, **Caring**, was the topic of today's session. For your child, this asset means: *Your parent(s) tell you it's important to help other people.*

Caring begins in the home. When parents meet their children's emotional needs, children are more able and free to meet others' needs by reaching out and helping others. When parents show they care for others, children follow their example. Caring children grow up to be caring adults, and the cycle continues.

There are two ways to show care for other people. Tell your child about both kinds. If possible, give your child personal experience in both kinds.

★ **In-Person Caring.** This includes spending time with people who need help, talking with them face-to-face, being with them, and interacting with them one-on-one. This kind of caring happens in a childcare center, a homeless shelter, a hospice, a home for elderly people, a food shelf, and other places where people go to get help.

★ **Indirect Caring.** This includes collecting money to give to charities, shelters, or other helping organizations. It includes collecting food, clothing, toys, personal care items (shampoo, toothpaste, soap), and other useful things and giving them to people or organizations to distribute to people in need.

Ideas to Try at Home

★ As a family, volunteer to work at a fundraiser, a food drive, a homeless shelter, or an animal shelter.

★ Spend time with a neighbor or an extended family member who lives alone.

★ Start a donations jar. Have family members put pocket change in the jar. (You might suggest that children contribute a percentage of their weekly allowance.) Every so often, count the money in the donations jar. Once it reaches an agreed-upon amount ($10? $25? $100?), have a family meeting to decide where to donate the money you've collected.

★ Broaden your definition of *caring* to include many different people—family members, neighbors, people in your community and country, people on the other side of the world.

For more ideas, check out a Volunteer Center near you. Call 1-800-VOLUNTEER (1-800-865-8683) or visit the Web site: *1-800-VOLUNTEER.org.* You also can visit Volunteer Match on the Web: *www.volunteermatch.org.* Enter your ZIP code and press "Search" to get a list of volunteer opportunities in your area.

Session 27: Equality and Social Justice

Backdrop

Write the name of the asset and its definition on the board.

> **Optional.** Write this quotation on the board: "This country will not be a good place for any of us to live in unless we make it a good place for all of us to live in."—Theodore Roosevelt

Outcomes

★ to help students add the Equality and Social Justice asset to their lives

★ to help students understand the meaning of *social justice*

★ to encourage students to think about and stand up for their values and beliefs

Preparation

★ Make two large signs, one that says "Agree" and another that says "Disagree."

★ Gather and create a list of statements that reflect values and beliefs. Your list may include some or all of the following, or other statements you prefer:

⭐ Share and share alike.

⭐ The time is always ripe to do right.

⭐ Actions speak louder than words.

⭐ All persons are born equal.

⭐ Anyone can grow up to be the president or leader of this country.

⭐ Where there's a will, there's a way.

⭐ Bullies never win.

⭐ The best things in life are free.

⭐ Live and let live.

⭐ Live free or die.

⭐ All children have the capacity to be both kind and cruel.

⭐ Standing for right when it is unpopular is a true test of moral character.

⭐ First and foremost, be true to yourself.

⭐ When in doubt, tell the truth.

⭐ Poor people work harder than rich people.

Materials

★ copies of the book *Knowing and Doing What's Right*

★ copies of the "Caring" tracker page (from the CD-ROM)

★ large paper bags, scissors, crayons or markers

★ copies of the "Agree or Disagree" and "Adding Assets at Home" handouts

1. Getting Started

Greeting. Have students say hello to someone near them.

Take 5. Hand out copies of the "Caring" tracker page and allow a few moments for students to complete them.

Two-Minute Partners. Have students form partners. Using the asset definition or the quotation on the board, ask the partners to each spend a minute describing what the words mean to him or her.

Preview. Tell students what they will do in this session. Make sure they have all necessary materials.

2. The Asset Question

Ask students: **What is *social justice?*** Begin a discussion with several definitions, including those on page 25 of the student book. Consider these definitions from leading human rights and peace activists:

★ "Social justice means moving towards a society where all hungry are fed, all sick are cared for, the environment is treasured, and we treat each other with love and compassion."—Medea Benjamin, founding director of Global Exchange and cofounder of CODEPINK: Women for Peace

★ "Social justice means complete and genuine equality of all people."—Paul George, director of Peninsula Peace and Justice Center

★ "Social justice means no kids going to bed hungry, no one without shelter or healthcare and a free and lively discussion and participation in the political direction and organization of our communities and nation."—Kirsten Moller, executive director and cofounder of Global Exchange

Invite students to contribute their own definitions. See if the group can agree on a definition.

3. Before the Story

Here's an activity to get students thinking about and debating their values and beliefs.

Agree or Disagree*

★ Tape up the two large signs (Agree/Disagree) on opposite sides of the room.

★ Tell students that you will read a statement. Students should take a moment to think about it, decide whether they agree or disagree, then go and stand by the appropriate sign.

★ Read the first statement from your prepared list. (***Example:*** "Share and share alike.") Allow time for students to move to the sign of their choice.

★ Invite students to give reasons why they agree or disagree with the statement. Say that if they hear a reason that changes their mind, they are free to move to the other sign.

Continue by reading and discussing as many statements as time allows.

Note: At this point in the session, you may either continue with the story or skip ahead to the session activity and return to the story later.

Standards/Objectives Highlights

Character Education	School has a range of strategies for diverse cultures, skills, and interests
Health	Students analyze the influence of culture and other factors on health
Social Studies	Students identify tensions between belief systems and policies and laws
Language Arts	Students read to build understanding of the ethical aspects of human experience
SEL Competencies	Students learn to achieve mutually satisfactory resolutions to conflict by addressing the needs of all concerned

*Adapted with permission from *Building Assets Is Elementary: Group Activities for Helping Kids Ages 8–12 Succeed* (Stand Up for What You Believe). Copyright © 2004 by Search Institute, Minneapolis, MN; 800-888-7828; www.search-institute.org. All rights reserved.

4. The Story

Read It. Read aloud and discuss Kia's story on pages 20–21 and 31–32 of the student book. You may want to stop reading at the bottom of page 21 and talk about why Kia feels confused about standing up for Isaac.

Story Questions for Discussion. Ask students:

★ What do you think of Kia's reaction to the phrase, "He's so retarded"? What do you do or say when someone uses that phrase?

★ Why does Ben call Kia "Miss Goody-Goody"? Even if the label was meant to be mean, do you think it "fits" Kia?

★ Why doesn't Isaac appreciate Kia standing up for him?

★ Do you think Kia stood up for Isaac just because she has a sister with a disability? Could she have other reasons, too?

★ What does Kia's mom mean when she says, "Life sure can be complicated"?

5. Asset-Building Activities At-a-Glance

Read over the activities on pages 22–30 of the student book and decide which ones are most suitable for your students. *Suggestions:*

★ Encourage students to make "I Believe . . . " lists. If they want, they can share their lists. See if they would like to create a "We Believe . . . " list for the whole classroom or group.

★ Ask volunteers to read the Universal Declaration of Human Rights and make a summary report to the group.

★ List on the board the freedoms we take for granted. Have students brainstorm other freedoms besides those named on pages 25–26 of the student book.

★ Suggest students work in pairs to look up definitions of *social justice,* write them in neat (or calligraphy) handwriting, and display them in the room.

★ Ask volunteers to visit the Amnesty International Web site *(www.amnestyusa.org),* check out AIKids, and report back to the group. Is this something your class would like to follow up on?

6. Session Activity

★ Hand out copies of "Agree or Disagree."

★ Read aloud the instructions so all students understand what to do.

★ Circulate as students work, helping them to express in words their feelings about these statements of belief.

★ If possible, display the completed handouts where others can see them—perhaps in a hall or on a bulletin board.

★ Hand out copies of "Adding Assets at Home."

7. Closing Question

Ask students: **What will you do to start adding the Equality and Social Justice asset to your life?** If there's time, encourage responses. Give an example of building this asset in your own life.

Preparation for Next Session

★ Make the book *Knowing and Doing What's Right* available to students if you would like them to read ahead the story and/or activity ideas for the Integrity asset (Session 28).

★ Gather suitable biographies of role models such as Rosa Parks, Martin Luther King Jr., Mother Teresa, Gandhi, and Abraham Lincoln.

Agree or Disagree

Now's your chance to say what's *really* on your mind about a value or belief you feel strongly about. You can choose a statement from the Agree/Disagree activity we did as a group or come up with your own statement.

1. Write the value or belief statement here:

_____

_____

_____

2. Write why you agree or disagree with it. Support your decision with one or two reasons:

_____

_____

_____

3. If you want, you can draw a picture or cartoon strip to illustrate your argument:

Session 27

Equality and Social Justice

Today your child learned about the **Equality and Social Justice** asset. For your child, this asset means: *Your parent(s) tell you it's important to speak up for equal rights for all people.*

Children today probably are more aware of *in*equality and social *in*justice than we grown-ups realize—or want to admit. They are constantly exposed to televised images of starving or suffering people. Many children know what poverty is, either from personal experience or because they have friends or classmates who live in poverty. And many have a sincere desire to help. You may want to share this example with your child:

After an 11-year-old boy named Trevor Ferrell saw a news story about people living on the streets, he begged his parents to take him downtown Philadelphia so he could give his own blanket and pillow to a homeless person. During the following weeks, he and his family (with help from classmates and neighbors) made nightly trips into the city to hand out food, clothing, and blankets. Today Trevor's Campaign includes homeless shelters and programs for people in need. More than 1,700 people have been helped because a young boy was moved by what he saw on television.

If you want to know more, visit the Trevor's Campaign Web site: *www.trevorscampaign.org.*

Ideas to Try as a Family

★ Talk as a family about equality and social justice. Does everyone know what those words mean? Or can you at least agree on what you think they mean?

★ Talk about "big stuff"—racism, sexism, ageism, poverty, hunger, discrimination. What do your children know about them? What have they heard? What have they experienced? What would they like to know?

★ Don't assume your kids are clueless; they hear all kinds of language and slurs in school and on the playground. Ask them what they have heard. Ask them how they feel about hurtful words.

★ Find a way to make your community a more just and equal place. Volunteer as a family at a soup kitchen, shelter, or food pantry.

★ Would family members be willing to give up certain foods to help feed the hungry? Eat vegetarian for a week; donate the money you would have spent on meat to a food shelf.

★ Learn about organizations that work for equality and social justice. Pick one to support. Children can contribute part of their allowance.

Session 28: Integrity

Backdrop

Write the name of the asset and its definition on the board.

> **Optional.** Write this quotation on the board:
> "I try to do the right thing at the right time."
> —Kareem Abdul-Jabbar

Outcomes

★ to help students add the Integrity asset to their lives

★ to help students identify when their actions match their beliefs

★ to help students act bravely and stand up for their beliefs

Preparation

Gather suitable biographies of role models such as Rosa Parks, Martin Luther King Jr., Mother Teresa, Gandhi, and Abraham Lincoln.

Materials

★ copies of the book *Knowing and Doing What's Right*

★ copies of the "Equality and Social Justice" tracker page (from the CD-ROM)

★ copies of the "Role Model Portrait" and "Adding Assets at Home" handouts

★ crayons or markers, glue

1. Getting Started

Greeting. Have students say hello to someone near them.

Take 5. Hand out copies of the "Equality and Social Justice" tracker page and allow a few moments for students to complete them.

Two-Minute Partners. Have students form partners. Using the asset definition or the quotation on the board, ask the partners to each spend a minute describing what the words mean to him or her.

Preview. Tell students what they will do in this session. Make sure they have all necessary materials.

2. The Asset Question

Make sure students know what it means to have *integrity.* Here's a simple definition: *Having a personal moral code and sticking to it no matter what.*

Ask students: **Is integrity something you have only when other people are watching? Or is it something you have all the time? How do you know?**

Talk about how integrity covers big things and small things. *Examples:* A person with integrity would not rob a bank. A person with integrity would not steal a dollar from a friend's desk, even if the friend wasn't around and there was no chance of getting caught or found out.

Optional Activity: Vocabulary

Word Origin. *Integrity* comes from the Latin *integer,* meaning soundness. Ask students to investigate more about the roots of this word and report to the group on ways in which the word *integrity* relates to Adam's story.

3. The Story

Read It. Read aloud and discuss Adam's story on pages 33–34 and 43–44 of the student book. You may want to stop at the bottom of page 34 and discuss Adam's conflict at this point in the story.

Story Questions for Discussion. Ask students:

★ How did Ricardo show his anger while playing catch at the start of the story?

★ Why was Ricardo trying to be in charge of Adam *and* his birthday party?

★ Have you ever felt the way Adam did when he admitted Ricardo was stubborn but still his friend? How did you handle that mixed feeling?

★ Why does Adam's decision to have fun at his own party, no matter what, show integrity?

★ If you could add a sentence to the story, how would you describe what *integrity* means to Adam?

4. After the Story

Turning the Tale. Suppose the story ended differently. After discussing Adam's story, have students role-play this scene:

★ Adam thinks about Ricardo's words and wonders if the party would be more fun if only boys were there. He decides to go to Ellie's house to try to talk her out of coming—but not in a direct way. Instead, Adam will hint that maybe she won't like being the only girl at his party. Maybe she'd rather come to dinner with his family on his birthday instead. What happens between Ellie and Adam?

If time allows, have students role-play the scene in several different ways.

5. Asset-Building Activities At-a-Glance

Read aloud some of the activities on pages 35–41 of the student book, or ask for volunteers to read them aloud. What activities appeal to students to do on their own or to do with a partner? *Suggestions:*

★ Have partners create portraits of each other's positive qualities. Display them around the room.

★ Have partners work together to identify people with integrity. They might be people they know or people they have heard about or learned about by reading, watching TV, or going to movies.

Standards/Objectives Highlights	
Character Education	School approaches behavior by emphasizing values and consequences
Health	Students demonstrate nonviolent strategies to manage or resolve conflict
Social Studies	Students describe the influence of attitudes and values on personal identity
Language Arts	Students use a variety of resources to gather and synthesize information
SEL Competencies	Students generate, implement, and evaluate positive and informed solutions to problems

★ Have students talk with neighbors about integrity, then report back to the group on what they learned.

You might also have students share stories of times when they stood strong and showed integrity.

6. Session Activity

★ Hand out copies of "Role Model Portrait." Read aloud the instructions so everyone understands what to do. Tell students they can work alone, with partners, or even in small groups, as long as they agree on a role model. If you were able to collect biographies of role models, make them available for students to use.

★ Circulate to help students decide on a role model, how to organize information, and the best way to portray this person.

★ Hand out copies of "Adding Assets at Home." Remind students that their parents or caregivers are the best resources for identifying other adults to support them.

7. Closing Question

Ask students: **What will you do to begin adding the Integrity asset to your life?** If there's time, encourage responses. Give an example of building this asset in your own life.

Preparation for Next Session

Make the book *Knowing and Doing What's Right* available to students if you would like them to read ahead the story and/or activity ideas for the Honesty asset (Session 29).

Role Model Portrait

A Person I Admire

Make a Role Model Portrait of Rosa Parks, Martin Luther King Jr., Mother Teresa, Gandhi, Abraham Lincoln, or someone else who is known for his or her outstanding integrity. Start by listing on scrap paper some things you already know about the person. Learn more about the person by reading books or articles or surfing the Web. In the space below, draw or paste a picture of the person. Add words, phrases, facts, and/or drawings that tell about his or her integrity.

Integrity

Today your child learned about the **Integrity** asset. For your child, this asset means: *Your parent(s) tell you it's important to stand up for your beliefs.* Students made portraits of people they admire—role models for what it means to have integrity. You might ask your child to tell you about the role model he or she chose.

Have a dialogue with your child about what it means to act on conviction. You might ask questions like these: **Is it easy or hard to stand up for something you believe in? What do you do when it's hard? Can you tell me about a time when you did this?** Encourage your child to keep acting on his or her convictions. Let your child know how proud you are of him or her.

Ideas and Activities to Try at Home

Help Your Child Build Integrity at Home.

★ Discuss with your child people he or she has read about or seen in the news. How do their actions show integrity?

★ Help your child make a list of things he or she stands for or against. Ask questions like: "Why are the things on your list important to you?" "How can you show that you are for or against something?"

★ Point out when your child says one thing but does another. Ask your child to point out when you do this, too.

★ Acknowledge when your child stands up for something or someone.

Role Model Integrity for Your Child.

★ Before you can model integrity for your child, you have to know what it is you believe in. Ask yourself: What do I value?

★ Get involved. Let your child see you and your beliefs in action.

★ Stand up for what you believe. Point out to your child when others do the same.

Quick Tip: Check your local library for a book called *What Do You Stand For? For Kids: A Guide to Building Character* by Barbara A. Lewis (Minneapolis: Free Spirit Publishing, 2005). Bring it home to share and discuss as a family.

Session 29: Honesty

Backdrop

Write the name of the asset and its definition on the board.

> **Optional.** Write this quotation on the board: "Always speak the truth—think before you speak."—Lewis Carroll

Outcomes

★ to help students add the Honesty asset to their lives

★ to encourage students to recognize ways in which they depart from the truth

★ to invite students to identify ways to build their "honesty muscles"

Materials

★ copies of the book *Knowing and Doing What's Right*

★ copies of the "Integrity" tracker page (from the CD-ROM)

★ copies of the "Script Starter" and "Adding Assets at Home" handouts

1. Getting Started

Greeting. Have students say hello to someone near them.

Take 5. Hand out copies of the "Integrity" tracker page and allow a few moments for students to complete them.

Two-Minute Partners. Have students form partners. Using the asset definition or the quotation on the board, ask the partners to each spend a minute describing what the words mean to him or her.

Preview. Tell students what they will do in this session. Make sure they have all necessary materials.

2. The Asset Question

Ask students: **Why is it sometimes hard to tell the truth?** Then ask: **Why is it sometimes easier to make up excuses or little white lies?** Invite students to share their favorite excuses. Write them on the board.

3. Before the Story

Have students role-play scenes in which excuses and little white lies get kids into "hot water." (Make sure they understand what "getting into hot water" means.) They should act out what happens as a result of the excuse/little white lie, and how to fix the situation. *Possible scenes:*

A. Sometime during the school day, you lose your science book. There's a science test tomorrow, and you need your book to study. You tell your teacher that someone stole your book.

B. You're supposed to pick up your little sister from junior kindergarten and walk home together. You forget and only remember when you are nearly home. You go back for her and end up getting home much later than expected. You tell your dad the teacher kept you after school and made you late.

C. Your best friend's birthday is a week away. You get him a great gift—something you know he'll really like. Only you really like it, too. In fact, you like it so much that you decide to keep it for yourself. At the party, you tell your friend that you forgot to bring his gift.

4. The Story

Read It. Read aloud and discuss Brianna's story on pages 45–46 and 53–54 of the student book. You may want to stop reading at the bottom of page 46 and talk about how Brianna might be feeling. She lied to her dad, her dad found out, her friends know something's up, and it looks like her weekend is ruined. Ask students: **If you were Brianna, how would you feel right now?**

Story Questions for Discussion. Ask students:

★ Brianna doesn't seem to have any regrets about how she left her room as she runs to join her friends. What does this tell you about Brianna's truth-telling habits?

★ What message does Brianna's dad send by coming to the court to get her instead of waiting for her to come home after the game?

★ Brianna says, "Well, Daddy, maybe I'm not as good of a picker-upper as you are. I can't help that!" What should she have said instead?

★ What does Brianna mean when she asks if she and her dad can start the day over?

★ Think of a time when you were caught in a lie. What did you say? What did you do? What happened as a result of your lie?

5. Asset-Building Activities At-a-Glance

Read over the activities from pages 47–52 of the student book. Write some or all of the following statements on the board and discuss them as a group. Do students understand what each statement means? Is this something they might want to try?

★ Be honest with your family.

★ Be honest with yourself.

★ Commit to the truth.

★ Be honest when you play games and sports.

★ Make a pact with your friends not to lie to each other.

Ask students to think of more ways to build their "honesty muscles." Add them to the list on the board.

6. Session Activity

★ Hand out copies of "Script Starter."

★ Have students work alone to make their lists. If they have trouble getting started, talk about how kids get into "hot water" when they lie and get caught. Ask students to share brief examples.

Standards/Objectives Highlights

Character Education	School offers an academic curriculum that provides challenges to promote character development
Health	Students choose a healthy option when making a decision
Social Studies	Students use change, conflict, and complexity to explain patterns of change and continuity
Language Arts	Students use spoken and written language to accomplish their own purposes
SEL Competencies	Students identify and label their feelings

★ When everyone has made his or her list, have students form small groups and vote on a list they think would make a good script.

★ Have each group present their list to the whole group and tell why they think it would make a good script. Have the whole group vote for one list.

★ Work with students to turn the list into a script, or assign this task to volunteers. Have students act it out for the group.

If possible, have students act out their script for another class or group.

7. Closing Question

Ask students: **What will you do to start adding the Honesty asset to your life?** If there's time, encourage responses. Give an example of building this asset in your own life.

Preparation for Next Session

Make the book *Knowing and Doing What's Right* available to students if you would like them to read ahead the story and/or activity ideas for the Responsibility asset (Session 30).

Script Starter

Think of a time when telling a lie got you into hot water. List all the details here. Don't hold anything back. Someone reading your list should know exactly what went on.

Where were you? _____

_____

_____

When did this happen? _____

_____

_____

What did you do? _____

_____

_____

What did you say? _____

_____

_____

Was anyone else involved? _____

_____

_____

What happened next? _____

_____

_____

Honesty

Today your child learned about the **Honesty** asset. For your child, this asset means: *Your parent(s) tell you it's important to be truthful.* Students wrote about and talked about times when lying got them into hot water. You may want to ask your child to share stories he or she heard (and told!).

As adults, we can teach our children the value of honesty by modeling it, talking about it, and explaining why it's important.

Ideas and Activities to Try at Home

Tips for Teaching Honesty

★ If someone gives you too much change, correct the situation immediately.

★ Admit and apologize when you haven't been totally honest.

★ Choose friends who are honest.

★ Avoid gossip.

★ Avoid saying one thing behind someone's back, another to his or her face. Children find this confusing—and it could land you in hot water when a child blurts out something that was never meant to be repeated.

★ Point out when characters in TV shows and movies are being dishonest. Are there any consequences for their dishonesty?

★ If you suspect that your child has lied, don't accuse him or her. Ask questions like, "Do you think I believe you right now?" or "Do you think I'm having a hard time believing you?" This will give your child time to think about what to say next—and the opportunity to be truthful. (Accusations make us defensive; questions invite reflection and allow us to save face.)

Discussion Questions to Try. Ask your child:

★ When was the last time it was hard for you to be honest? Tell me about it.

★ What's the worst thing that can happen when you lie?

★ Do you ever worry that telling the truth might hurt someone else's feelings?

★ What can we do at home to make our family more honest?

Session 30: Responsibility

Backdrop

Write the name of the asset and its definition on the board.

> **Optional.** Write this quotation on the board: "You are the only one responsible for your own actions."—Holly Lisle

Outcomes

★ to help students add the Responsibility asset to their lives

★ to help students accept the responsibility opportunities found at school

★ to help students begin to understand that responsibility is built upon self-respect and bravery

Materials

★ copies of the book *Knowing and Doing What's Right*

★ copies of the "Honesty" tracker page (from the CD-ROM)

★ large paper bags, paper, poster board, scissors, crayons or markers

★ copies of the "Notes for a Responsibility Bazaar" and "Adding Assets at Home" handouts

1. Getting Started

Greeting. Have students say hello to someone near them.

Take 5. Hand out copies of the "Honesty" tracker page and allow a few moments for students to complete them.

Two-Minute Partners. Have students form partners. Using the asset definition or the quotation on the board, ask the partners to each spend a minute describing what the words mean to him or her. Or ask students to talk about what they think *responsible* means.

Preview. Tell students what they will do in this session. Make sure they have all necessary materials.

2. The Asset Question

Ask students: **What kinds of things are babies responsible for? How about two-year-olds? How about your parents or other grown-ups who take care of you?** Guide students to see that taking on more responsibilities is part of growing up.

3. Before the Story

There are many types of responsibilities. Begin a discussion of different types by drawing five large concentric circles on the board. Label each one, like this:

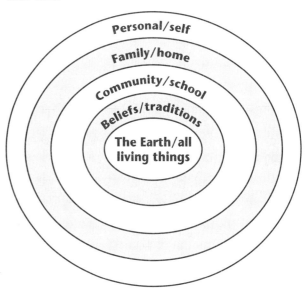

Personal/self
Family/home
Community/school
Beliefs/traditions
The Earth/all living things

As you draw each circle, invite students to describe their responsibilities in each area. *Examples:*

★ Personal/self: taking care of myself; being a good person

★ Family/home: treating family members with love and respect

★ Community/school: being a contributing member of a community; doing my school-work; participating in class discussions

★ Beliefs/traditions: respecting and following the beliefs I've been taught and the traditions I've grown up with

★ The Earth/all living things: respecting our planet and life itself

4. The Story

Read It. Read aloud and discuss Erik's story on pages 55–56 and 64–65 of the student book. You may want to stop reading at the bottom of page 56 and talk about how serious responsibility can be. What could happen to five-year-old David when the two older boys ride off and leave him alone? Do you think Erik and Spencer thought about that ahead of time? Tell students that *acting responsibly* involves thinking about the possible consequences of our actions.

Story Questions for Discussion. Ask students:

★ When Erik tries to get David to come home, it turns into an argument. What if Erik had used different words with David? What words would you have used?

★ Is being "the boss" of someone the same as being responsible? Why or why not?

★ How did Erik's mother act when Erik came home without David? How do you think she was feeling?

★ Erik didn't seem to be worried about David—until they all went looking for him. Why was he worried then?

★ What was the first thing Erik did when they found David? Have you ever tried to make an excuse for something you did or shouldn't have done? Was Erik taking responsibility for his behavior?

★ Do you think Erik will be more responsible in the future?

Optional Activity: Writing Skill

What If . . . ? Have students write a version of Erik's story in which Erik acts responsibly.

Standards/Objectives Highlights	
Character Education	School gives opportunities for moral action
Health	Students identify health-related situations that might require a thoughtful decision
Social Studies	Students learn to explain how people respond differently based on shared values and beliefs
Language Arts	Students participate as creative members of literacy communities
SEL Competencies	Students establish and work toward the achievement of short- and long-term pro-social goals

5. Asset-Building Activities At-a-Glance

Read over the activities on pages 57–63 of the student book and decide which ones are most suitable for your students. *Suggestions:*

★ Have students list their responsibilities. Discuss whether they seem to have too many or too few.

★ Have students copy the "7 Ways to Show You're Responsible" list to take home as a reminder.

★ Acknowledge how easy it is to make excuses or play the blame game. Talk about times when students have made excuses for not doing their homework, or blamed someone else for not completing an assignment or project on time.

★ Ask students for ideas on how everyone can be more responsible in the classroom. Write their ideas on the board. Save them or have students create a Responsibilities Poster to display in the classroom.

★ Discuss the rules students follow in their neighborhoods.

★ Invite students to tell about a time when they shared a responsibility with a friend.

6. Session Activity

★ Hand out copies of "Notes for a Responsibility Bazaar."

★ Explain that a *bazaar* can be any kind of a gathering or shop where a variety of goods are sold. Students will create a Responsibility Bazaar to put different ideas about responsibility on display—not for sale, but for learning, sharing, and fun.

★ Allow students to work individually or in groups to prepare their contributions—whatever they prefer. Circulate as they work, offering help where needed.

★ If possible, invite another class or group to visit your bazaar.

★ Hand out copies of "Adding Assets at Home."

7. Closing Question

Ask students: **What will you do to start adding the Responsibility asset to your life?** If there's time, encourage responses. Give an example of building this asset in your own life.

Preparation for Next Session

★ Make the book *Knowing and Doing What's Right* available to students if you would like them to read ahead the story and/or activity ideas for the Healthy Lifestyle asset (Session 31).

★ If possible, bring in a pedometer to show students.

Notes for a Responsibility Bazaar

What do you want to say or show others about responsibility? **Ideas:** Write a poem, paragraph, story, saying, or skit about responsibility. Draw a picture or comic strip. Make a list, poster, map, or chart.

Use this space for notes or sketches.

ReSponSibility

Today your child learned about the **Responsibility** asset. For your child, this asset means: *Your parent(s) tell you it's important to be responsible for your own behavior.* Students talked about different types of responsibilities they have—to themselves, at home, at school, and in the world.

To help our children grow into responsible adults, we need to give them practice being responsible at home. Does your child have a chores chart? Does your child know what you expect of him or her? Do you have a daily things-to-do list? If you do, you might share it with your child as an example of how it helps you stay organized and meet your responsibilities.

More Ways to Teach Responsibility at Home

★ Show your child, in small steps, all the parts of a task you want or expect him or her to do. Allow your child time to grow into taking full responsibility for the task.

★ Encourage all members of the family to maintain their own chores charts, to-do lists, or responsibilities lists.

★ Come up with small ways to reward your child for being responsible. Something as simple as adding a star or a sticker to a chores chart can encourage responsible behavior (and make a child's day).

★ Celebrate in a big way when your child's efforts have conquered big tasks.

★ Try not to nag or rescue your kids when they "forget" to be responsible or do a chore. Let natural consequences take their course (unless, of course, those consequences will put your child at risk). A child who runs out of socks to wear will learn to put dirty socks in the laundry basket. If a small toy disappears from the yard, the child will learn to put toys away.

★ Keep your expectations realistic and allow for mistakes.

★ Give your child more responsibility as he or she matures. If you're not sure what's appropriate for your child, read a book on child development or ask an expert—like your school counselor. Other parents can be experts, too.

★ Model responsibility. When you make a promise, keep it. When you say you'll do something, do it. When you fail to keep a promise or a commitment, don't make excuses. Try to make things right and do better in the future.

Session 31: Healthy Lifestyle

What this asset means to the child: Your parent(s) tell you it's important to have good health habits and an understanding of healthy sexuality.

Backdrop

Write the name of the asset and its definition on the board.

> **Optional.** Write this quotation on the board: "It is never too early to start taking care of yourself."—Jane Brody

Outcomes

★ to help students add the Healthy Lifestyle asset to their lives

★ to make students more aware of their lifestyle choices

★ to encourage students to get some exercise every day

Preparation

If possible, have on hand a pedometer to show the students.

Materials

★ copies of the book *Knowing and Doing What's Right*

★ copies of the "Responsibility" tracker page (from the CD-ROM)

★ copies of the "Every Step Counts" and "Adding Assets at Home" handouts

1. Getting Started

If time and circumstances allow, begin the session with a walk—around the building, around the block, or wherever works for you and your group.

Greeting. Have students say hello to someone near them.

Take 5. Hand out copies of the "Responsibility" tracker page and allow a few moments for students to complete them.

Two-Minute Partners. Have students form partners. Using the asset definition or the quotation on the board, ask the partners to each spend a minute describing what the words mean to him or her.

Preview. Tell students what they will do in this session. Make sure they have all necessary materials.

2. The Asset Question

Ask students: **What's a lifestyle?** Responses may include:

★ the way a person lives, as shown in the person's activities, interests, opinions, and friends

★ how a person expresses himself or herself—clothes, hair style, jewelry, personal space, way of speaking

★ living according to one's values, attitudes, and beliefs

★ the choices a person makes—friends, food, clothes, entertainment

★ a way of looking at the world

3. Before the Story

To prepare students for reading the story, invite them to write in their own notebooks, just for themselves, the three most important things about their own lifestyle. Explain that they won't have to show or share this with anyone.

4. The Story

Read It. Read aloud and discuss Zoe's story on pages 66–67 and 78–79 of the student book. You may want to stop at the bottom of page 67 and talk specifically about the dilemma Zoe is facing at this point. Invite students to share how they've dealt with similar dilemmas in their own lives. Have they ever been called "chicken"? Have they ever done something to avoid being called "chicken"?

Note: You may want to reread "A message for you" on page 70 of *Knowing and Doing What's Right* to see if you need to address the topic of a family's lifestyle with your student group or privately with any student.

Story Questions for Discussion. Ask students:

★ At the start of the story, Mandy and Zoe are looking at a fashion magazine. What do they learn from an ad they see there? How does the ad influence them? (Talk briefly about the power of advertising to shape our decisions and actions.)

★ Why do you think "the words don't come" when Zoe wants to tell Mandy to forget the whole idea of trying to smoke?

★ Zoe thinks about her parents before trying the cigarette. What does this tell you about Zoe's relationship with her parents?

★ Zoe worries that Mandy will know if she "wimps out." What does this tell you about Zoe's relationship with Mandy? (Talk briefly about the power of negative peer pressure.)

★ How does Zoe feel when she takes a puff of the cigarette?

★ What did you think when Mandy told Zoe, "Come on, can't you take a joke?"

★ If you were Zoe, would you tell your parents what happened? Why or why not?

5. Asset-Building Activities At-a-Glance

Read aloud some of the activities on pages 68–77 of the student book, or ask for volunteers to read them aloud. What activities appeal to the students to do on their own, with a partner, or in a small group? Ask volunteers to mention some of the activities they would like to try to do in the coming days. These may include:

★ Take walks in the neighborhood and try to take the stairs more often, instead of elevators or escalators.

★ Challenge yourself to get up to walking 10,000 steps a day. See if you can buy or borrow a pedometer. (Some pedometers are very inexpensive—a few dollars or less.)

Standards/Objectives Highlights

Character Education	School sets expectations for moral action inside and outside school
Health	Students list healthy options to health-related issues or problems
Social Studies	Students seek ethical solutions to problems that arise when values come into conflict
Language Arts	Students research issues and interests by generating questions and posing problems. They communicate their discoveries
SEL Competencies	Students effectively convey and follow through with their decision not to engage in unwanted or unsafe conduct

★ Check into what it will take for you to add exercise to your daily life.

★ Avoid temptations. Challenge each other to avoid temptations. Help each other to avoid temptations.

★ Get all of your questions out—about body changes, food, exercise, crushes, strong feelings, sex, or whatever. Find an adult you trust. Ask if you can talk.

★ Role-play saying no with your friends.

6. Session Activity

★ Introduce the idea of walking and counting steps as an exercise for staying fit.

★ Ask students to guess about how many steps they walk on a normal day.

★ Hand out copies of "Every Step Counts." Tell students they will keep track of their steps for three hours, one hour at a time (or in shorter increments, if that seems more realistic). They will use these amounts to calculate about how many steps they walk on a normal day.

★ Students can take their sheets with them and report back later—perhaps the next time you meet as a group.

★ Remind students that walking is good for them, but they shouldn't go overboard with walking or counting steps.

★ Hand out copies of "Adding Assets at Home."

7. Closing Question

Ask students: **What will you do to begin adding the Healthy Lifestyle asset to your life?** If there's time, encourage responses. Give an example of building this asset in your own life.

Preparation for Next Session

★ Make the book *Making Choices and Making Friends* available to students if you would like them to read ahead the story and/or activity ideas for the Planning and Decision Making asset (Session 32).

★ Think of an important personal goal you reached or are working toward that you would feel comfortable sharing with students. Review your process for reaching that goal—your steps toward the goal—so you can share that with students as well. What else can you use to illustrate the concepts of *process* and *steps?*

Every Step Counts

Keep track of your steps for three hours—one hour at a time. It can be tricky to count every step, so do the best you can. (If you have a pedometer, it will count your steps for you.) Then fill in the information below to figure out about how many steps you walked in the whole day.

1. Number of steps I walked during one morning hour: _____

2. Number of steps I walked during one afternoon hour: _____

3. Number of steps I walked during one evening hour: _____

4. Add these three numbers to get a total of _____ steps in three hours.

5. Divide the total by 3 to get an **average** of _____ steps per hour.

6. The time I woke up on this day: _____

7. The time I went to bed on this day: _____

8. The total number of hours I was awake: _____

9. Multiply my total awake hours _____ by my **average** steps per hour _____ to get a grand total of about _____ steps in one day.

Healthy Lifestyle

Today your child learned about the **Healthy Lifestyle** asset. For your child, this asset means: *Your parent(s) tell you it's important to have good health habits and an understanding of healthy sexuality.*

Students heard and discussed a story about two friends. One talked the other into trying to smoke a cigarette. You can probably guess that this happens a lot. In fact, studies have shown that friends are the main reason young people start smoking. Kids can become addicted to nicotine after smoking just two cigarettes!

Where do you want your child to learn lifestyle choices? From friends, or from you? From TV, movies, magazines, and advertising, or from you? It's not always easy to talk to our kids about good health habits, and it's even harder to talk with them about healthy sexuality. But if we don't do it, someone else will.

We like these tips from "Talking with Kids About Tough Issues," a national campaign by Children Now *(www.childrennow.org)* and the Kaiser Family Foundation *(www.kff.org)*. You can read the full text at *www.talkingwithkids.org.*

How to Talk with Your Kids About Anything

1. Start early.
2. Initiate conversations with your child . . .
3. . . . even about sex and relationships.
4. Create an open environment.
5. Communicate your values.
6. Listen to your child.
7. Try to be honest.
8. Be patient.
9. Use everyday opportunities to talk.
10. Talk about it again. And again.

Remember that kids watch and notice what their parents do. It may seem as if they're not paying attention, but they are! When you choose a healthy lifestyle, you're setting a good example for your child. Ask yourself: Am I getting enough exercise? Eating right? Taking care of myself? Modeling healthy, positive ways to show affection? Take some time to examine your own beliefs, values, and views about health and sexuality. What do you want your child to learn from you?

> **Quick Tip:** Researchers have found that when children are exposed to healthy lifestyles and healthy sexual attitudes, they're more likely to make these things part of their lives.

Making Choices and Making Friends: The Social Competencies Assets

★ The **Social Competencies Assets** are **Internal Assets.**

★ **Internal Assets** are values, skills, and self-perceptions that kids develop internally, with help from caring adults.

★ The **Social Competencies Assets** are about helping kids develop the skills they need to interact effectively with others, to make difficult decisions, and to cope with new situations. They're about making plans, making friends, and getting along with all kinds of people while avoiding risky situations and resolving conflicts nonviolently.

The Social Competencies Assets are:

32. Planning and decision making—Child thinks about decisions and is usually happy with the results of her or his decisions.

33. Interpersonal competence—Child cares about and is affected by other people's feelings, enjoys making friends, and, when frustrated or angry, tries to calm herself or himself.

34. Cultural competence—Child knows and is comfortable with people of different racial, ethnic, and cultural backgrounds and with her or his own cultural identity.

35. Resistance skills—Child can stay away from people who are likely to get her or him in trouble and is able to say no to doing wrong or dangerous things.

36. Peaceful conflict resolution—Child attempts to resolve conflict nonviolently.

Session 32: Planning and Decision Making

> **What this asset means to the child:** You think about the choices you make, and you're usually happy with your decisions. You know how to plan ahead.

Backdrop

Write the name of the asset and its definition on the board.

> **Optional.** Write this quotation on the board: "Every intersection in the road of life is an opportunity to make a decision."—Duke Ellington

Note: Write the session backdrop quotation on the board when it is appropriate for your students. Always write the name of the asset and its definition on the board.

Outcomes

* to help students add the Planning and Decision Making asset to their lives

* to help students understand the importance of planning

* to invite students to set a goal and spell out steps for reaching it

Preparation

Think of an important personal goal you reached or are working toward that you would feel comfortable sharing with students. Review your process for reaching that goal—your steps toward the goal—so you can share that with the students as well. What else can you use to illustrate the concepts of *process* and *steps?*

Materials

* copies of the book *Making Choices and Making Friends*

* copies of the "Healthy Lifestyle" tracker page (from the CD-ROM)

* copies of the "Plan the Steps to Your Goal" and "Adding Assets at Home" handouts

1. Getting Started

Greeting. Have students say hello to someone near them.

Take 5. Hand out copies of the "Healthy Lifestyle" tracker page and allow a few moments for students to complete them.

Note: Make sure students know it's always appropriate to share feelings or an experience related to this asset or any other one. Sometimes, share your own examples as well.

Two-Minute Partners. Have students form partners. Using the asset definition or the quotation on the board, ask the partners to each spend a minute describing what the words mean to him or her. Or ask students to tell each other about a good decision they have made.

Preview. Tell students what they will do in this session. Make sure they have all necessary materials.

2. The Asset Question

Ask students: **What's the point of having plans? Why not just decide to do whatever you want, whenever you want?** Guide students toward seeing that *planning* is a big help in controlling what happens in all kinds of situations. Explain by saying that you probably wouldn't invite friends to your birthday party without first having some kind of plan in place. Your plan would cover the when and where of the party, how many people to invite, what kind of food to serve, which games to play, and more. Parties (and other important events) can't happen without a plan.

Tell students about an important personal goal you reached or are working toward. Share the steps you took (or are taking).

3. Before the Story

Discuss what it means to work as partners, a team, or a group. In situations like these, each person has to do his or her part for things to work out as planned. Ask: **Have you ever been involved in a group project where it was hard for people to work together or get the assignment done? Or have you ever been on a team that struggled with teamwork?** Invite students to share their own stories.

Note: Allow the story to be the central focus of each session.

4. The Story

Read It. Read aloud and discuss Graham and Leon's story on pages 6–8 and 17–18 of the student book. You may want to stop reading at the bottom of page 8 and ask if students can predict the problem that will occur in this story.

Story Questions for Discussion. Ask students:

★ Does the plan that the boys agreed on at the beginning of the story *sound* like it will work? Why or why not?

★ How did Graham tackle his part of the project? What does this tell you about him?

★ Why do you think Leon has trouble doing his part of the project?

★ Do you think Graham is a good planner? What about Leon?

★ Did Graham's friend Jenna give him good advice? Why or why not?

★ How did Graham's solution to his problem with Leon turn out? Why do you think it worked?

**Optional Activity:
Reading Comprehension**

Steps in a Process. Review Graham and Leon's story. Have students pay close attention to what happens after the boys set their goals for the project. Chart the various steps and events on the board, starting with "Leon and Graham Make a Plan" and ending with "Leon and Graham's New Plan." Guide students to see that there was nothing wrong with the first plan. It probably would have worked, if Leon had behaved differently.

Standards/Objectives Highlights

Character Education	School takes steps to help students practice core values so that they become habitual patterns of behavior
Health	Students can predict the potential outcomes of options when making a health-related decision
Social Studies	Students use knowledge of facts and concepts to inform decision-making
Language Arts	Students research issues by generating ideas, questions, and posing problems; they communicate their discoveries
SEL Competencies	Students establish and work toward the achievement of short- and long-term pro-social goals

5. Asset-Building Activities At-a-Glance

Read over the activities from pages 9–15 of the student book and decide which ones are most suitable for your students. *Suggestions:*

At Home: Be a Planner.

★ Write about how you plan your day (not just school and homework but the fun stuff, too).

★ Share one of your goals with the group. Tell about the steps you have already taken, or are taking now, to reach it.

★ List ways to get into the habit of writing down goals, plans, wishes, and steps.

★ Write about a time when you made a decision you later regretted. What would you do differently next time? Talk to a grown-up at home about this experience.

With Friends: Be a Good Listener.

★ Be a friend who can help with plans and who can be depended on to follow through.

★ Learn to listen when a friend talks to you about a decision he or she is trying to make. Don't give advice right away, unless you're asked to. Offer your support or suggest adults who might help.

★ Help support a friend who is making a decision by working on a Pros and Cons list with him or her.

6. Session Activity

★ Hand out copies of "Plan the Steps to Your Goal."

★ Read aloud the instructions so all students understand what to do.

★ Hand out copies of "Adding Assets at Home."

7. Closing Question

Ask students: **What will you do to start adding the Planning and Decision Making asset to your life?** If there's time, encourage responses. Give an example of building this asset in your own life.

Preparation for Next Session

★ Make the book *Making Choices and Making Friends* available to students if you would like them to read ahead the story and/or activity ideas for the Interpersonal Competence asset (Session 33).

★ Have ready a list of six or more feelings for students to act out in a game of Feelings Charades. You might choose feelings that you have observed in some of your students and want other students to become more aware of. Write each feeling on a separate slip of paper.

Plan the Steps to Your Goal

Goals help you get somewhere in life, but it's important to set *smart* goals—ones that are within your reach. Write a goal in the space below, making sure it's one that is *positive, specific,* and *realistic:*

_____

Now that you have a goal, identify at least three steps you have to take to reach it. Write each step and a deadline for each step in a footprint below:

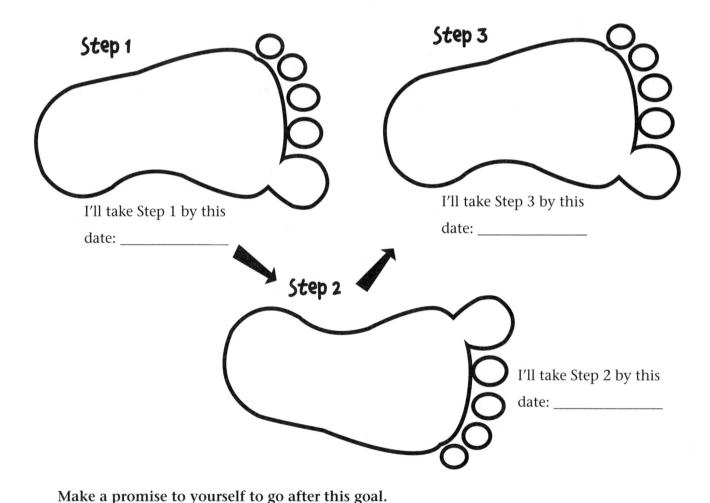

Step 1

I'll take Step 1 by this

date: _____

Step 3

I'll take Step 3 by this

date: _____

Step 2

I'll take Step 2 by this

date: _____

Make a promise to yourself to go after this goal.

I pledge to try to reach my goal. Signed _____

Congratulations! You are now on your way to achieving your goal.

ADDING ASSETS AT HOME

Planning and Decision Making

Today your child was introduced to the **Social Competencies Assets.** They are about forming the skills and attitudes children need to succeed in the world. We want our children to be capable of managing their behavior in a range of social situations; to have friends—and keep them; to respect other people's differences; and to resolve conflicts peacefully. Put simply, our goal for them is to be well-equipped to cope with life's challenges and to develop into healthy, competent adults.

The first of the social competencies assets is **Planning and Decision Making.** For your child, this asset means: *You think about the choices you make, and you're usually happy with your decisions. You know how to plan ahead.* Children who have this asset are more likely to get better grades in school, feel more independent, and think through the consequences of their actions.

Ideas and Activities to Try at Home

★ Share with your child stories about plans and decisions you have made. What goals have you worked toward, and what steps have you taken to reach your goals? You probably weren't always successful. What did you do when you experienced a setback?

★ Ask your child if he or she has a goal in mind. This might be a school-related goal ("I want to do well on the science test"), a personal goal ("I want to learn how to play the piano"), or a goal about the future ("Someday I want to work with animals"). Help your child plan realistic steps toward his or her goal. Then do what you can to help your child take the first step.

★ Have family meetings to talk about plans that affect the whole family. Get everyone involved. Even very young children can have something to contribute, and knowing that you seek and value their contributions is a tremendous self-esteem booster.

★ Learning to make good decisions takes practice. Give your child plenty of age-appropriate opportunities to make decisions at home. View each decision as another step toward becoming a competent, confident adult.

★ Help your child understand that choices have consequences. Play the "What If?" game. *Example:* "What if you decide to watch TV instead of study for your test? What might happen?"

★ Create a chores chart for your child—or your whole family. This will help everyone plan ahead.

★ Allow your child to make choices about daily plans, including snacks, meals, clothing, playtime, homework time, etc. Offer guidance when necessary.

★ Give your child the opportunity to plan a social occasion with a friend. Let your child come up with a fun activity to try or a new place to go. Have him or her help prepare any snacks or meals.

★ Buy a calendar or planner for your child to use. Help him or her fill in daily, weekly, and monthly activities.

Session 33: Interpersonal Competence

What this asset means to the child: You care about other people and their feelings. You enjoy making friends. When you feel angry or frustrated, you try to calm yourself down.

Backdrop

Write the name of the asset and its definition on the board.

> **Optional.** Write this quotation on the board: "I praise loudly. I blame softly."—Catherine II

Outcomes

★ to help students add the Interpersonal Competence asset to their lives

★ to teach students how to calm themselves when stressed or angry

★ to help students understand the power of words to communicate feelings

Preparation

Have ready a list of six or more feelings for students to act out in a game of Feelings Charades. You might choose feelings that you have observed in some of your students and want other students to become more aware of. Write each feeling on a separate slip of paper.

Materials

★ copies of the book *Making Choices and Making Friends*

★ copies of the "Planning and Decision Making" tracker page (from the CD-ROM)

★ copies of the "Write It Right" and "Adding Assets at Home" handouts

1. Getting Started

Greeting. Suggest students say hello to someone near them in a new way.

Take 5. Hand out copies of the "Planning and Decision Making" tracker page and allow a few moments for students to complete them.

Two-Minute Partners. Have students form partners. Using the asset definition or the quotation on the board, ask the partners to each spend a minute describing what the words mean to him or her. If you use the quote, discuss what it means to "blame softly" but "praise loudly."

Preview. Tell students what they will do in this session. Make sure they have all necessary materials.

2. The Asset Question

Ask students: **What do you mean when you say someone is *competent* in a skill?** Talk at first about easily recognized skills—such as being competent in music, sports, crafts, or school subjects. Then ask how they would describe a person who is competent in *relating to other people*. Ask: **How might a person with this type of skill act toward others? How might he or she treat friends and classmates?**

3. Before the Story

Talk about emotions that we are all familiar with: feeling angry, anxious, frustrated, or upset. Ask students: **How do you know when someone might be experiencing one of these emotions— what are the signs?** Answers might include: a worried expression, groaning, yelling, crossed arms, stomping a foot, whining, or lashing out at others.

Ask students if they are familiar with a game called *charades*. If they are not, briefly explain how it is played: You act out a word or phrase using body language and facial expressions, but no words or other verbal sounds. Teach students a few common gestures in charades:

★ To show that the word has three syllables, lay three fingers on your arm.

★ To indicate the length of a word, use your thumb and forefinger to indicate a short word, both arms to indicate a long word.

★ To communicate "sounds like," cup one hand behind your ear.

Ask for volunteers to act out feelings. Give each volunteer one of the feelings slips you prepared earlier and allow a moment or two for students to prepare. Have each student act out his or her feeling for the group. Afterward, talk briefly about how easy (or hard) it was to communicate a feeling, and how easy (or hard) it was to guess a feeling.

4. The Story

Read It. Read aloud and discuss Maria, Jordy, and Bel's story on pages 19–21 and 32–34 of the student book. You may want to stop reading at the bottom of page 21 and talk about how Belinda got her way.

Story Questions for Discussion. Ask students:

★ **The first part of the story uses words like** *challenges, racing,* **and** *rush.* **What kind of mood do those words create?**

★ How does Maria feel when Bel calls her "Miss Slowpoke"?

★ When Maria and Jordy don't give in right away, Bel's face gets red and her eyes squint. What do these signs tell Maria and Jordy about how Bel is feeling and what she might do next?

★ Have you ever been caught saying not-so-nice things about a friend, the way Maria and Jordy are? How did you feel?

★ Have you ever overheard friends saying not-so-nice things about you? What did that feel like?

★ What happens at the end of the story? (Everyone apologizes.) Did everyone need to say they were sorry, not just Bel? Do you think the apologies helped?

5. Asset-Building Activities At-a-Glance

Note: Knowing how to calm oneself down when one is angry or frustrated is such an important life skill that you should teach it directly during this session, even if this limits the time you have available for other activities.

Standards/Objectives Highlights

Character Education	School infuses character education throughout the school day
Health	Students identify how peers can influence healthy and unhealthy behaviors
Social Studies	Students develop empathy and skepticism regarding attitudes, values, and behaviors of people
Language Arts	Students adjust their spoken and written language to communicate effectively with various audiences
SEL Competencies	Students believe that others deserve to be treated with kindness and compassion

Read aloud the activity on pages 25–26 of the student book, or communicate it to the students in your own words. Tell students they will breathe in *deeply* through the nose while you count to five. Then they will breathe out *slowly* through the mouth while you count backwards from five. Demonstrate breathing deeply and slowly. Tell students they can close their eyes if they want to.

Have students breathe in and out ten times while you count out loud. Then have them breathe in and out ten times while counting silently in their heads. Afterward, ask how everyone feels. Calm? Relaxed? More ready to deal with whatever the day brings? Encourage students to use this technique the next time they sit down to take a test, the next time they start to get into an argument with a sibling or friend, or anytime they feel stressed, upset, or about to lose their temper.

If time allows, briefly review other asset-building activities from pages 22–30 of the student book:

★ Talk about your feelings with a family grown-up.

★ Start a feelings journal.

★ Build a feelings vocabulary.

★ Make a new friend at school today.

★ Read aloud and discuss "A special message for boys" on page 30.

6. Session Activity

★ Hand out "Write It Right."

★ Read aloud the opening paragraph so students know what to do. (You may wish to reread certain parts of the story in the student book to remind students of vocabulary words that were introduced.)

★ Help students understand that relationships with other people inspire powerful feelings, and that it can help to express these feelings through words (spoken or written). Understanding feelings is an important step in developing interpersonal competence.

★ Circulate as students work and offer help where needed.

★ Hand out copies of "Adding Assets at Home."

7. Closing Question

Ask students: **What will you do to start adding the Interpersonal Competence asset to your life?** If there's time, encourage responses. Give an example of building this asset in your own life.

Preparation for Next Session

★ Make the book *Making Choices and Making Friends* available to students if you would like them to read ahead the story and/or activity ideas for the Cultural Competence asset (Session 34).

★ If possible, bring snack foods (tortilla chips with salsa, pita bread and hummus) to share, or choose fruits and vegetables from other regions to try. Plan to talk about your own culture and background, or share photos or mementos from places you have visited in other parts of the world.

★ Have available maps, atlases, and/or globes so students can look up the names and locations of countries around the world. If possible, have a large map available, plus sticky notes and string (if needed).

write It Right

Words have power in them. Using them correctly makes your writing and speaking strong. Look at some of the words and phrases below, which were used in Maria, Jordy, and Bel's story. The words help express strong feelings or actions.

Vocabulary Words

closest challenge rush calm cheats beams shouts

Write the vocabulary word that fits into each sentence:

1. To Amy, Jannell was more than a good friend—she was her _____ friend.

2. Paul is so angry, he _____ the signals to his team.

3. It wasn't easy, but Tedra stayed _____ when her friend challenged her.

Phrases

No fair! twist my arm temper tantrums give in

Pick the phrase that fits the mood:

4. Hey! It's my turn! _____

5. Okay, I'll do it—you don't have to _____

6. Even if she pressures me, this time I won't _____

On a separate sheet of paper, write a sentence to answer each of the following questions. Use the underlined word or phrase in your sentence.

1. When might you need to <u>shout</u>?

2. Why do some people throw <u>temper tantrums</u>?

3. Tell about a time when you felt like you had to <u>give in</u>.

4. Have you ever seen people <u>cheat</u> to win a game or get their way?

Interpersonal Competence

Today your child learned about the **Interpersonal Competence** asset. For your child, this asset means: *You care about other people and their feelings. You enjoy making friends. When you feel angry or frustrated, you try to calm yourself down.*

Because children often *make* friends easily, this asset may seem simple. Yet *being* a friend involves many additional skills. Children need to know how to express their own feelings. They also need to know how to "read" other people's feelings. Children who can *empathize* with others—who can understand and even identify with their feelings—get along better with friends and classmates, have fewer behavior problems in and out of school, and have higher self-esteem.

Ideas and Activities to Try at Home

★ Invite people to your home for meals. Vary the guests—friends, neighbors, your child's friends, your child's teacher, people you know from your faith community or workplace. Model the social skills of hospitality and conversation. Make sure your child is included in the conversation—especially if the guest is your child's friend or teacher, but even if the guest is one of your coworkers.

★ Give your child practice in meeting people, starting conversations, asking questions, and finding similar interests.

★ Help your child if his or her relationship with a friend isn't going smoothly. Ask questions; offer gentle guidance.

Ways to Build Empathy in Your Child

★ Invite your child to share his or her feelings. Model and share your own feelings as appropriate.

★ When you are out in public places, people watch together. Guess what kind of mood people are in by the way they walk or talk.

★ Find out what is easiest for your child—being empathetic, being sensitive, or making friends. Build on your child's strengths and interests.

★ When your child says or does things that hurt other people's feelings, talk with your child about how his or her behavior affects others.

Session 34: Cultural Competence

What this asset means to the child: You know and are comfortable with people of different races, ethnic backgrounds, and cultures. You're also comfortable with your own cultural identity.

Backdrop

Write the name of the asset and its definition on the board.

> **Optional.** Write this quotation on the board: "It's easy to hate a stereotype, hard to hate someone you know."—Lynn Duvall

Outcomes

★ to help students add the Cultural Competence asset to their lives

★ to invite students to share and appreciate aspects of their own culture and other students' cultures

★ to demonstrate the diversity that exists within your group

Preparation

Bring snack foods (tortilla chips with salsa, pita bread and hummus) to share, or choose fruits and vegetables from other regions to try. Plan to talk about your own culture and background, or share photos or mementos from places you have visited in other parts of the world.

Have available maps, atlases, and/or globes so students can look up the names and locations of countries around the world. If possible, have a large map available, plus sticky notes and string (if needed).

Materials

★ copies of the book *Making Choices and Making Friends*

★ copies of the "Interpersonal Competence" tracker page (from the CD-ROM)

★ copies of the "Where in the World" and "Adding Assets at Home" handouts

1. Getting Started

Greeting. Have students say hello to someone near them.

Take 5. Hand out copies of the "Interpersonal Competence" tracker page and allow a few moments for students to complete them.

Two-Minute Partners. Have students form partners. Using the asset definition or the quotation on the board, ask the partners to each spend a minute describing what the words mean to him or her.

Preview. Tell students what they will do in this session. Make sure they have all necessary materials.

2. The Asset Question

Ask students: **What does the word *culture* mean?** Share one or both of these definitions:

★ The values, traditions, customs, and arts shared by a group of people who are unified by race, ethnicity, language, nationality, or religion.

★ A set of learned beliefs, values, and behaviors that members of a society share. These ways are passed on from generation to generation.

Invite students to talk about their cultural background or some of their family traditions. Meanwhile, hand out the treats you brought to class. Share photos and mementos from your travels.

3. Before the Story

Use this activity to explore with students how it feels to be included in and excluded from a group.*

★ In a large space, have students form a circle. Quickly survey what the students are wearing and use their clothing as a basis for asking certain participants to leave the circle. For example, you might ask anyone wearing shorts or anyone wearing the color blue to leave the circle. (Use general clothing features that do not distinguish economic class or cultural groups.)

★ Ask students still in the circle to join hands. Have those outside of the circle take turns trying to push their way into the circle (but not roughly). If some succeed in getting through, they may join hands with the others. Continue until a few students have pushed into the circle.

★ Have everyone rejoin the larger circle and repeat the activity, using different clothing types to dismiss participants. This time, students outside the circle can simply tap a person on the shoulder to rejoin the circle— they don't have to push their way in.

End the activity with a brief discussion. Ask:

★ How did it feel to have to leave the circle?

★ How did it feel to try to keep others out of the circle?

★ How did it feel to try to break through the circle?

★ How did it feel when you could rejoin the circle just by tapping someone on the shoulder?

★ What did you learn from this activity?

4. The Story

Read It. Read aloud and discuss Diego's story on pages 35–36 and 47–49 of the student book. You may wish to stop reading at the bottom of page 36 to give some background on artist Diego Rivera.

Note: Diego Rivera is considered the greatest Mexican painter of the 20th century. He was born in 1886 and began to draw at a young age; he took drawing courses as a teen and, as a young man, began exhibiting his paintings. He is most famous for his murals.

Story Questions for Discussion. Ask students:

★ How is Diego feeling at the start of the story? Why is he feeling that way?

Standards/Objectives Highlights

Character Education	School implements a wide range of strategies to accommodate the diverse cultures and needs of students
Health	Students identify the influence of culture on health practice and behaviors
Social Studies	Students articulate the implications of cultural diversity, as well as cohesion, within and across groups
Language Arts	Students read from many genres to build understanding of the ethical and aesthetic aspects of human experience
SEL Competencies	Students understand that individual and group differences complement each other and make the world more interesting

---

*Adapted with permission from *Building Assets Is Elementary: Group Activities for Helping Kids Ages 8–12 Succeed* (Selective Circles). Copyright © 2004 by Search Institute, Minneapolis, MN; 800-888-7828; www.search-institute.org. All rights reserved.

★ Do you ever talk with a parent or other family grown-up about your feelings? Who's the easiest person to talk to about feelings in your family?

★ Why is Diego worried about being "too different"? Is being "different" a bad thing or a good thing?

★ Does being named after a famous Mexican artist make Diego proud of his heritage? What makes *you* proud of *your* heritage?

★ Does it take courage for Diego to invite kids to his home for dinner?

★ Are there special dishes your family makes that you think your friends would like to try? Why did Diego's friends enjoy making empanadas with Diego's dad?

★ What do you think will happen next with Diego and his new friends?

5. Asset-Building Activities At-a-Glance

Read aloud some of the activities on pages 37–46 of the student book, or ask for volunteers to read them aloud. What activities appeal to the students? Ask volunteers to mention some they might like to try in the coming days. These may include:

★ Track down information about where your family is from and who your ancestors are. Bring it in to share with the group.

★ Ask a parent if you can try one new food from a different culture each week. Learn to cook a new food every month. Bring in the recipes to share with the group.

★ Have a group discussion about stereotypes.

★ Come up with ways to speak out at school if you see someone telling racist jokes or excluding people because of their ethnic or cultural background. Write a list of phrases you might use to tell someone that his or her jokes are offensive.

★ Find a pen pal or email pal. You might do this as a group project.

★ Consider how you might get to know more people in your neighborhood—especially people who may speak a different language or have a background that is different from your own.

6. Session Activity

★ Divide the class into small groups. Hand out "Where in the World?"

★ Read aloud the instructions so all students understand what to do.

★ Display the maps around the room. If you have a larger map available, have students transfer their information so the whole class is represented on a single map. If the map is not meant to be written on, use sticky notes and strings.

★ Hand out copies of "Adding Assets at Home."

7. Closing Question

Ask students: **What will you do to begin adding the Cultural Competence asset to your life?** If there's time, encourage responses. Give an example of building this asset in your own life.

Preparation for Next Session

★ Make the book *Making Choices and Making Friends* available to the students if you would like them to read ahead the story and/or activity ideas for the Resistance Skills asset (Session 35).

★ Contact a high school in your area. Ask an administrator or teacher to recommend two students who can role-play resistance skills in front of your group—saying no to doing things that are dangerous or wrong, resisting negative peer pressure, modeling self-respect, and staying true to themselves. Provide the list of "12 Role Plays to Try" from pages 60–61 of the student book, or have the visiting students make up their own role plays (and run them by you first for appropriateness). If it's not possible to bring in older students to do the role plays, ask volunteers from your group to choose several from the list on pages 60–61 of the student book and practice them ahead of time. They will perform them for the whole group during the session.

where in the world?

What continent were you born on? What country were you born in? Find them on the map and label them. *Examples:* Continent: Africa. Country: Somalia. Do this for everyone in your group. Draw lines connecting each person's birthplace. After all, you're connected *now* by being in the same group—and in the same room.

From *A Leader's Guide to The Adding Assets Series for Kids: Activities and Strategies for Positive Youth Development* by Ann Redpath, Ed.D., Pamela Espeland, and Elizabeth Verdick, copyright © 2007. Free Spirit Publishing Inc., Minneapolis, MN; www.freespirit.com. This page may be photocopied for individual, classroom, and small group work only. For other uses, call 866-703-7322.

ADDING ASSETS AT HOME

Cultural Competence

Today your child learned about the **Cultural Competence** asset. For your child, this asset means: *You know and are comfortable with people of different races, ethnic backgrounds, and cultures. You're also comfortable with your own cultural identity.*

Many people have broadened their cultural horizons through enjoyment of the arts—especially music. "Through music," musician Vince Gill has said, "you learn not to care about the color of someone's skin." Historian Barbara Jordan once commented, "We, as human beings, must be willing to accept people who are different from ourselves." Our world is rapidly becoming more diverse. Most parents want their children to have experience with and be comfortable with people of different racial, ethnic, and cultural backgrounds.

Even so, children often gravitate toward those who look like themselves. They may naturally form friendships with children of the same gender, age, race, or religion. You can help your child understand that the world is larger and more diverse (and interesting!) than imagined. Encourage your child to develop an appreciation for different cultures, to respect all people, and to treat each person with tolerance and equality.

Ideas and Activities to Try at Home

* Celebrate the customs and rituals of your own heritage.

* Help your child feel proud—but not superior—about his or her cultural, ethnic, or racial identity.

* Show your child how to use a globe, an atlas, and maps. Expose him or her to legends and stories from different parts of the world. Study the flags of other nations and find pictures of their money, stamps, and heroes.

* Experience music from different countries and cultures—go to the library to borrow CDs, or find out about local ethnic festivals that may offer live music.

* Be aware of any stereotypes you may have that your child could pick up on.

* Discuss with your child how different cultures are portrayed in books, television, videos, and movies. Are the portrayals accurate? Are any stereotypes used? How can someone distinguish between what's real and what's generalized?

Session 35: Resistance Skills

What this asset means to the child: You stay away from people who could get you into trouble. You can say no to doing things that are dangerous or wrong.

Backdrop

Write the name of the asset and its definition on the board.

> **Optional.** Write this quotation on the board: "The greatest oak was once a little nut who held its ground."—Anonymous

Outcomes

★ to help students add the Resistance Skills asset to their lives

★ to help students realize the power of the word *no*

★ to identify ways to overcome negative peer pressure

Preparation

Contact a high school in your area. Ask an administrator or teacher to recommend two students who can role-play resistance skills in front of your group—saying no to doing things that are dangerous or wrong, resisting negative peer pressure, modeling self-respect, and staying true to themselves. Provide the list of "12 Role Plays to Try" from pages 60–61 of the student book, or have the visiting students make up their own role plays (and run them by you first for appropriateness). If it's not possible to bring in older students to do the role plays, ask volunteers from your group to choose several from the list on pages 60–61 of the student book and practice them ahead of time. They will perform them for the whole group during this session.

Materials

★ copies of the book *Making Choices and Making Friends*

★ copies of the "Cultural Competence" tracker page (from the CD-ROM)

★ copies of the "My Supporters" and "Adding Assets at Home" handouts

1. Getting Started

Greeting. Have students say hello to each other.

Take 5. Hand out copies of the "Cultural Competence" tracker page and allow a few moments for students to complete them.

Two-Minute Partners. Have students form partners. Using the asset definition or the quotation on the board, ask the partners to each spend a minute describing what the words mean to him or her.

Preview. Tell students what they will do in this session. Make sure they have all necessary materials.

2. The Asset Question

Ask students: **Why is it hard sometimes to say that simple little word *no*?** Ask volunteers to talk about a time when they were pressured to do something dangerous or wrong. How did they resist? If they went along, what were the consequences?

Note: You may want to reread "A message for you" on page 54 of *Making Choices and Making Friends* to see if you need to address the topic of resistance skills with your student group or privately with any student you feel is currently troubled by negative peer pressure.

3. Before the Story

Introduce the high school students (or volunteers from your group) who will be doing the role plays. Have them perform the role plays, and allow time for questions after each scenario. Ask students if they have other ideas for what to say and do in each situation.

4. The Story

Read It. Read aloud and discuss Maddie and Krista's story on pages 50–52 and 63–64 of the student book. You may want to stop reading at the bottom of page 52 and ask students to predict what they think Krista and Maddie will do.

Story Questions for Discussion. Ask students:

★ At the beginning of the story, Maddie isn't sure why she and Krista were even invited to Alexia's party. By the end of the story, the answer became clearer. Why do *you* think Alexia invited them?

★ At the start of the story, Maddie really wants to be accepted into Alexia's group. Why is this so important to her? Do you think she feels the same way at the end of the story? Why or why not?

★ Krista jumps in and volunteers to do a dare before Maddie. Why do you think she does this?

★ Have you ever been in a situation like the one Maddie and Krista find themselves in? Tell us about it and what you did.

★ What do Maddie and Krista learn from this experience?

★ Do you think Maddie cares anymore about being part of Alexia's group? Why or why not?

★ If Krista had gone ahead and cut the flowers, would that have made her part of Alexia's group? Why or why not?

5. Asset-Building Activities At-a-Glance

Read over the activities from pages 53–62 of the student book and decide which ones are most suitable for your students. *Suggestions:*

At Home.

★ Remind yourself often of your unique and special qualities.

★ Talk with family grown-ups, older siblings, and cousins about different ways to say no to negative peer pressure. Ask them to share their personal stories of being "tested."

At School.

★ Find kids who take school seriously. Hang out with them.

Standards/Objectives Highlights

Character Education	School takes deliberate steps to help students understand what core values mean in everyday behavior and why some behaviors are right and others wrong
Health	Students demonstrate refusal skills to avoid or reduce health risks
Social Studies	Students explain and apply concepts such as power, role, status, justice, and influence to the examination of persistent issues and social problems
Language Arts	Students employ a wide range of strategies to communicate appropriately with different audiences for different purposes
SEL Competencies	Students effectively convey and follow through with their decision not to engage in unwanted conduct

★ Be a friend who can help others say no when the time arises.

★ With friends, role-play saying no. The more practice you get, the easier it will be to say it in real life when you need to.

6. Session Activity

★ Hand out copies of "My Supporters."

★ Read aloud the instructions so everyone knows what to do.

★ Hand out copies of "Adding Assets at Home."

Optional Activity: Story Telling Skill

Invent a New Ending. Have students invent versions of Maddie and Krista's story that end differently. In one version, Krista cuts the flowers. In another, she asks Maddie to cut the flowers. In another, the neighbor who owns the rose bushes looks out her window and sees the girls in her garden. In another . . . ? Have students explore the dramatic possibilities of various endings. They can write them, describe them to the group, sketch them, or act them out.

7. Closing Question

Ask students: **What will you do to start adding the Resistance Skills asset to your life?** If there's time, encourage responses. Give an example of building this asset in your own life.

Preparation for Next Session

★ Make the book *Making Choices and Making Friends* available to students if you would like them to read ahead the story and/or activity ideas for the Peaceful Conflict Resolution asset (Session 36).

★ Find out if your school, district, or organization has a peer mediation program in place. If it does, gather information to share with your students.

My Supporters

Who can help you stand strong when you face challenges in life? Who can you count on for help and support? (Think of family, relatives, teachers, neighbors, or others.) List their names here. Find out their contact information, including their phone numbers, addresses, or email addresses so you can easily get in touch with them. An adult at home can help you get this information, if needed. Once you've filled it out, keep this sheet in a handy place so you can call on your supporters when you need them.

Name of My Supporter: _____

Contact Information: _____

_____

Name of My Supporter: _____

Contact Information: _____

_____

Name of My Supporter: _____

Contact Information: _____

_____

Name of My Supporter: _____

Contact Information: _____

_____

Name of My Supporter: _____

Contact Information: _____

_____

Name of My Supporter: _____

Contact Information: _____

_____

Session 35

Resistance Skills

Today, your child was introduced to the **Resistance Skills** asset. For your child, this asset means: *You stay away from people who could get you into trouble. You can say no to doing things that are dangerous or wrong.*

While we want to teach our children resistance skills, we also must teach them the values that underlie their choices. As children learn to resist negative behaviors and stay out of trouble, they also will be learning what to *value*—what to say *yes* to.

Ideas to Try at Home

★ Demonstrate resistance skills for your child. Talk with your child about things to say no to—pressure to take a negative risk, to do something dangerous, to break a rule. Make your expectations clear. Children really do listen to what their parents say!

★ Make your home a place where your child feels comfortable expressing his or her feelings, values, and opinions.

★ Talk with your child about times when you were pressured to do something dangerous or wrong. What did you do? If you went along, what were the consequences?

★ As you watch television programs and movies together, point out examples of negative peer pressure, kids getting others into trouble, and using resistance skills.

★ Teach your child the difference between being *passive*, being *aggressive*, and being *assertive*. Being passive means going along and not standing up for yourself. Being aggressive means being pushy and demanding. When you're assertive, you stand up for your rights and beliefs in positive, respectful ways. Teach and model assertiveness skills.

★ Know who your child's friends are. Make sure that your child spends time at your home with friends and doesn't always go to their homes so you can observe their play. Talk with your child about his or her friends. Do they have resistance skills? Do they respect themselves? Do they stay out of trouble?

Session 36: Peaceful Conflict Resolution

> **What this asset means to the child:** You try to resolve conflicts in a peaceful way, without using harsh words or violent actions.

Backdrop

Write the name of the asset and its definition on the board.

> **Optional.** Write this quotation on the board: "Go and talk things over. Words can do magic." —Leo Lionni

Outcomes

★ to help students add the Peaceful Conflict Resolution asset to their lives

★ to help students understand that conflict is normal

★ to teach students ways to resolve conflicts without aggression

Preparation

★ Find out if your school, district, or organization has a peer mediation program in place. If it does, gather information to share with your students.

★ Review the breathing exercise from Session 33: Interpersonal Competence so you can teach it again if needed. (Find it on pages 25–26 of the student book or page 206 of this Leader's Guide.) Think of several conflict-themed role plays for students to try. Write them on the board. *Examples:*

★ One student calls a classmate a rude name

★ Two friends start arguing about who gets to have the first turn

★ Siblings get into an argument about who does more chores

★ A group of students won't let other kids join in their game at recess

Materials

★ copies of the book *Making Choices and Making Friends*

★ copies of the "Resistance Skills" tracker page (from the CD-ROM)

★ copies of the "Dignity Stance" and "Adding Assets at Home" handouts

1. Getting Started

Greeting. Suggest students say hello to someone near them in a peaceful way. *For example:* "Hi. Everything cool with you?"

Take 5. Hand out copies of the "Resistance Skills" tracker page and allow a few moments for students to complete them.

Two-Minute Partners. Have students form partners. Using the asset definition or the quotation on the board, ask the partners to each spend a minute describing what the words mean to him or her.

Preview. Tell students what they will do in this session. Make sure they have all necessary materials.

2. The Asset Question

Ask students: **What is conflict?** (*A misunderstanding, disagreement, or fight between two or more people. You also can experience conflict within yourself. Example:* "Should I hang out with this person or someone else?") Let students know that conflicts are a normal part of life and bound to happen—they can't always be avoided. Explain that there are positive and negative ways to handle a conflict. Emphasize that we always have *choices* about what we say or how we act during a conflict.

4. The Story

Read It. Read aloud and discuss Keisha's story on pages 65–66 and 76–77 of the student book.

Story Questions for Discussion. Ask students:

★ Keisha's brothers are playing football together when all of a sudden they start to fight. What caused the disagreement? Why did the argument get physical?

★ Why does Keisha kick one of her brothers? What do you think of her actions?

★ Keisha's dad reminds her of a conversation they had earlier about resolving conflicts peacefully. Imagine that conversation. What do you think Keisha's dad said? What do you think she learned?

★ What does Keisha say that makes her brothers stop arguing? How do you think they feel hearing their younger sister say these words?

★ Have you ever handled a conflict peacefully, like Keisha did? Tell us about it.

★ The characters in this story apologize for their actions afterward. How important do you think apologies are? Why?

5. Asset-Building Activities At-a-Glance

Read aloud some of the activities on pages 67–74 of the student book, or ask for volunteers to read them aloud. Ask volunteers to mention some of the activities they would like to try in the coming days. These might include:

★ Write "I feel___ when you ___. I need____" on a slip of paper or a note card. Keep it in your backpack or pocket as a reminder of how I-messages work.

★ Practice using I-messages with your friends and family.

★ Have a family meeting to resolve an ongoing conflict (or try to resolve it).

★ Learn about famous peacemakers like Nelson Mandela, Mother Teresa, and Martin Luther King Jr. by checking out books from the library or visiting Web sites. Share what you learn with others.

★ Read the "Tips for Peaceful Conflict Resolution." Copy them on a piece of paper and carry them in your notebook. Read them from time to time so you're ready to use them if a conflict comes up at home or at school.

Standards/Objectives Highlights	
Character Education	School does not tolerate peer cruelty or any form of violence, and deals with it effectively when it occurs
Health	Students demonstrate nonviolent strategies to manage or resolve conflict
Social Studies	Students apply knowledge of how groups work to meet individual needs and promote the common good
Language Arts	Students use a variety of information resources to gather and synthesize information to create and communicate knowledge
SEL Competencies	Students generate, implement, and evaluate positive and informed solutions to problems

If you gathered information about a peer mediation program, share it with your students. Ask if anyone would like to get involved. If students seem interested, follow through.

6. Session Activity

★ Hand out copies of "Dignity Stance."

★ Tell students they are going to learn a new way to handle conflict: being assertive but not aggressive. Talk about the difference between the two. When you're assertive, you stand up for your rights and beliefs in positive, respectful ways. When you're aggressive, you're pushy, demanding, and ready to argue or fight. Using Keisha's story as an example, point out how Billy, Jerome, and Keisha are all aggressive during different points in the story. At the end, Keisha is assertive and the conflict is resolved peacefully.

★ Ask students to practice the breathing exercise they learned in Session 33. Re-teach it if needed. Remind them that breathing this way can help them calm down and think more clearly during times of conflict or stress.

★ Read over the handout so students understand what is meant by the *dignity stance*. Divide students into partners or small groups and have them practice this body language.

★ Have students role-play the ideas written on the board. Students should try the dignity stance as they act out each scene. If there's time, come up with more role plays for practice.

★ Hand out copies of "Adding Assets at Home."

7. Closing Question

Ask students: **What will you do to start adding the Peaceful Conflict Resolution asset to your life?** If there's time, encourage responses. Give an example of building this asset in your own life.

Preparation for Next Session

★ Make the book *Proud to Be You* available to students if you would like them to read ahead the story and/or activity ideas for the Personal Power asset (Session 37).

★ Ask students to start thinking about this question: **What does *personal power* mean to you?** Have them write a brief definition to bring to the next session.

The Dignity Stance

Stand tall with your head held high.

Make direct eye contact.

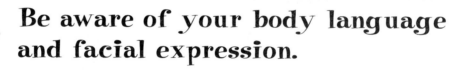

Use a firm, steady tone of voice.

Be aware of your body language and facial expression.

When you walk away, do it with pride.

Peaceful Conflict Resolution

Today your child was introduced to the **Peaceful Conflict Resolution** asset. For your child, this asset means: *You try to resolve conflicts in peaceful ways, without using harsh words or violent actions.*

In today's media-driven world, children are bombarded with images of violence and aggression in video games, on television, and in movies. They may start to see aggressive behavior as "normal" and act out what they see on the screen. You are a powerful force in teaching your child a better way. Learning the skills of conflict resolution will give your child the tools he or she needs to be assertive, empathize with others, and walk away from fights. You will see a difference at home, and your child will feel more confident at school.

As Mahatma Gandhi said, "Nonviolence is a plant of slow growth." It takes time for children to learn the skills of thinking before they act and taking personal responsibility for solving conflict. You can help your child by practicing the skills frequently at home.

Ideas and Activities to Try at Home

★ Encourage family members to state their needs without blaming others. Use I-messages ("I need you to speak in a calm voice") instead of You-messages ("You yell too much!"). Give each person a chance to tell his or her side of the story.

★ Teach your child how to compromise. Everyone involved in a conflict should get some of what he or she wants ("win-win").

★ When you don't handle a conflict well, stop, cool down, admit it, and apologize. Start over.

★ Limit your child's exposure to violent TV shows, movies, and video/computer games.

★ Let your child know you are a source of support. Ask questions like "Are you dealing with any conflicts at school or with friends?" and "How can I help you? Do you want to tell me about them?" Suggest that maybe together you can come up with ways to handle the conflicts.

Session 36

Proud to Be You:
The Positive Identity Assets

★ The **Positive Identity Assets** are **Internal Assets**.

★ **Internal Assets** are values, skills, and self-perceptions that kids develop internally, with help from caring adults.

★ The **Positive Identity Assets** are about encouraging kids to form a strong sense of their own power, purpose, worth, and promise. Kids need to believe that they matter in the world—and to feel that they have some control over the things that happen to them.

The Positive Identity Assets are:

37. Personal power—Child feels she or he has some influence over things that happen in her or his life.

38. Self-esteem—Child likes and is proud to be the person she or he is.

39. Sense of purpose—Child sometimes thinks about what life means and whether there is a purpose for her or his life.

40. Positive view of personal future—Child is optimistic about her or his personal future.

Session 37: Personal Power

What this asset means to the child: You feel that you have some control over things that happen in your life.

Backdrop

Write the name of the asset and its definition on the board.

> **Optional.** Write this quotation on the board: "You are in control of your life. Don't ever forget that."—Barbara Hall

Note: Write the session backdrop quotation on the board when it is appropriate for your students. Always write the name of the asset and its definition on the board.

Outcomes

★ to help students add the Personal Power asset to their lives

★ to help students understand the meaning of personal power

★ to help students determine whether they have and use personal power

Preparation

Remind students that at the end of the last session, you asked them to start thinking about the question: **What does *personal power* mean to you?** and to write a brief definition. Say that if they didn't get around to writing a definition, they can take a moment to write one now.

Materials

★ copies of the book *Proud to Be You*

★ copies of the "Peaceful Conflict Resolution" tracker page (from the CD-ROM)

★ copies of the "Power Quiz" and "Adding Assets at Home" handouts

1. Getting Started

Greeting. Suggest students greet each other warmly.

Take 5. Hand out copies of the "Peaceful Conflict Resolution" tracker page and allow a few moments for students to complete them.

Note: Make sure students know it's always appropriate to share feelings or an experience related to this asset or any other one. Sometimes, share your own examples as well.

Two-Minute Partners. Have students form partners. Using the asset definition or the quotation on the board, ask the partners to each spend a minute describing what it means to have control over your life.

Preview. Tell students what they will do in this session. Make sure they have all necessary materials.

2. The Asset Question

Ask students: **Do you feel that you have some control over things that happen in your life?** Invite students to share examples of things they feel they have *some* control over, and things they feel they have *no* control over.

3. Before the Story

Help students understand what personal power means—and doesn't mean. Draw two columns on the board. Write "Personal Power Is . . . " at the top of one column, "Personal Power Isn't . . . " at the top of the other. Invite students to share the definitions they wrote earlier. Write them on the board.

In short, you want students to understand that personal power isn't about being bigger, stronger, smarter, richer, or more popular than other people, or about bossing them around. It's about feeling secure and confident inside yourself, making choices and decisions, and being responsible for your own behavior and feelings.

Note: Allow the story to be the central focus of each session.

4. The Story

Read It. Read aloud and discuss Danny's story on pages 6–7 and 20–22 of the student book. You may want to stop reading at the bottom of page 7 and ask students: **If you met Danny on the playground—a kid who's kind of short, overweight, not very good at sports, and almost always picked last for teams—would you think, "There's someone who has personal power"? Why or why not?** Remind students that personal power is something you have on the *inside*. It might not be obvious to other people right away.

Story Questions for Discussion. Ask students:

★ When Danny mutters, "Jake the Jock, in command," what does this tell you about how Jake usually acts? What does it tell you about Danny?

★ What does it mean to be one of the "unchosen"? How does it feel? Have you ever been in this situation?

★ What are Danny's strengths? (A sense of humor, his ability to keep things in perspective, his realistic awareness of his own abilities, and his friendship with Amanda, among others.)

★ Danny has a chance to bring two runners home—and win the game for his team. Then what happens, and what does he do instead?

★ What do you think of Danny's decision to help his friend—and lose the game?

★ Who else admires Danny for his decision?

5. Asset-Building Activities At-a-Glance

Have key words and phrases from some of the activities from pages 8–18 of the student book written on the board. Ask volunteers to read them aloud. Which activities do they think they might try during the next day or two? *Examples:*

★ Be an *optimist*. Look on the bright side.

★ Tune in to your *inner voice*. Use positive self-talk.

★ Build a skill.

★ Get some exercise every day.

	Standards/Objectives Highlights
Character Education	School provides students with opportunities for moral action
Health	Students demonstrate effective verbal and nonverbal communication skills to enhance health
Social Studies	Students study the ways human beings view themselves in and over time
Language Arts	Students adjust their spoken and written language to communicate effectively with various audiences for different purposes
SEL Competencies	Students accurately perceive situations in which a decision is to be made and assess factors that might influence responses

★ Take on more responsibility at home.

★ Smile!

If time allows, explore the topic of positive self-talk with students. Read aloud the "5 Things to Tell Yourself When Things Go Wrong" on page 10 of the student book. Ask students: **What do YOU tell yourself when things go wrong?**

If you have a computer in your classroom with Internet access, check out the *www.kidshealth.org/kid* Web site. Type the word *fear* in the Search box, then scroll down the list of search results. Do any of the articles seem especially suitable for your group? You might want to print out copies and make them available for students to read. Do the same for the word *worry*.

6. Session Activity

★ Hand out copies of "Power Quiz." Read aloud the opening paragraph so all students know what to do.

★ Hand out copies of "Adding Assets at Home."

7. Closing Question

Ask students: **What will you do to start adding the Personal Power asset to your life?** If there's time, encourage responses. Give an example of building this asset in your own life.

Preparation for Next Session

★ Make the book *Proud to Be You* available to students if you would like them to read ahead the story and/or activity ideas for the Self-Esteem asset (Session 38).

★ Have available small spiral-bound note-books, one for each student.

★ Visit your school media center or local public library and gather examples of diaries or journals that are appropriate for your students to page through during this session. ("Appropriate," of course, means non-steamy!) *Examples: Anne Frank: The Diary of a Young Girl,* books from Scholastic's "Dear Dumb Diary" series by Jim Benton, books from the "Princess Diaries" series by Meg Cabot, the delightful *Diary of a Spider* and *Diary of a Worm* by Doreen Cronin, illustrated by Harry Bliss—whatever you can find. Some are fictional but all are written in journal/diary form.

Power Quiz

Even though you're just a kid, even though the adults in your life still tell you what to do and you pretty much have to do what they say, you still have *personal power*. Remember that personal power means having some control over things that happen in your life. It means feeling secure and confident inside yourself. It means making choices and decisions. It means being responsible for your own behavior and feelings.

Read each pair of statements and check the one that is most true for you. When you're through, turn the page upside-down to discover which statements show personal power.

1. ☐ **a.** I would walk out of a movie (or stop watching it at home) if I thought it was trashy and a waste of time.

☐ **b.** I would watch it all the way through.

2. ☐ **a.** I would make friends with a new kid even if my other friends told me not to.

☐ **b.** I would ignore the new kid to keep my friends happy.

3. ☐ **a.** I usually look for what's wrong with things.

☐ **b.** I try to look on the bright side of things.

4. ☐ **a.** When I do well on a test, I think, "That was lucky!"

☐ **b.** When I do well on a test, I think, "I studied hard, and I deserved to do well."

5. ☐ **a.** I try to get my friends to like the same people and things I do.

☐ **b.** I know I can't control what other people like or don't like.

6. ☐ **a.** If things don't go my way, I try again.

☐ **b.** If things don't go my way, I give up.

7. ☐ **a.** If I'm having a bad day and I need a hug, I ask my mom or dad to hug me.

☐ **b.** If I'm having a bad day, I keep it to myself.

8. ☐ **a.** I wait to see what other people think before giving my opinion about something.

☐ **b.** I have my own opinions, but I'm willing to hear what other people have to say.

9. ☐ **a.** I do my best to dress like the popular kids at school, even though it's sometimes hard to keep up.

☐ **b.** I have my own personal style.

10. ☐ **a.** I try to get my chores done before being told.

☐ **b.** I do my chores when my parents tell me to do them.

1.a, 2.a, 3.b, 4.b, 5.b, 6.a, 7.a, 8.b, 9.b, 10.a

ADDING ASSETS AT HOME

Personal Power

Your child is learning about the **Positive Identity** assets. These four assets support your efforts to instill a positive sense of self in your child. This asset category ties in closely with the first category—the Support assets. Responding to your child's successes and mistakes with love and support builds your child's sense of positive identity.

Today your child learned about the **Personal Power** asset. For your child, this asset means: *You feel that you have some control over things that happen in your life.*

Signs of Personal Power to Watch for and Encourage in Your Child.

★ Optimism. In general, your child looks on the bright side of life. She expects good things to happen.

★ A sense of having some control. When good things happen for him, he believes he helped to make them happen. Good things aren't just "luck" or "accidents." On the other hand, when bad things happen, he doesn't blame himself. Instead, he looks for ways to make things better.

★ A sense that she matters in the world—that she can make a difference. When she comforts a friend, offers to help with a chore, or insists that she donate her allowance to a stop-the-hunger drive, she knows that her actions and decisions count.

Tips for Boosting Your Child's Personal Power.

★ Be your child's cheering section. Say, "I know you can do it if you try!" and "I knew you could do it if you tried!" What if he fails? Say, "I'm glad you tried!"

★ Be alert for times when your child says things like, "I didn't mean to do it!" or "So-and-so made me do it!" Each one is a teachable moment. Point out that your child is responsible for her own actions and choices.

★ Talk with your child about things we can and can't control. We can't "make" someone else happy. We can't "make" someone like us or stop teasing us. We don't have that kind of power over others.

★ Finally, whenever possible, give your child some control over choices and decisions made at home. Not only does this build personal power, it's also good practice for growing up.

Session 38: Self-Esteem

What this asset means to the child: You like yourself, and you're proud to be the person you are.

Backdrop

Write the name of the asset and its definition on the board.

> **Optional.** Write this quotation on the board: "There is no one alive who is Youer than You." —Dr. Seuss

Outcomes

★ to help students add the Self-Esteem asset to their lives

★ to make sure students understand what self-esteem is (and isn't)

★ to help students form the journaling habit

Preparation

★ Visit your school media center or local public library and gather examples of diaries or journals that are appropriate for your students to page through during this session. ("Appropriate," of course, means non-steamy!) *Examples: Anne Frank: The Diary of a Young Girl,* books from Scholastic's "Dear Dumb Diary" series by Jim Benton, books from the "Princess Diaries" series by Meg Cabot, the delightful *Diary of a Spider* and *Diary of a Worm* by Doreen Cronin, illustrated by Harry Bliss—whatever you can find. Some are fictional but all are written in journal/diary form.

★ Write on the board several journaling prompts from page 29 of the student book, or create your own journaling prompts for your students to try.

Materials

★ copies of the book *Proud to Be You*

★ copies of the "Personal Power" tracker page (from the CD-ROM)

★ small spiral-bound notebooks, one for each student

★ copies of the "Journaling Tips & Tricks" and "Adding Assets at Home" handouts

1. Getting Started

Greeting. Suggest students say hello to someone near them.

Take 5. Hand out copies of the "Personal Power" tracker page and allow a few moments for students to complete them.

Two-Minute Partners. Have students form partners. Using the asset definition or the quotation on the board, ask the partners to each spend a minute describing what the words mean to him or her. You might also ask how many know who Dr. Seuss is.

Preview. Tell students what they will do in this session. Make sure they have all necessary materials.

2. The Asset Question

Ask students: **Is there such a thing as too much self-esteem?** You should be able to tell from the students' responses whether they know the real meaning of self-esteem. To clarify, read aloud or paraphrase "A message for you" on page 34 of the student book.

3. Before the Story

Have students tell their partners *one* thing they like about each other—and *one* thing they like about themselves. Invite volunteers to share what they said. Ask students: **How does it feel to boost each other up? How does it feel to boost yourself up?**

4. The Story

Read It. Read aloud and discuss Lisa's story on pages 23–25 and 41–42 of the student book. You may want to stop reading at the bottom of page 25 and talk about why Lisa wanted to write in her journal for a while.

Story Questions for Discussion. Ask students:

★ Do you know what Lisa means when she says "I just had an Alexander day"? Has anyone ever read *Alexander and the Terrible, Horrible, No Good, Very Bad Day*? (Briefly describe the book, or have a student describe it.)

★ What do you think is the *worst* thing that happened to Lisa that day?

★ What does Lisa's dad say and do to help her feel better?

★ What does Lisa do to help herself feel better?

★ Have you ever written in a journal?

5. Asset-Building Activities At-a-Glance

Review the activities on pages 26–39 of the student book and select some you think your students might want to try over the next several days. Write ideas on the board. *Examples:*

★ Write things you like about your siblings (or other family members) on sticky notes and post them around your home.

★ Make a "proud-of-me" list.

★ Take care of your body. Wash your hands—lots!

★ Make a new friend.

★ Treat younger kids with respect

★ Celebrate someone's birthday.

6. Session Activity

★ Read aloud or paraphrase the "Keep Journals About Your Life" activity on pages 27–28 of the student book. Tell students that today everyone will start a journal about his or her life—and you hope that everyone will form the journaling habit.

Standards/Objectives Highlights

Character Education	School provides students with varied opportunities for engaging in moral action in the community and to be positively affected by them
Health	Students explain how media influences thoughts, feelings, and health behaviors
Social Studies	Students relate such factors as physical capabilities, learning, motivation, personality, perception, and behavior to individual development
Language Arts	Students apply a variety of information resources to gather and synthesize information and to create and communicate knowledge
SEL Competencies	Students recognize and understand their obligation to engage in ethical, safe, and legal behaviors

★ Give each student a small spiral-bound note-book and a copy of the "Journaling Tips & Tricks" handout.

★ Tell students they can journal about any-thing they want. Point them toward the journaling prompts written on the board. Say they can use one of those if they want to, or if they can't think of anything else. Allow them to look through the examples of diaries and journals you brought to class.

★ Circulate while they work—not to read what they're writing, but to offer encouragement.

★ Hand out copies of "Adding Assets at Home."

7. Closing Question

Ask students: **What will you do to start adding the Self-Esteem asset to your life?** If there's time, encourage responses. Give an example of building this asset in your own life.

Preparation for Next Session

★ Make the book *Proud to Be You* available to students if you would like them to read ahead the story and/or activity ideas for the Sense of Purpose asset (Session 39).

★ Read the "Two People with Purpose" stories on pages 51 and 52 of *Proud to Be You*. Collect more information about Michael Fox and Ann Belles to share with students. You might find some of Dr. Fox's newspaper columns or more details about his life. Ann Belles is often featured in newspaper and magazine articles and on television news programs. Print out interesting articles you find and have them available for students who want to know more about these passionate, committed, purposeful people.

★ Gather a selection of dictionaries, thesauruses, and rhyming dictionaries for students to use. They will write poems during the next session, and some may want to try rhyming the lines.

Journaling Tips & Tricks

There's just one journaling RULE you need to follow: **Date every entry!** Why? Because otherwise, when you look back at your journal later, you might not remember when you wrote a particular entry. Part of the fun of journaling is tracking how your thoughts and feelings, attitudes and goals change over the years. You won't be able to do that unless you **date every entry.**

Here are some journaling TIPS and TRICKS you can try.

★ Don't worry about grammar, spelling, and punctuation. Just write.

★ Don't JUST write. Draw, sketch, scribble, doodle, and/or paint with watercolor. (There's an old saying: "A picture is worth a thousand words.")

★ Don't worry about cross-outs, smudges, splotches, or wrinkles.

★ Use rubber stamps. If you can, find a rubber stamp set. You can use it to stamp initials, words, even whole sentences.

★ Paste in photos, clippings, postcards, copies of emails or letters you wrote (or received), printouts of instant messages, ticket stubs from movies you enjoyed or fun places you visited—what else do you want to keep? Later on, these things will remind you of times in your life.

★ Create collages.

★ Write your favorite poem.

★ Write the words to your favorite song.

★ Write your favorite quotes.

★ Write about your hopes, dreams, goals, and big plans for the future.

★ Write about sad times and good times.

★ You might want to keep your journal by your bed so you can write down your dreams as soon as you wake up.

★ Carry your journal everywhere so you can write in it whenever.

★ Be true to yourself. Write only for you self. You don't have to share your journal with anyone else . . . unless you want to.

Session 38

ADDING ASSETS AT HOME

Self-Esteem

Today your child learned about the **Self-Esteem** asset. For your child, this asset means: *You like yourself, and you're proud to be the person you are.*

Often, people are confused about what self-esteem really means. It's worth repeating here what the student book, *Proud to Be You,* says on this topic:

> Some kids (and adults) are confused about what self-esteem really means. It doesn't mean thinking about yourself all the time. It doesn't mean bragging about yourself, showing off, or being stuck-up. It doesn't mean putting other people down because you think you're better than they are. It's not about flattery and empty praise.
>
> Self-esteem means feeling strong and secure inside yourself. It means feeling good about your values and beliefs, your skills and abilities, how you treat others, and the good things you do. Also, it's not possible to have "too much self-esteem." In fact, the more you have, the better!

Here are four reasons why you need self-esteem:

1. Self-esteem gives you the courage to take positive risks. You know that if you fail, it's not the end of the world.

2. Self-esteem gives you the strength to resist negative risks and peer pressure. You respect yourself too much to do something dumb.

3. Self-esteem makes you strong. You can cope with whatever life throws your way.

4. Self-esteem makes you *resilient*. That means you can bounce back from problems, mistakes, disappointments, and failures.

Quick Tips for Building Self-Esteem in Children.

★ Tell them you love them—regularly and often.

★ Show them you love them.

★ Spend time with them.

★ Find something special about them to celebrate.

★ Treat them with respect.

★ Listen without interrupting.

★ Talk without yelling.

★ When your child makes mistakes or bad choices, separate the deed from the doer. The *choice* is bad, not the child.

In the words of Jean Illsley Clark: "Let children know we are glad they were born."

Session 39: Sense of Purpose

What this asset means to the child: You sometimes think about what life means and whether your life has a purpose.

Backdrop

Write the name of the asset and its definition on the board.

> **Optional.** Write this quotation on the board: "I've come to believe that each of us has a personal calling that's as unique as a fingerprint—and that the best way to succeed is to discover what you love."—Oprah Winfrey

Outcomes

★ to help students add the Sense of Purpose asset to their lives

★ to invite students to think about some of life's big questions

★ to encourage students to think about their own purpose and describe it in a creative way

Preparation

★ Collect more information about Michael Fox and Ann Belles to share with students. (See pages 51 and 52 of *Proud to Be You*.) You might find some of Dr. Fox's newspaper columns or more details about his life. Ann Belles is often featured in newspaper and magazine articles and on television news programs. Print out interesting articles you find and have them available for students who want to know more about these passionate, committed, purposeful people.

★ Gather a selection of dictionaries, thesauruses, and rhyming dictionaries for students to use. They will write poems during the session, and some may want to try rhyming the lines.

Materials

★ copies of the book *Proud to Be You*

★ copies of the "Self-Esteem" tracker page (from the CD-ROM)

★ copies of the "Me, the Name I Call Myself: A Name Poem" and "Adding Assets at Home" handouts

1. Getting Started

Greeting. Have students say hello to someone near them.

Take 5. Hand out copies of the "Self-Esteem" tracker page and allow a few moments for students to complete them.

Two-Minute Partners. Have students form partners. Using the asset definition or the quotation on the board, ask the partners to each spend a minute describing what the words mean to him or her. Or ask students to describe one thing they'd like to do in their life.

Preview. Tell students what they will do in this session. Make sure they have all necessary materials.

2. The Asset Question

Ask students: **What does it mean to have a purpose? How does it feel to have a purpose?** You might offer some synonyms for *purpose*—a *reason*, an inner *drive*, a sense of *direction, meaning, motivation*, maybe *hope*. Say that it helps to find purpose in everything we do; otherwise, what's the point of doing it?

Note: You may want to reread "A message for you" on page 47 of *Proud to Be You* to see if you need to address the topic of sadness with your student group or privately with any student you feel may be struggling with sadness or pain.

237

3. Before the Story

Ask students if they know anyone who seems to have a strong sense of purpose. Is there someone they admire? Someone who seems to be here on planet Earth for a particular reason? Someone they can't imagine doing anything but what he or she is doing? You might mention that some people seem born to be great leaders, great athletes, great musicians, or great writers. They're living their purpose. Some people believe their main purpose is to be a mom, or a dad, or a teacher. Some people think it's enough to live a good, responsible life. That's their purpose.

Read aloud the "Two People with Purpose" stories on pages 51–52 of the student book. Share with students some of the additional information you gathered about Michael Fox and Ann Belles. Make it available after the session for interested students to continue exploring on their own.

4. The Story

Read It. Read aloud and discuss Art's story on pages 43–45 and 57–59 of the student book. You may want to stop at the bottom of 45 and ask students why they think Art headed for the woods after school.

Story Questions for Discussion. Ask students:

★ Why does getting an F on his science test make Art feel so terrible? Have you ever had a big shock like that in a subject you really like?

★ While Art is on the bus watching the storm, he notices how the wind bends the tree branches at odd angles. What does this tell you about Art's observation skills? Do you think this is an important quality for a future scientist to have?

★ When Art sees the baby bird in the grass, he looks for clues. What does he see? What does he learn?

★ What does Art's mom mean when she says, "Well, *this* is science"?

★ Do you think something like an F on a test should totally change someone's sense of purpose?

★ Does Art have his sense of purpose back at the end of the story? How can you tell?

Standards/Objectives Highlights

Character Education	School takes steps to help everyone appreciate core values, reflect upon them, desire to embody them, and become committed to them
Health	Students predict the potential outcomes of each option when making a health-related decision
Social Studies	Students identify and describe ways ethnic and national cultures influence individuals' daily lives
Language Arts	Students apply strategies to interpret texts; they draw on prior experience, their interactions with others, and their knowledge of word meaning
SEL Competencies	Students believe others deserve to be treated with kindness and compassion and feel motivated to contribute to the common good

Optional Activity: Reading Skill

Predict. To *predict* means to tell what you think might happen next in a story or an article based on what has already happened. Making predictions helps students realize that texts make sense and that they progress logically. Predictions also help students make connections between information from their own experience and that of the text.

Ask students: **What do you predict Art and his mom will talk about when they get back to the house? Looking into the future, what do you predict Art might do with his life?**

5. Asset-Building Activities At-a-Glance

Read aloud some of the activities on pages 46–55 of the student book, or ask for volunteers to read them aloud. What activities appeal to the students to do on their own or to do with a partner or in a small group? These may include:

★ Make and share "passion plans."

★ Talk about ways to respect the Earth and all who live here. Pick one and make it a passion.

★ Start a scrapbook about people who do good things in the world.

★ Collect more stories about people with purpose.

★ Try to find purpose in everything you're learning in school—even the dull, boring subjects, or the really hard subjects.

★ Interview people to learn their sense of purpose. Report back to the group.

6. Session Activity

★ Hand out copies of "Me, the Name I Call Myself: A Name Poem." Read aloud the introduction and the examples so everyone knows what to do. Circulate and offer help while students work. Encourage them to use the dictionaries, thesauruses, and rhyming dictionaries you brought to class.

★ Hand out copies of "Adding Assets at Home."

7. Closing Question

Ask students: **What will you do to begin adding Sense of Purpose asset to your life?** If there's time, encourage responses. Give an example of building this asset in your own life.

Preparation for Next Session

★ Make the book *Proud to Be You* available to students if you would like them to read ahead the story and/or activity ideas for the Positive View of Personal Future asset (Session 40).

★ If there is no mirror in your room, arrange to bring one in.

Me, the Name I Call Myself: A Name Poem

Think about **YOU.** Think about your talents, your interests, skills, and favorite things to do. Think about your purpose in life. Think about the letters of your name. You're about to write a poem that brings them all together. Here are two examples:

T om is my name—like the drum (tom tom!)

O is for orchestra—I play in one

M usician is what I want to become!

S tella is the name my parents gave me

T hat's also another name for STAR

E very night I

L ove to

L ook up at the sky . . . someday I will be an

A stronaut and fly!

> Your poem doesn't have to rhyme . . . but it can if you want it to.
>
> Start each line with a letter of your name. Remember, this poem is all about **YOU.**

\line
\line
\line
\line
\line
\line
\line
\line
\line
\line
\line

Sense of Purpose

Today your child read about and discussed the **Sense of Purpose** asset. For your child, this asset means: *You sometimes think about what life means and whether your life has a purpose.*

Students wrote name poems to celebrate themselves, their talents and abilities, and their sense of purpose. If your child brought his or her poem home, you might ask to see it, or ask your child to tell you about it.

We all have the same number of hours in a day. Many of us believe that we have one life to live on this Earth (although some religious traditions include a belief in reincarnation). We might ask ourselves what the poet Mary Oliver asks in her poem "The Summer Day":

Tell me, what is it you plan to do with your one wild and precious life?

Without passion or purpose, life can seem pointless. We usually think of passion and purpose as belonging to adults. But children can—and should—have a reason to get up in the morning and something to be excited about.

Conversation Starters to Try at Home

★ What matters to you?

★ What do you really care about?

★ What's your biggest dream?

★ Why do you think you're here on Earth?

★ What is your favorite thing to do—and how can I help you do it?

The great teacher Joseph Campbell told his students to "follow your bliss"—to go where your body and soul want you to go. When we model for our children what it means to have a sense of purpose in life, we give them permission to do the same.

Session 40: Positive View of Personal Future

What this asset means to the child: You feel hopeful about your own future.

Backdrop

Write the name of the asset and its definition on the board.

> **Optional.** Write this quotation on the board: "The best thing about the future is that it comes one day at a time."—Abraham Lincoln

Outcomes

★ to help students add the Positive View of Personal Future asset to their lives

★ to invite students to imagine their future selves in a positive light

★ to inspire hope in students

Preparation

If there is no mirror in your room, bring one in and position it where students can easily approach it and see themselves in it.

Materials

★ copies of the book *Proud to Be You*

★ copies of the "Sense of Purpose" tracker page (from the CD-ROM)

★ copies of the "Mirror, Mirror on the Wall" and "Adding Assets at Home" handouts

★ art materials for self-portraits—crayons, colored markers, magazines with pictures, tape, glue, scissors

1. Getting Started

Greeting. Have students greet each other.

Take 5. Hand out copies of the "Sense of Purpose" tracker page and allow a few moments for students to complete them.

Two-Minute Partners. Have students form partners. Using the asset definition or the quotation on the board, ask the partners to each spend a minute describing what the words mean to him or her. Or ask students to describe one thing they look forward to in the future.

Preview. Tell students what they will do in this session. Make sure they have all necessary materials.

2. The Asset Question

Ask students: **When you try to imagine your future, how do you feel?** Tell students that today's session is all about feeling hopeful about what the future will bring.

3. Before the Story

Ask students if they have watched reporters interview people on television. Explain that you're about to have your own interview show. A reporter will interview five people—but not the way they are today. He or she will interview their future selves.

Pull tables, desks, and chairs together to create a "Larry King"-type set. Ask for a volunteer to be the reporter/interviewer. Ask for five volunteers to be the interview subjects. If you get a lot of volunteers for each role, have students write their names on slips of paper, then draw names out of a sack, box, or hat.

Once you have identified your reporter and interview subjects, allow them to move to another part of the room. Tell them their job is to come up with an interesting five- or ten-minute television show. Each subject must decide on a future self to be. The reporter must come up with a list of questions to ask. *Examples:* "What is your career?" "How did you decide what you wanted to be and do?" "What's the secret of your success?" "What's the most important thing you've ever done?"

While the group prepares their show, you might talk with the other students about their plans for the future. After the group has performed their show, thank them for giving you a peek into the future.

4. The Story

Read It. Read aloud and discuss Janelle's story on pages 60–62 and 75–77 of the student book. You may want to stop reading at the bottom of page 62 and talk about why Janelle thinks no one understands what she's going through.

Story Questions for Discussion. Ask students:

★ Why has Janelle decided not to go out for the dance team?

★ What does Janelle's brother Ian do for her?

★ Does Ian stick his nose into Janelle's business? Is that sometimes an okay thing to do? Has it ever happened to you?

★ How does Janelle feel about Ian's actions at first? How does she feel later in the story?

★ Have you ever been pressured to do something you weren't sure you were up to? What's it like when our friends and family have real faith in us?

★ How does Janelle's view of her future as a dancer change?

5. Asset-Building Activities At-a-Glance

Read over the activities on pages 63–73 of the student book and decide which ones your students might enjoy doing. *Suggestions:*

★ Write a story about your future self. Don't hold back. Dream big!

★ Make a real effort to be *optimistic*— to look on the bright side.

★ Read about famous people who overcame problems to find success.

★ Visit some career-related Web sites and learn what it takes to be a . . . what? Your choice.

★ Collect quotes that make you smile (or think).

★ Talk with your friends about your hopes for the future.

6. Session Activity

★ Hand out copies of "Mirror, Mirror on the Wall." Read aloud the introduction so everyone knows what to do.

Standards/Objectives Highlights

Character Education	School sets clear expectations for students to engage in moral action both inside and outside school
Health	Students describe how the school and community can support personal health practices and behaviors
Social Studies	Students use chronology, causality, change, conflict, and complexity to explain patterns of change and continuity
Language Arts	Students develop a respect for diversity in language use across cultures
SEL Competencies	Students generate, implement, and evaluate positive and informed solutions to problems

★ Give students time to create their self-portraits.

★ Invite volunteers to do a brief show-and-tell of their self-portraits.

★ Display them around the room.

★ Hand out copies of "Adding Assets at Home."

7. Closing Question

Ask students: **What will you do to start adding the Positive View of Personal Future asset to your life?** If there's time, encourage responses. Give an example of building this asset in your own life.

Preparation for Next Session

★ Ask students to bring a hat to the next session. Tell them they will be decorating their hats.

★ Have extra hats (like baseball-style caps) available for students who forget to bring their own.

★ If you can have a parade at the end of the closing session, arrange to have an audience. Perhaps your students can parade through another classroom or two, down the hall, across a playground during recess—or up the aisle at your place of worship.

★ Bring treats for the class, or ask students to bring something to share with the group.

See also the *Note* on page 9.

Mirror, Mirror on the wall

Look at yourself in a mirror. Don't "see" your hair, your clothes, or any of the flaws you think you have. "See" your true self—your inner self. Then "see" your future self—the wonderful person you could be in a year from now, or five years, or ten years, or fifty years. What have your eyes seen? What have your ears heard? What have your hands done? What ideas have gone through your head? What words have come out of your mouth?

Draw your future self. Or, if you don't want to draw, write a description of your future self.

Session 40

Positive View of Personal Future

Today your child learned about the **Positive View of Personal Future** asset. For your child, this asset means: *You feel hopeful about your own future.*

You may have noticed that all of the Developmental Assets are hopeful. The simplest definition of the assets is "good things every young person needs in his or her life." This positive outlook sets the assets apart from other approaches to helping kids succeed in life. Instead of saying, "Here's what's wrong with kids today," the assets say, "Here are the right things we can and should be doing for kids." Rather than focusing on problems, the assets spell out solutions.

Hope keeps us going, even when times are difficult or unbearable. There's no better example of how hope works than Viktor Frankl. Imprisoned at Auschwitz for three horrifying years, he survived and wrote a deeply moving, thought-provoking book, *Man's Search for Meaning.* Despite Frankl's suffering, he held on to hope, as evident in these words from his book:

He or she who has a *why* to live for can bear with almost any *how*.

**Everything can be taken from a person but one thing:
the last of human freedoms—to choose one's attitude in any given set of
circumstances, to choose one's own way.**

If Frankl can emerge from a Nazi death camp with his hope intact, then surely we can remain optimistic despite the challenges, disappointments, and difficulties we face. By modeling optimism for our children, we give them hope as well.

Ways to Teach and Model Hope at Home

★ Focus on solutions instead of problems.

★ Try to find something positive about everything—even if you have to look very hard.

★ Invite your child to tell you his or her dreams for the future. Never dismiss a dream as "silly" or "impossible."

★ Your child is probably not unaware of world events that may seem hopeless. Where there's famine, point out that many people are working to end hunger in the world (maybe including you and your family). Where there's war, explain that many people are committed to peace.

★ Look forward to your future and your child's future with joyful anticipation.

Closing Session: Happy Endings Make Good Beginnings

Optional. Write this quotation on the board: "Dream the biggest dream for yourself. Hold the highest vision of life for yourself."—Duke Ellington

Outcomes

★ to invite students to evaluate their progress in adding assets to their lives

★ to ask students to evaluate the Adding Assets course

★ to celebrate

Note: See "Before the Closing Session" on page 9 for preparation information.

Materials

★ copies of the tracker page for the preceding session's asset (from the CD-ROM; this might be the "Positive View of Personal Future" page for Session 40, or it might be a different tracker page, depending on which session you chose to end with)

★ copies of "Add Up Your Assets," "Adding Assets: Student's Course Evaluation," "Adding Assets: Parent/Caregiver's Course Evaluation," and "My Asset Promise to Myself"

★ art materials for making and decorating asset hats—colored paper, felt or other fabrics, markers, crayons, scissors, glitter, tape, glue

★ the Student Trackers

★ treats to share

The Session

1. Greet students and welcome them back to class. Tell them how much you have enjoyed being with them and helping them add assets to their lives. Have students greet each other.

2. Hand out copies of the tracker page for the preceding session's asset. Allow a few moments for students to complete them and add them to their binders.

3. Ask students to spend a few quiet moments looking over their Student Trackers and any notes they wrote to themselves during the course.

4. Hand out copies of the "Add Up Your Assets" checklist. Allow a few moments for students to complete the checklist.

5. Invite students to look through their Student Trackers and find the "Check It Out" checklist they completed at the start of the course. Have them compare the two checklists. Do they notice a difference? Most will probably say that they have more assets now than they did then.

6. Hand out copies of "Adding Assets: Student's Course Evaluation." Allow a few moments for students to complete them. Make sure students know they don't have to write their names on the evaluations. Say that they can leave them on your desk or table, writing-side-down, at the end of the session.

7. Hand out copies of "My Asset Promise to Myself." Let students look it over before adding it to their Student Tracker. If students want to share their promise, spend a few moments in discussion.

8. Tell students: **Work is done. Time for fun!** Spend the next block of time decorating hats. Students might want their hats to represent one of the assets, or all of the assets, or a particular asset category. Leave this up to them. Let them work in pairs or groups if they want. If appropriate, have music playing in the background.

9. When students have finished decorating their hats, have a parade. Walk through the school, building, or playground. Afterward, return to your classroom and enjoy the treats you brought to share.

10. As students leave, give them copies of "Adding Assets: Parent/Caregiver's Course Evaluation" to bring home. Let them bring their Student Trackers home as well.

Add up your Assets

Put a checkmark next to each statement that seems true for you.

- [ ] **1.** I feel loved and supported in my family.

- [ ] **2.** I can talk to my parent(s). I feel comfortable asking them for advice.

- [ ] **3.** There are other adults besides my parent(s) who give me support and encouragement.

- [ ] **4.** I have neighbors who know me and care about me.

- [ ] **5.** I get along well with teachers and other kids at my school. I feel that school is a caring, encouraging place to be.

- [ ] **6.** My parent(s) are actively involved in helping me succeed in school.

- [ ] **7.** I feel that adults in my community value and appreciate me.

- [ ] **8.** I am included in decisions at home and in my community.

- [ ] **9.** I have chances to help others in my community.

- [ ] **10.** I feel safe at home, at school, and in my neighborhood.

- [ ] **11.** My family has clear and consistent rules and consequences for my behavior. They keep track of me and know where I am all or most of the time.

- [ ] **12.** My school has clear rules and consequences for behavior.

- [ ] **13.** My neighbors keep an eye on kids in the neighborhood.

- [ ] **14.** The adults in my family behave in positive, responsible ways. They set good examples for me to follow. So do other adults I know.

- [ ] **15.** My best friends behave in positive, responsible ways. They are a good influence on me.

- [ ] **16.** My parent(s) and teachers expect me to do my best at school and in other activities.

- [ ] **17.** I do something with music, art, drama, or creative writing two or more times a week.

- [ ] **18.** I go to an organized after-school activity or community program for kids two or more times a week.

- [ ] **19.** I go to a religious program or service once a week or more.

- [ ] **20.** On most days, I spend some time with my parent(s). I spend some time doing things at home besides watching TV or playing video games.

- [ ] **21.** I want to do well in school, and I try my best.

- [ ] **22.** I like to learn new things in and out of school.

- [ ] **23.** I usually hand in my homework on time.

- [ ] **24.** I care about and feel connected to the teachers and other adults at my school.

- [ ] **25.** I like to read, and I read for fun on most days of the week.

- [ ] **26.** My parent(s) tell me it's important to help other people.

- [ ] **27.** My parent(s) tell me it's important to speak up for equal rights for all people.

- [ ] **28.** My parent(s) tell me it's important to stand up for my beliefs.

- [ ] **29.** My parent(s) tell me it's important to be truthful.

- [ ] **30.** My parent(s) tell me it's important to be responsible for my own behavior.

- [ ] **31.** My parent(s) tell me it's important to have good health habits and an understanding of healthy sexuality.

- [ ] **32.** I think about the choices I make, and I'm usually happy with my decisions. I know how to plan ahead.

- [ ] **33.** I care about other people and their feelings. I enjoy making friends. When I feel angry or frustrated, I try to calm myself down.

- [ ] **34.** I know and am comfortable with people of different races, ethnic backgrounds, and cultures. I'm also comfortable with my own cultural identity.

- [ ] **35.** I stay away from people who could get me into trouble. I can say no to doing things that are dangerous or wrong.

- [ ] **36.** I try to resolve conflicts in a peaceful way, without using harsh words or violent actions.

- [ ] **37.** I feel that I have some control over things that happen in my life.

- [ ] **38.** I like myself, and I'm proud to be the person I am.

- [ ] **39.** I sometimes think about what life means and whether my life has a purpose.

- [ ] **40.** I feel hopeful about my own future.

Add up your assets. How many checkmarks do you have?_____

Adding Assets: Student's Course Evaluation

1. I will keep my Student Tracker and look at it

once a week   every month   once a year   never

(circle one)

to remind me of the assets I have and the assets I need.

2. I will keep my list of assets someplace where I can see it every day.

TRUE   FALSE

(circle one)

3. The asset I am proudest of having is: _____

4. The asset I want most to add to my life is: _____

5. The ONE thing I learned in this course and will always remember is: _____

_____

6. Here's what I liked BEST about this course: _____

_____

7. Here's what I liked LEAST about this course: _____

_____

8. I wish we had done MORE of this: _____

_____

9. I think we did TOO MUCH of this: _____

_____

10. Here are my ideas for making this course better: _____

_____

_____

_____

ADDING ASSETS: PARENT/CAREGIVER'S COURSE EVALUATION

1. Please look at the checklists your child completed at the beginning and the end of this course. (Ask to see your child's Student Tracker. Look for "Check It Out" and "Add Up Your Assets.") What do you think about your child's responses? _____

_____

_____

2. Did your child bring home some of the "Adding Assets at Home" handouts?

Circle one: **YES**   **NO**

If **YES,** did the handouts give you good ideas for conversations or activities with your child?

Circle one: **YES**   **NO**

If you can, please give an example or two: _____

_____

_____

3. Did your child talk with you about any of the activities we did during the sessions?

Circle one: **YES**   **NO**

If **YES,** which of the activities do you feel were most helpful (or most fun) for your child?

_____

_____

4. Do you believe the Adding Assets course benefited your child?

Circle one: **YES**   **NO**

Please explain: _____

_____

_____

5. If we teach this course again, what do you think we should tell parents about it?

_____

_____

6. Do you have any other comments or suggestions you would like to share? Please write them here—and continue on the back of the page if needed.

_____

_____

_____

Please return this form to _____ by _____ .
$\qquad$ (teacher's name) $\qquad$ (date)

THANK YOU!

My Asset Promise to Myself

1. I will choose and think about TWO assets that I'm very proud of having in my life and in myself.

2. I will choose and focus on TWO assets that I really want to add to my life.

3. I will try to keep learning more about why the assets are important to me.

4. I will share with my family and friends what I know about the assets and what I'm trying to do to add assets.

5. This is what the assets mean to me:

I believe that everyone can build assets—including me.

I believe that asset building goes on all the time.

I believe that I have a future full of hope.

Appendix:
National Standards Charts

	Character Education Quality Standards	
Principle No.	**Principle**	**Asset/Session**
Principle 1	Effective character education promotes core ethical values as the basis of good character.	
1.1	The school staff and parent community have agreed on the core ethical values they wish to promote in their character education initiative.	1, 12, 19, 24
1.2	The school has defined its core ethical values in terms of behaviors that can be observed in the school, family, and community.	1, 4, 5, 11, 12, 14, 16, 17, 21, 22, 32, 33, 35, 39
1.3	The school has made deliberate and effective efforts to make its core ethical values, the justification for them, and their behavioral definitions widely known throughout the school and parent community.	2, 3, 4, 5, 6, 11, 12, 13, 16, 20, 22, 24, 34, 36, 39
Principle 2	Effective character education defines "character" comprehensively to include thinking, feeling, and behavior.	1
2.1	The school takes deliberate and effective steps to help students acquire a developmentally appropriate understanding of what the core values mean in everyday behavior and grasp the reasons why some behaviors are right and others wrong.	5, 10, 12, 15, 16, 19, 26, 31, 35, 36, 37, 39
2.2	The school takes deliberate and effective steps to help everyone appreciate the core values, reflect upon them, desire to embody them, and become committed to them.	2, 7, 9, 16, 19, 23, 24, 25, 30, 32, 39, 40
2.3	The school takes deliberate and effective steps to help students practice the core values so that they become habitual patterns of behavior.	1, 3, 8, 9, 10, 12, 16, 18, 20, 21, 22, 31
Principle 3	Effective character education uses a comprehensive, intentional, and proactive approach to character development.	7, 19
3.1	The school is intentional and proactive in addressing character at all grade levels.	3, 12, 21, 26, 30, 31, 37
3.2	Character education is regularly integrated into all aspects of classroom life.	3, 7, 12, 14, 24, 36, 37
3.3	Character education is infused throughout the school day to include sports and extra-curricular activities; core values are upheld by adults and taken seriously by students throughout the school environment.	5, 8, 18, 22, 23, 24, 33, 37
Principle 4	Effective character education creates a caring school community.	
4.1	The school makes it a high priority to foster caring attachments between adults and students.	2, 6, 7, 12, 14, 18, 24, 26
4.2	The school makes it a high priority to help students form caring attachments to each other.	5, 8, 12, 15, 22, 26, 33, 36
4.3	The school does not tolerate peer cruelty or any form of violence and takes steps to prevent peer cruelty and violence, and deal with it effectively when it occurs.	10, 12, 15, 16, 19, 21, 28, 30, 31, 33, 35, 36, 38, 39
4.4	The school makes it a high priority to foster caring attachments among adults within the school community.	3, 6, 12, 14, 18, 24, 26
Principle 5	Effective character education provides students with opportunities for moral action.	9, 15, 19, 30, 31, 35, 36, 37
5.1	The school sets clear expectations for students to engage in moral action both inside and outside the school.	4, 9, 13, 23, 30, 31, 38, 40
5.2	The school provides students with repeated and varied opportunities for engaging in moral action within the school, and the students engage in these opportunities and are positively affected by them.	7, 12, 15, 31, 35, 36
5.3	The school provides students with repeated and varied opportunities for engaging in moral action in the larger community, and the students engage in these opportunities and are positively affected by them.	3, 4, 7, 8, 13, 14, 18, 22, 31, 36, 38
Principle 6	Effective character education includes a meaningful and challenging academic curriculum that respects all learners, develops their character, and helps them succeed.	21, 22, 27, 29, 35

Character Education Quality Standards (2003 revision) from Character Education Partnership.

Appendix

Principle No.	Principle	Asset/Session
6.1	The academic curriculum provides meaningful and appropriate challenges to students that promote character development throughout the curriculum.	2, 12, 21, 25, 28
6.2	The school implements a wide range of strategies to accommodate the diverse cultures, skills, interests, and needs of students.	5, 16, 22, 25, 27, 34, 40
6.3	Teachers make connections between core values and academic content.	2, 23
Principle 7	Effective character education strives to develop students' self-motivation.	17
7.1	The school explicitly values students engaging in moral action for its own sake.	1, 9, 16, 19, 35, 36, 37
7.2	Staff recognize and celebrate good character by emphasizing social rather than material recognition (behavior modification rewards).	21, 22, 27, 31, 33, 35, 38
7.3	The school's approach to behavior management emphasizes core values within constructive discussion, explanation, and consequences.	1, 10, 16, 21, 28, 29, 30, 35, 39
Principle 8	Effective character education engages the school staff as a learning and moral community that shares responsibility for character education and attempts to adhere to the same core values that guide the education of students.	1, 3, 30
8.1	All professional school staff are included in planning, receiving staff development for, and carrying out the schoolwide character education effort.	12, 14, 24, 39
8.2	Support staff have been included in planning, receiving staff development for, and carrying out the schoolwide character education effort.	12, 14, 24, 36
8.3	Staff model the core values in their interaction with students and each other, and students perceive that they do.	1, 7, 24, 28, 33, 36, 40
Principle 9	Effective character education fosters shared moral leadership and long-range support of the character education initiative.	31, 40
9.1	The character education program has leaders, including the school principal, who champion the character education effort.	5
9.2	There is a leadership group (a committee or task force) inclusive of staff, students, and parents that guides the ongoing planning and implementation of the character education program and encourages the involvement of the whole school in character-related activities.	6, 12, 21, 24, 33, 34, 40
9.3	Students are explicitly involved in creating and maintaining a sense of community and in other leadership roles that contribute to the character education effort.	3, 4, 5, 7, 8, 9, 12, 18, 19, 21, 26, 33, 34, 36
Principle 10	Effective character education engages families and community members as partners in the character-building effort.	1, 2, 7, 11, 18, 20
10.1	The school recognizes the pivotal role that parents, extended families, religious institutions, youth organizations, and the immediate community play in the moral upbringing of children.	1, 2, 3, 4, 6, 7, 8, 11, 13, 14, 20, 25, 30, 34
10.2	The school and its faculty regularly exchange communications with parents and guardians, provide suggestions and activities that help them reinforce the core values, and offer workshops and resources on character education and general parenting skills.	1, 6, 7, 8, 11, 14, 20, 23, 24
Principle 11	Effective character education assesses the character of the school, the school staff's functioning as character educators, and the extent to which students manifest good character.	
11.1	The school staff, in collaboration with the appropriate governance bodies, regularly assess the character of the school as a moral community to determine its degree of success.	12, 16, 21, 36
11.2	The staff periodically report on their efforts to implement character education, as well as on their growth as character educators.	24, 30, 39
11.3	The school assesses student progress in developing an understanding of and an emotional attachment and commitment to the qualities of good character; behavior is assessed in ways that reflect core values.	17, 24, 26, 31, 36, 39

Character Education Quality Standards (2003 revision) from Character Education Partnership.

Standard No.	National Health Education Standards	Asset/Session
	Standard	
Standard 1	Students will comprehend concepts related to health promotion and disease prevention to enhance health.	
1.1	Describe the relationship between healthy behaviors and personal health.	1, 2, 11, 12, 13, 14, 15, 16, 20, 31, 35, 37, 38
1.2	Identify examples of emotional, intellectual, physical, and social health.	21, 22, 27, 31, 33, 35, 38
1.3	Describe ways in which a safe and healthy school and community environment can promote personal health.	5, 6, 30, 31, 35, 39, 40
1.4	Describe ways to prevent common childhood injuries and health problems.	31, 35
1.5	Describe when it is important to seek health care.	31, 34, 35, 36, 38
Standard 2	Students will analyze the influence of family, peers, culture, media, technology, and other factors on health behaviors.	17, 22, 27, 29, 31, 39, 40
2.1	Describe how family influences personal health practices and behaviors.	1, 6, 11, 20, 21, 31, 32, 35, 38
2.2	Identify the influence of culture on health practices and behaviors.	27, 31, 34, 36, 39
2.3	Identify how peers can influence healthy and unhealthy behaviors.	5, 15, 18, 23, 31, 33, 35, 37, 38
2.4	Describe how the school and community can support personal health practices and behaviors.	3, 4, 5, 12, 13, 18, 24, 31, 35, 39, 40
2.5	Explain how media influences thoughts, feelings, and health behaviors.	25, 28, 31, 38
2.6	Describe ways technology can influence personal health.	
Standard 3	Students will demonstrate the ability to access valid information and products and services to enhance health.	
3.1	Identify characteristics of valid health information, products, and services.	38
3.2	Locate resources from home, school, and community that provide valid health information.	4, 5, 19, 20, 21, 22, 23, 24, 28, 31, 35, 37, 38
Standard 4	Students will demonstrate the ability to use interpersonal communication skills to enhance health and avoid or reduce health risks.	3, 14, 28, 31, 35
4.1	Demonstrate effective verbal and non-verbal communication skills to enhance health.	22, 26, 31, 37
4.2	Demonstrate refusal skills to avoid or reduce health risks.	19, 31, 35, 38
4.3	Demonstrate non-violent strategies to manage or resolve conflict.	19, 20, 28, 31, 35, 36, 39, 40
4.4	Demonstrate how to ask for assistance to enhance personal health.	24, 32, 37
Standard 5	Students will demonstrate the ability to use decision-making skills to enhance health.	2, 3, 31, 32
5.1	Identify health-related situations that might require a thoughtful decision.	2, 4, 16, 30, 31, 32, 38
5.2	Analyze when assistance is needed when making a health-related decision.	3, 32
5.3	List healthy options to health-related issues or problems.	31
5.4	Predict the potential outcomes of each option when making a health-related decision.	16, 32, 39
5.5	Choose a healthy option when making a decision.	28, 31
5.6	Describe the outcomes of a health-related decision.	32, 38

National Health Education Standards from American Alliance for Health, Physical Education, Recreation and Dance.

Standard No.	Standard	Asset/Session
Standard 6	Students will demonstrate the ability to use goal-setting skills to enhance health.	15, 16, 18, 19, 21, 22, 30, 31, 32, 35, 37, 38, 39
6.1	Set a personal health goal and track progress toward its achievement.	18, 22, 30, 31, 32, 37, 39
6.2	Identify resources to assist in achieving a personal health goal.	17, 18, 19, 20, 22, 25, 26, 29, 31, 32, 39
Standard 7	Students will demonstrate the ability to practice health-enhancing behaviors and avoid or reduce health risks.	1, 2, 19, 31, 32, 35, 37, 38, 39, 40
7.1	Identify responsible personal health behaviors.	
7.2	Demonstrate a variety of healthy practices and behaviors to maintain or improve personal health.	31
7.3	Demonstrate a variety of behaviors to avoid or reduce health risks.	31
Standard 8	Students will demonstrate the ability to advocate for personal, family, and community health.	1, 2, 4, 6, 11, 13, 30, 31
8.1	Express opinions and give accurate information about health issues.	
8.2	Encourage others to make positive health choices.	15, 30, 31

National Health Education Standards from American Alliance for Health, Physical Education, Recreation and Dance.

From *A Leader's Guide to The Adding Assets Series for Kids: Activities and Strategies for Positive Youth Development* by Ann Redpath, Ed.D., Pamela Espeland, and Elizabeth Verdick, copyright © 2007. Free Spirit Publishing Inc., Minneapolis, MN; www.freespirit.com. This page may be photocopied for individual, classroom, and small group work only. For other uses, call 866-703-7322.

Curriculum Standards for Social Studies

Standard No.	Standard	Asset/Session
Culture/Standard 1	Social studies programs should include experiences that provide for the study of culture and cultural diversity, so that the learner can:	4
1.a	compare similarities and differences in the ways groups, societies, and cultures meet human needs and concerns;	3, 7, 13, 14, 19, 27, 34, 37
1.b	explain how information and experiences may be interpreted by people from diverse cultural perspectives and frames of reference;	19, 22, 27, 34
1.c	explain and give examples of how language, literature, the arts, architecture, other artifacts, traditions, beliefs, values, and behaviors contribute to the development and transmission of culture;	7, 12, 16, 17, 25, 27, 30, 34, 39
1.d	explain why individuals and groups respond differently to their physical and social environments and/or changes to them on the basis of shared assumptions, values, and beliefs;	3, 6, 7, 8, 22, 30, 34, 36, 39
1.e	articulate the implications of cultural diversity, as well as cohesion, within and across groups.	4, 5, 27, 34, 38, 39
Time, Continuity, & Change/Standard 2	Social studies programs should include experiences that provide for the study of the ways human beings view themselves in and over time, so that the learner can:	7, 16, 17, 22, 25, 28, 29, 37, 38
2.a	demonstrate an understanding that different scholars may describe the same event or situation in different ways but must provide reasons or evidence for their views;	34, 36, 39
2.b	identify and use key concepts such as chronology, causality, change, conflict, and complexity to explain, analyze, and show connections among patterns of historical change and continuity;	13, 22, 23, 28, 32, 40
2.c	identify and describe selected historical periods and patterns of change within and across cultures, such as the rise of civilizations, the development of transportation systems, the growth and breakdown of colonial systems, and others;	25, 27
2.d	identify and use processes important to reconstructing and reinterpreting the past, such as using a variety of sources, providing, validating, and weighing evidence for claims, checking for credibility of sources, and searching for causality;	27
2.e	develop critical sensitivities such as empathy and skepticism regarding attitudes, values, and behaviors of people in different historical contexts;	3, 16, 27, 33, 36, 37, 38, 39
2.f	use knowledge of facts and concepts drawn from history, along with methods of historical inquiry, to inform decision-making about and action-taking on public issues.	7, 10, 16, 32, 37
People, Places & Environments/Standard 3	Social studies programs should include experiences that provide for the study of people, places, and environments, so that the learner can:	4, 22, 37
3.a	elaborate mental maps of locales, regions, and the world that demonstrate understanding of relative location, direction, size, and shape;	4
3.b	create, interpret, use, and distinguish various representations of the earth, such as maps, globes, and photographs;	4, 34
3.c	use appropriate resources, data sources, and geographic tools such as aerial photographs, satellite images, geographic information systems (GPS), map projections, and cartography, to generate, manipulate, and interpret information such as atlases, data bases, grid systems, charts, graphs, and maps;	6, 22
3.d	estimate distance, calculate scale, and distinguish other geographic relationships such as population density and spatial distribution patterns;	4

Expectations of Excellence: Curriculum Standards for Social Studies (Silver Spring, MD: National Council for the Social Studies, 1994).

Appendix

Standard No.	Standard	Asset/Session
3.g	describe how people create places that reflect cultural values and ideals as they build neighborhoods, parks, shopping centers, and the like;	3, 4, 7, 13, 16, 25, 30, 34, 40
3.h	examine, interpret, and analyze physical and cultural patterns and their inter-actions, such as land use, settlement patterns, cultural transmission of customs and ideas, and ecosystem changes;	19, 27, 31, 34, 39, 40
3.i	describe ways that historical events have been influenced by, and have influ-enced, physical and human geographic factors in local, regional, national, and global settings.	4, 13, 35
Individual Development & Identity/Standard 4	Social studies programs should include experiences that provide for the study of individual development and identity, so that the learner can:	1
4.a	relate personal changes to social, cultural, and historical contexts;	4, 7, 16, 19, 22, 27, 32, 33, 34, 40
4.b	describe personal connections to place—as associated with community, nation, and world;	3, 4, 19, 20, 26, 30, 34, 40
4.c	describe the ways family, gender, ethnicity, nationality, and institutional affiliations contribute to personal identity;	1, 2, 6, 11, 20, 25, 32, 35, 37
4.d	relate such factors as physical endowment and capabilities, learning, motivation, personality, perception, and behavior to individual development;	1, 11, 16, 17, 18, 21, 22, 32, 33, 38
4.e	identify and describe ways regional, ethnic, and national cultures influence individuals' daily lives;	4, 7, 8, 21, 27, 31, 34, 39
4.f	identify and describe the influence of perception, attitudes, values, and beliefs on personal identity;	2, 5, 6, 11, 21, 22, 26, 27, 28, 29, 35, 36, 37, 38, 39, 40
4.g	identify and interpret examples of stereotyping, conformity, and altruism;	34, 38
4.h	work independently and cooperatively to accomplish goals.	1, 4, 5, 9, 16, 18, 31, 32, 34, 38, 39, 40
Individuals, Groups, & Institutions/Standard 5	Social studies programs should include experiences that provide for the study of interactions among individuals, groups, and institutions, so that the learner can:	1, 20, 27
5.a	demonstrate an understanding of concepts such as role, status, and social class in describing the interactions of individuals and social groups;	18, 20, 22, 24, 27, 38
5.b	analyze group and institutional influences on people, events, and elements of culture;	3, 7, 30, 34
5.c	describe the various forms institutions take and the interactions of people with institutions;	4, 8, 9, 11, 12, 14, 19, 33, 34, 36
5.d	identify and analyze examples of tensions between expressions of individuality and group or institutional efforts to promote social conformity;	1, 6, 10, 15, 29, 34, 35, 36, 38
5.e	identify and describe example of tensions between belief systems and government policies and laws;	27, 36
5.f	describe the role of institutions in furthering both continuity and change;	16, 19, 20, 27, 40
5.g	apply knowledge of how groups and institutions work to meet individual needs and promote the common good.	5, 10, 11, 12, 30, 36, 40
Power, Authority, & Governance/Standard 6	Social studies programs should include experiences that provide for the study of how people create and change structures of power, authority, and governance, so that the learner can:	
6.a	examine persistent issues involving the rights, roles, and status of the individual in relation to the general welfare;	12, 13, 27, 35, 36, 38, 40

Expectations of Excellence: Curriculum Standards for Social Studies (Silver Spring, MD: National Council for the Social Studies, 1994).

Standard No.	Standard	Asset/Session
6.b	describe the purpose of government and how its powers are acquired, used, and justified;	27
6.c	analyze and explain ideas and governmental mechanisms to meet needs and wants of citizens, regulate territory, manage conflict, and establish order and security;	29, 30
6.d	describe the ways nations and organizations respond to forces of unity and diversity affecting order and security;	30
6.f	explain conditions, actions, and motivations that contribute to conflict and cooperation within and among nations;	27, 32, 36
6.g	describe and analyze the role of technology in communications, transportation, information-processing, weapons development, or other areas as it contributes to or helps resolve conflicts;	15
6.h	explain and apply concepts such as power, role, status, justice, and influence to the examination of persistent issues and social problems.	5, 10, 27, 33, 35, 36, 39, 40
Production, Distribution, & Consumption/Standard 7	Social studies programs should include experiences that provide for the study of how people organize for the production, distribution, and consumption of goods and services, so that the learner can:	
7.c	explain the difference between private and public goods and services;	8, 9
7.f	explain and illustrate how values and beliefs influence different economic decisions;	8, 9, 15, 27, 34
7.h	compare basic economic systems according to who determines what is produced, distributed, and consumed.	27
Science, Technology, & Society/Standard 8	Social studies programs should include experiences that provide for the study of relationships among science, technology, and society, so that the learner can:	
8.a	examine and describe the influence of culture on scientific and technological choices and advancement, such as in transportation, medicine, and warfare;	2
8.b	show through specific examples how science and technology have changed people's perceptions of the social and natural world, such as in their relationship to the land, animal life, family life, and economic needs, wants, and security;	1, 22
8.c	describe examples in which values, beliefs, and attitudes have been influenced by new scientific and technological knowledge, such as the invention of the printing press, conceptions of the universe, applications of atomic energy, and genetic discoveries;	21, 22, 40
8.d	explain the need for laws and policies to govern scientific and technological applications, such as in the safety and well-being of workers and consumers and the regulation of utilities, radio, and television;	
8.e	seek reasonable and ethical solutions to problems that arise when scientific advancements and social norms or values come into conflict.	27, 30, 31, 36, 40
Global Connections/ Standard 9	Social studies programs should include experiences that provide for the study of global connections and interdependence, so that the learner can:	
9.a	describe instances in which language, art, music, belief systems, and other cultural elements can facilitate global understanding or cause misunderstanding;	16, 25
9.b	analyze examples of conflict, cooperation, and interdependence among groups, societies, and nations;	3, 27, 39, 40

Expectations of Excellence: Curriculum Standards for Social Studies (Silver Spring, MD: National Council for the Social Studies, 1994).

Curriculum Standards for Social Studies continued

Standard No.	Standard	Asset/Session
9.c	describe and analyze the effects of changing technologies on the global community;	4
9.d	explore the causes, consequences, and possible solutions to persistent, contemporary and emerging global issues, such as health, security, resource allocation, economic development, and environmental quality;	30, 31
9.f	demonstrate understanding of concerns, standards, issues, and conflicts related to universal human rights.	9, 34, 35, 36, 39, 40
Civic Ideas & Practices/ Standard 10	Social studies programs should include experiences that provide for the study of the ideals, principles, and practices of citizenship in a democratic republic, so that the learner can:	8, 9, 21, 22
10.a	examine the origins and continuing influence of key ideals of the democratic republican form of government, such as individual human dignity, liberty, justice, equality, and the rule of law;	36
10.b	identify and interpret sources and examples of the rights and responsibilities of citizens;	8, 9, 22, 27, 28, 30, 34, 35, 39, 40
10.d	practice forms of civic discussion and participation consistent with the ideals of citizens in a democratic republic;	27
10.e	explain and analyze various forms of citizen action that influence public policy decisions;	27
10.g	analyze the influence of diverse forms of public opinion on the development of public policy and decision-making;	32
10.j	examine strategies designed to strengthen the "common good," which consider a range of options for citizen action.	9, 13, 16, 19, 20, 22, 27, 30, 34, 35, 36, 37, 39, 40

Expectations of Excellence: Curriculum Standards for Social Studies (Silver Spring, MD: National Council for the Social Studies, 1994).

Standards for the English Language Arts

Standard No.	Standard	Asset/Session
Standard 1	Students read a wide range of print and non-print texts to build an understanding of texts, of themselves, and of the cultures of the United States and the world; to acquire new information; to respond to the needs and demands of society and the workplace; and for personal fulfillment. Among these texts are fiction and nonfiction, classic and contemporary works.	13, 16, 17, 21, 22, 23, 25, 26, 28, 30, 32, 33, 34, 36, 37, 38, 39, 40
Standard 2	Students read a wide range of literature from many periods in many genres to build an understanding of the many dimensions (e.g., philosophical, ethical, and aesthetic) of human experience.	16, 19, 22, 25, 27, 34, 36, 37, 38, 39, 40
Standard 3	Students apply a wide range of strategies to comprehend, interpret, evaluate, and appreciate texts. They draw on their prior experience, their interactions with other readers and writers, their knowledge of word meaning and of other texts, their word identification strategies, and their understanding of textual features (e.g., sound-letter correspondence, sentence structure, context, and graphics).	1, 3, 11, 13, 15, 22, 25, 26, 28, 29, 33, 39
Standard 4	Students adjust their use of spoken, written, and visual language (e.g., conventions, style, and vocabulary) to communicate effectively with a variety of audiences and for different purposes.	2, 3, 4, 6, 7, 8, 9, 17, 22, 23, 25, 27, 32, 33, 34, 36, 37, 39
Standard 5	Students employ a wide range of strategies as they write and use different writing process elements appropriately to communicate with different audiences for a variety of purposes.	4, 7, 8, 12, 17, 19, 22, 23, 27, 30, 34, 35, 36, 37, 38, 39, 40
Standard 6	Students apply knowledge of language structure, language conventions (e.g., spelling and punctuation), media techniques, figurative language, and genre to create, critique, and discuss print and non-print texts.	1, 11, 17, 21, 22, 31, 38
Standard 7	Students conduct research on issues and interests by generating ideas and questions, and by posing problems. They gather, evaluate, and synthesize data from a variety of sources (e.g., print and non-print texts, artifacts, and people) to communicate their discoveries in ways that suit their purpose and audience.	4, 5, 6, 7, 8, 18, 19, 21, 22, 30, 31, 32, 34, 38, 39, 40
Standard 8	Students use a variety of technological and information resources (e.g., libraries, databases, computer networks, and video) to gather and synthesize information and to create and communicate knowledge.	1, 8, 9, 10, 14, 15, 22, 24, 27, 28, 29, 36, 37, 38
Standard 9	Students develop an understanding of and respect for diversity in language use, patterns, and dialects across cultures, ethnic groups, geographic regions, and social roles.	4, 5, 9, 10, 13, 22, 27, 34, 39, 40
Standard 10	Students whose first language is not English make use of their first language to develop competency in the English language arts and to develop understanding of content across the curriculum.	23, 26, 27, 34, 36, 38
Standard 11	Students participate as knowledgeable, reflective, creative, and critical members of a variety of literacy communities.	1, 3, 4, 5, 7, 15, 17, 25, 30, 34, 36, 37, 38, 39, 40
Standard 12	Students use spoken, written, and visual language to accomplish their own purposes (e.g., for learning, enjoyment, persuasion, and the exchange of information).	1, 4, 5, 6, 16, 19, 20, 21, 22, 23, 28, 29, 33, 37, 38, 39, 40

SEL (Social and Emotional Learning) Competencies

Standard No.	Standard	Asset/Session
1. Self Awareness		
1.1	**Identifying emotions:** Identifying and labeling one's feelings	1, 2, 5, 7, 11, 12, 14, 15, 16, 21, 22, 29, 33, 37, 38
1.2	**Recognizing strengths:** Identifying and cultivating one's strengths and positive qualities	1, 2, 3, 4, 5, 6, 8, 9, 13, 14, 16, 18, 22, 28, 31, 35, 39
2. Social Awareness		
2.1	**Perspective-taking:** Identifying and understanding the thoughts and feelings of others	2, 4, 6, 7, 8, 9, 12, 14, 15, 19, 26, 27, 33, 34, 37
2.2	**Appreciating diversity:** Understanding that individual and group differences complement each other and make the world more interesting	2, 3, 4, 5, 12, 13, 14, 15, 19, 24, 25, 26, 27, 34, 36
3. Self Management		
3.1	**Managing emotions:** Monitoring and regulating feelings so they aid rather than impede the handling of situations	1, 2, 3, 8, 9, 11, 16, 21, 22, 23, 27, 32, 33, 36, 37, 38
3.2	**Goal setting:** Establishing and working toward the achievement of short- and long-term pro-social goals	3, 5, 6, 8, 12, 14, 16, 18, 21, 22, 23, 30, 31, 32, 33, 36, 37, 39, 40
4. Responsible Decision Making		
4.1	**Analyzing situations:** Accurately perceiving situations in which a decision is to be made and assessing factors that might influence one's response	2, 3, 4, 7, 8, 9, 10, 11, 12, 15, 21, 22, 28, 32, 37, 39, 40
4.2	**Assuming personal responsibility:** Recognizing and understanding one's obligation to engage in ethical, safe, and legal behaviors	1, 2, 3, 4, 5, 6, 8, 9, 10, 12, 13, 15, 19, 23, 26, 27, 30, 31, 35, 38
4.3	**Respecting others:** Believing that others deserve to be treated with kindness and compassion and feeling motivated to contribute to the common good	1, 2, 3, 4, 5, 7, 8, 9, 12, 15, 19, 20, 24, 26, 27, 33, 34, 36, 37, 39
4.4	**Problem solving:** Generating, implementing, and evaluating positive and informed solutions to problems	3, 9, 14, 16, 17, 18, 21, 22, 28, 32, 35, 36, 37, 40
5. Relationship Skills		
5.1	**Communication:** Using verbal and nonverbal skills to express oneself and promote positive and effective exchanges with others	2, 6, 8, 9, 11, 12, 14, 15, 16, 24, 25, 33, 36, 38
5.2	**Building relationships:** Establishing and maintaining healthy and rewarding connections with individuals and groups	3, 6, 7, 9, 12, 13, 14, 17, 18, 19, 20, 24, 31, 33, 35, 36, 37
5.3	**Negotiation:** Achieving mutually satisfactory resolutions to conflict by addressing the needs of all concerned	1, 2, 5, 6, 9, 10, 11, 12, 13, 16, 20, 22, 27, 28, 31, 36, 40
5.4	**Refusal:** Effectively conveying and following through with one's decision not to engage in unwanted, unsafe, unethical, or unlawful conduct	2, 4, 6, 10, 12, 15, 19, 31, 32, 35, 37, 40

SEL (Social and Emotional Learning) Competencies from Collaborative for Academic, Social, and Emotional Learning (CASEL), University of Illinois at Chicago.

Correlation of National Standards to Developmental Assets

Asset	Character Education Quality Standards	SEL (Social and Emotional Learning) Competencies	National Health Education Standards	Curriculum Standards for Social Studies	Standards for the English Language Arts
1	**Family support**—Family life provides high levels of love and support.	1.1, 1.2, 2, 2.3, 7.1, 7.3, 8, 8.3, 10, 10.1	1.1, 1.2, 3.1, 4.2, 4.3, 5.3	1.1, 2.1, 7, 8	4, 4.c, 4.d, 4.h, 5, 5.d, 8.b	3, 6, 8, 11, 12
2	**Positive family communication**—Parent(s) and child communicate positively. Child feels comfortable seeking advice and counsel from parent(s).	1.3, 2.2, 4.1, 6.1, 6.3, 10, 10.1	1.1, 1.2, 2.1, 2.2, 3.1, 4.1, 4.2, 4.3, 5.1, 5.3, 5.4	1.1, 5, 5.1, 7, 8	4.c, 4.f, 8.a	4
3	**Other adult relationships**—Child receives support from adults other than her or his parent(s).	1.3, 2.3, 3.1, 3.2, 4.4, 5.3, 8, 9.3, 10.1	1.2, 2.2, 3.1, 3.2, 4.1, 4.2, 4.3, 4.4	2.4, 4, 5, 5.2	1.a, 1.d, 2.e, 3.g, 4.b, 5.b, 9.b	3, 4, 11
4	**Caring neighborhood**—Child experiences caring neighbors.	1.2, 1.3, 5.1, 5.3, 9.2, 9.3, 10.1	1.2, 2.1, 2.2, 4.1, 4.2, 4.3, 5.2, 5.4	2.4, 3.2, 5.1, 8	1, 1.e, 3, 3.a, 3.b, 3.d, 3.g, 3.l, 4.a, 4.e, 4.h, 5.c	4, 5, 7, 9, 11, 12
5	**Caring school climate**—Relationships with teachers and peers provide a caring, encouraging school environment.	1.2, 1.3, 2.1, 3.3, 4.2, 6.2, 9.1, 9.3	1.1, 1.2, 2.2, 3.2, 4.2, 4.3, 5.3	1.3, 2.3, 2.4	1.e, 4.f, 4.h, 5.g, 6.h	7, 9, 11, 12
6	**Parent involvement in schooling**—Parent(s) are actively involved in helping the child succeed in school.	1.3, 4.1, 4.4, 10.1	1.2, 2.1, 4.2, 5.1, 5.2, 5.3, 5.4	1.3, 2.1, 3.2, 8	1.d, 3.c, 4.c, 4.f, 5.d	4, 7, 12
7	**Community values children**—Child feels valued and appreciated by adults in the community.	2.2, 3, 3.2, 4.1, 5.2, 5.3, 8.3, 9.3, 10, 10.1	1.1, 2.1, 3.2, 4.1, 4.3, 5.2		1.a, 1.c, 1.d, 2, 2.f, 3.g, 4.a, 4.b, 4.e, 5.b	4, 5, 7, 11
8	**Children as resources**—Child is included in decisions at home and in the community.	2.2, 2.3, 5, 5.1, 7.1, 9.3	1.2, 2.1, 3.1, 4.1, 4.2, 4.3, 4.4, 5.1, 5.2, 5.3		4.h, 5.c, 7.c, 7.f, 9.f, 10, 10.b, 10.j	4, 5, 8, 9
9	**Service to others**—Child has opportunities to help others in the community.	2.2, 2.3, 5, 5.1, 7.1, 9.3	1.2, 2.1, 3.1, 4.1, 4.2, 4.3, 4.4, 5.1, 5.2, 5.3		4.h, 5.c, 7.c, 7.f, 9.f, 10, 10.b, 10.j	4, 5, 8, 9
10	**Safety**—Child feels safe at home, at school, and in her or his neighborhood.	2.1, 2.3, 4.3, 7.3	4.1, 4.2, 5.3, 5.4		2.f, 5.d, 5.g, 6.h	8, 9

Appendix

Asset		Character Education Quality Standards	SEL (Social and Emotional Learning) Competencies	National Health Education Standards	Curriculum Standards for Social Studies	Standards for the English Language Arts
11	**Family boundaries**—Family has clear and consistent rules and consequences and monitors the child's whereabouts.	1.2, 1.3, 10, 10.1	1.1, 3.1, 4.1, 5.1, 5.3	1.1, 2.1, 8	4.c, 4.d, 4.f, 5.c, 5.g	3, 6
12	**School boundaries**—School provides clear rules and consequences.	1.1, 1.2, 1.3, 2.1, 2.3, 3.2, 4.1, 4.2, 4.3, 4.4, 5.2, 6.1, 8.1, 8.2, 9.2, 9.3, 11.1	1.1, 2.1, 2.2, 3.2, 4.1, 4.2, 4.3, 5.1, 5.2, 5.3, 5.4	1.1, 2.4	1.c, 5.c, 5.g, 6.a	5
13	**Neighborhood boundaries**—Neighbors take responsibility for monitoring the child's behavior.	1.3, 3.1, 5.1, 5.3, 10.1	1.2, 2.2, 4.2, 5.2, 5.3	1.1, 2.4, 8	1.a, 2.b, 3.g, 3.l, 6.a, 10.j	1, 3
14	**Adult role models**—Parent(s) and other adults in the child's family, as well as nonfamily adults, model positive, responsible behavior.	1.2, 3.2, 4.1, 4.4, 5.3, 8.1, 8.2, 10.1	1.1, 1.2, 2.1, 3.2, 4.4, 5.1, 5.2	1.1, 4	1.a, 5.c	8
15	**Positive peer influence**—Child's closest friends model positive, responsible behavior.	2.1, 4.2, 4.3, 5, 5.2	1.1, 2.1, 4.1, 4.2, 4.3, 5.1, 5.4	1.1, 6, 8.2	5.d, 6.g, 7.f	3, 8, 11
16	**High expectations**—Parent(s) and teachers expect the child to do her or his best at school and in other activities.	1.2, 1.3, 2.1, 2.2, 2.3, 4.3, 6.2, 7.1, 7.3, 11.1	1.1, 1.2, 3.1, 3.2, 4.4, 5.1, 5.3	1.1, 2.3, 5.1, 5.4, 6	1.c, 2, 2.e, 2.f, 3.g, 4.a, 4.b, 4.d, 4.h, 5.f, 9.a, 10.j	1, 2, 12
17	**Creative activities**—Child participates in music, art, drama, or creative writing two or more times per week.	1.2, 7, 11.3	4.4, 5.2	6.2	1.c, 2, 4.d	4, 5, 7, 11
18	**Child programs**—Child participates two or more times per week in cocurricular school activities or structured community programs for children.	2.3, 3.3, 4.1, 4.4, 5.3, 9.3, 10	1.2, 3.2, 4.4, 5.2	2.3, 2.4, 6, 6.1, 6.2	4.d, 4.h, 5.a	7
19	**Religious community**—Child attends religious programs or services one or more times per week.	1.1, 2.1, 2.2, 3, 4.3, 5, 7.1, 9.3	2.1, 2.2, 4.2, 4.3, 5.2, 5.4	3.2, 4.2, 4.3, 6, 6.2, 7	1.a, 1.b, 3.h, 4.a, 4.b, 5.c, 5.f, 10.j	2, 5, 7, 12
20	**Time at home**—Child spends some time most days both in high-quality interaction with parent(s) and doing things at home other than watching TV or playing video games.	1.3, 2.3, 10, 10.1	4.3, 5.2, 5.3	1.1, 2.1, 3.2, 4.3, 6.2	4.c, 5, 5.a, 5.f, 10.j	12

Correlation of National Standards to Developmental Assets continued

Asset		Character Education Quality Standards	SEL (Social and Emotional Learning) Competencies	National Health Education Standards	Curriculum Standards for Social Studies	Standards for the English Language Arts
21	Achievement motivation—Child is motivated and strives to do well in school.	1.2, 2.3, 3.1, 4.3, 6, 6.1, 7.2, 7.3, 9.2, 9.3, 11.1	1.1, 3.1, 3.2, 4.1, 4.4	1.2, 2.1, 3.2, 6	4.d, 4.e, 4.f, 8.c, 10	1, 6, 7, 12
22	Learning engagement—Child is responsive, attentive, and actively engaged in learning at school and enjoys participating in learning activities outside of school.	1.2, 1.3, 2.3, 3.3, 4.2, 5.3, 6, 6.2, 7.2	1.1, 1.2, 3.1, 3.2, 4.1, 4.4, 5.3	1.2, 2, 3.2, 4.1, 6, 6.1, 6.2	1.b, 1.d, 2, 2.b, 3, 3.c, 4.a, 4.b, 4.d, 4.f, 5.a, 8.b, 8.c, 10, 10.b, 10.j	1, 2, 3, 4, 5, 6, 7, 8, 9, 12
23	Homework—Child usually hands in homework on time.	2.2, 3.3, 5.1, 6.3	3.1, 3.2, 4.2	2.3, 3.2	2	1, 4, 5, 10, 12
24	Bonding to adults at school—Child cares about teachers and other adults at school.	1.1, 1.3, 2.2, 3.2, 3.3, 4.1, 4.4, 8.1, 8.2, 8.3, 9.2, 11.2, 11.3	2.2, 4.3, 5.1, 5.2	2.4, 3.2, 4.4	2.b, 2.d, 5.a	8
25	Reading for pleasure—Child enjoys and engages in reading for fun most days of the week.	2.2, 6.1, 6.2, 10.1	2.2, 5.1	2.5, 6.2	1.c, 2, 2.c, 3.g, 4.c, 9.a	1, 2, 3, 11
26	Caring—Parent(s) tell the child it is important to help other people.	2.1, 3.1, 4.1, 4.2, 4.4, 9.3, 11.3	2.1, 2.2, 4.2, 4.3	4.1, 6.2	4.f	1, 3, 10
27	Equality and social justice—Parent(s) tell the child it is important to speak up for equal rights for all people.	6, 7.2	2.1, 2.2, 3.1, 4.2, 4.3, 5.3	1.2, 2, 2.2	1.a, 1.b, 1.c, 1.e, 2.c, 2.e, 3.h, 4.a, 4.b, 4.e, 4.f, 5, 5.a, 5.e, 5.f, 6.a, 6.b, 6.f, 6.h, 7.f, 7.h, 8.e, 9.b, 10.b, 10.d, 10.e, 10.j	4, 5, 7, 11
28	Integrity—Parent(s) tell the child it is important to stand up for one's beliefs.	4.3, 6.1, 7.3, 8.3	1.2, 4.1, 4.4, 5.3	2.5, 3.2, 4, 4.3, 5	2, 2.b, 4.f, 10.b	1, 3, 8, 12
29	Honesty—Parent(s) tell the child it is important to tell the truth.	7.3	1.1	2, 6.2	2, 4.f, 5.d, 6.c	3, 8, 12
30	Responsibility—Parent(s) tell the child it is important to accept personal responsibility for behavior.	6, 7.3, 10.1, 11.2	3.2, 4.2	1.3, 5.1, 6, 6.1, 8, 8.2	1.c, 1.d, 3.g, 5.b, 5.g, 6.c, 6.d, 8.e, 9.d, 10.b, 10.j	1, 5, 7, 10

Appendix

Asset		Character Education Quality Standards	SEL (Social and Emotional Learning) Competencies	National Health Education Standards	Curriculum Standards for Social Studies	Standards for the English Language Arts
31	Healthy lifestyle—Parent(s) tell the child it is important to have good healthy habits and an understanding of healthy sexuality.	2.1, 2.2, 2.3, 3.1, 4.3, 5, 5.1, 5.2, 5.3, 7.2, 9, 11.3	1.2, 3.2, 4.2, 5.2, 5.3, 5.4	1.1, 1.2, 1.3, 1.4, 1.5, 2, 2.1, 2.2, 2.3, 2.4, 2.5, 3.2, 4, 4.1, 4.2, 4.3, 5.1, 5.3, 5.5, 6, 6.1, 6.2, 7, 8, 8.2	3.h, 4.e, 4.h, 8.e, 9.d	6, 7
32	Planning and decision making—Child thinks about decisions and is usually happy with the results of her or his decisions.	1.2, 2.2	3.1, 3.2, 4.1, 4.4, 5.4	2.1, 4.4, 5, 5.1, 5.2, 5.4, 5.6, 6.1, 6.2, 7, 7.2, 7.3	2.b, 2.f, 4.a, 4.b, 4.c, 4.d, 4.h, 6.f, 10.g	1, 4, 7
33	Interpersonal competence—Child cares about and is affected by other people's feelings, enjoys making friends, and, when frustrated or angry, tries to calm herself or himself.	1.2, 3.3, 4.2, 4.3, 7.2, 8.3, 9.2, 9.3	1.1, 2.1, 3.1, 3.2, 4.3, 5.1, 5.2	1.2, 2.3, 5, 6	2.e, 4.a, 4.b, 4.d, 5.c, 6.h	1, 3, 4, 12
34	Cultural competence—Child knows and is comfortable with people of different racial, ethnic, and cultural backgrounds and with her or his own cultural identity.	1.3, 6.2, 9, 9.2, 9.3, 10.1	2.1, 2.2, 4.3	1.5, 2.2	1.a, 1.b, 1.c, 1.d, 1.e, 2.a, 3.b, 3.g, 3.h, 4.a, 4.b, 4.e, 4.g, 4.h, 5.b, 5.c, 5.d, 7.f, 9.f, 10.b, 10.j	1, 2, 4, 5, 7, 9, 10, 11
35	Resistance skills—Child can stay away from people who are likely to get her or him in trouble and is able to say no to doing wrong or dangerous things.	1.2, 2.1, 4.3, 5, 5.2, 6, 7.1, 7.2, 7.3	1.2, 4.2, 4.4, 5.2, 5.4	1.1, 1.2, 1.3, 1.4, 1.5, 2.1, 2.3, 2.4, 3.2, 4.2, 4.3, 6, 7	3.l, 4.c, 4.f, 5.c, 5.d, 6.e, 6.h, 9.f, 10.b, 10.j	1, 5
36	Peaceful conflict resolution—Child attempts to resolve conflict nonviolently.	1.3, 2.1, 3.2, 4.2, 4.3, 5, 5.2, 5.3, 8.2, 8.3, 9.3, 11.1, 11.3	2.2, 3.1, 3.2, 4.3, 4.4, 5.1, 5.2, 5.3	1.5, 2.2, 4.3	1.d, 2.a, 2.e, 4.f, 5.c, 5.d, 5.e, 5.g, 6.a, 6.f, 6.h, 8.e, 9.f, 10.a, 10.j	1, 2, 4, 5, 8, 10
37	Personal power—Child feels she or he has some influence over things that happen in her or his life.	2.1, 3.1, 3.2, 3.3, 5, 7.1	1.1, 2.1, 3.1, 3.2, 4.1, 4.3, 4.4, 5.4	1.1, 2.3, 3.2, 4, 4.1, 4.4, 6, 6.1, 7	1.a, 2, 2.e, 2.f, 3, 4.c, 4.f, 10.j	1, 2, 4, 5, 8, 11, 12
38	Self-esteem—Child likes and is proud to be the person she or he is.	4.3, 5.1, 5.3, 7.2	1.1, 3.1, 4.2, 5.1	1.1, 1.2, 1.5, 2.1, 2.3, 2.5, 3.1, 3.2, 4.2, 5.1, 5.6, 6, 7	1.e, 2, 2.e, 4.d, 4.f, 4.g, 4.h, 5.a, 5.c, 5.d, 6.a	1, 2, 5, 6, 7, 10, 11, 12
39	Sense of purpose—Child sometimes thinks about what life means and whether there is purpose for her or his life.	1.2, 1.3, 2.1, 2.2, 4.3, 7.3, 8, 8.1, 11.2, 11.3	1.2, 3.2, 4.1, 4.3	1.3, 2, 2.2, 2.4, 4.3, 5.4, 6, 6.1, 6.2, 7	1.c, 1.d, 1.e, 2.a, 2.e, 3.h, 4.e, 4.h, 6.h, 9.b, 9.f, 10.b, 10.j	1, 2, 3, 4, 7, 9, 11, 12
40	Positive view of personal future—Child is optimistic about her or his personal future.	2.2, 5.1, 6.4, 8.3, 9.2	3.2, 4.1, 4.4, 5.2, 5.3 5.4	1.3, 2, 2.4, 4.3, 7	2.b, 3.g, 3.h, 4.a, 4.b, 4.f, 4.h, 5.f, 5.g, 6.a, 6.h, 8.c, 8.e, 9.b, 9.f, 10.b, 10.j	1, 2, 5, 7, 9, 11, 12

Books

10-Minute Life Lessons for Kids: 52 Fun and Simple Games and Activities to Teach Your Child Honesty, Trust, Love, and Other Essential Virtues by Jamie C. Miller (New York: Harper Collins, 1998). Playful, easy-to-understand activities help parents teach children moral lessons they won't forget.

365 Ways to Raise Great Kids: Activities for Raising Bright, Caring, Honest Respectful, and Creative Children by Sheila Ellison and Barbara Ann Barnett (Naperville, IL: Sourcebooks, Incorporated, 1998). A resource for parents and educators filled with engaging, creative ways to help build self-esteem and strength of character in children.

Building Assets Is Elementary: Group Activities for Helping Kids Ages 8–12 Succeed by Search Institute (Minneapolis: Search Institute, 2004). Promoting creativity, time-management skills, kindness, manners, and more, this flexible activity book includes over 50 easy-to-use group exercises for the classroom or youth group.

Character Building Activities for Kids: Ready-to-Use Character Education Lessons & Activities for the Elementary Grades by Darlene Mannix (San Francisco: Jossey-Bass, 2002). Includes more than 140 lessons (with reproducibles) for developing character traits such as honesty, generosity, and fairness.

Character Matters: How to Help Our Children Develop Good Judgment, Integrity, and Other Essential Virtues by Thomas Lickona (New York: Touchstone, 2004). An award-winning psychologist offers more than 100 practical strategies for helping kids build strong personal character.

Great Books for Girls: More Than 600 Books to Inspire Today's Girls and Tomorrow's Women and *Great Books for Boys: More Than 600 Books for Boys 2 to 14* by Kathleen Odean (New York: Ballantine, 2002 and 1998). Annotated recommendations from a former Caldecott and Newbery Award committee member.

Great Places to Learn: How Asset-Building Schools Help Students Succeed by Neal Starkman, Peter C. Scales, and Clay Roberts (Minneapolis: Search Institute, 1999). With practical ideas, explanations, and stories, this book helps educators turn their schools into asset-building schools. Includes reproducible handouts, charts, lists, and assessment tools.

How to Parent So Children Will Learn by Sylvia B. Rimm, Ph.D. (New York: Three Rivers Press, 1997). Advice on setting limits, selecting appropriate rewards and punishments, decreasing arguments and power struggles, encouraging appropriate independence, guiding children toward good study habits, helping them improve their test-taking skills, and more.

The Life-Smart Kid: Teaching Your Child to Use Good Judgment in Every Situation by Lawrence J. Greene (Rocklin, CA: Prima Publications, 1995). Discover practical ways to help young people develop critical thinking and decision-making skills.

More Than Just a Place to Go: How Developmental Assets Can Strengthen Your Youth Program by Search Institute (Minneapolis: Search Institute, 2004). Helps youth programs integrate the Developmental Assets into their programs. Includes examples from successful and diverse programs. Companion to the 29-minute VHS video of the same title.

Parents Do Make a Difference: How to Raise Kids with Solid Character, Strong Minds, and Caring Hearts by Michele Borba (New York: Jossey-Bass, 1999). Based on nationwide research and pilot programs in elementary schools, this book combines simple steps to reinforce positive self-esteem in kids.

Pass It On at School: Activity Handouts for Creating Caring Schools by Search Institute (Minneapolis: Search Institute, 2003). This handy book offers 74 tip sheets and handout masters to help educators and parents promote a healthy, asset-building school environment.

Powerful Teaching: Developmental Assets in Curriculum and Instruction edited by Judy Taccogna, Ed.D. (Minneapolis: Search Institute, 2003). Following five guiding principals, this book instructs educators on how to foster asset-building in everything they do—from structuring lessons to interacting with students.

The Power of Positive Talk: Words to Help Every Child Succeed by Douglas Bloch, M.A., with Jon Merritt, M.S. (Minneapolis: Free Spirit Publishing, 2003). Affirmations can heal hurts, build self-esteem, and empower us to face life with confidence and courage. This book helps kids and adults learn affirmations for many situations and challenges.

What Kids Need to Succeed: Proven, Practical Ways to Raise Good Kids by Peter L. Benson, Ph.D., Judy Galbraith, M.A., and Pamela Espeland (Minneapolis: Free Spirit Publishing, 1994). More than 900 specific, concrete suggestions help adults help children build Developmental Assets at home, at school, and in the community.

What Young Children Need to Succeed: Working Together to Build Assets from Birth to Age 11 by Jolene L. Roehlkepartain and Nancy Leffert, Ph.D. (Minneapolis: Free Spirit Publishing, 2000). Hundreds of practical, concrete ideas help adults build Developmental Assets for children in four different age groups: birth to 12 months, ages 1–2, 3–5, and 6–11. Includes inspiring true stories from across the United States.

Web sites

Alliance for Youth
www.americaspromise.org
Founded in 1997, this organization is committed to fulfilling five promises to American Youth: Every child needs caring adults, safe places, a healthy start, marketable skills, and opportunities to serve.

Center for the 4th & 5th Rs (Respect and Responsibility)
www.cortland.edu/character/index.asp
A regional, state, and national resource in character education, founded by Dr. Thomas Lickona. Subscribe to the free online newsletter.

Children Lead
www.childrenlead.com
A division of LeadershipVillage.com, this site offers daily tips and informative articles about parenting for character and leadership.

Connect for Kids
www.connectforkids.org
Tips, articles, resources, volunteer opportunities, and more for adults who want to improve the lives of children in their community and beyond. Includes the complete text of Richard Louv's book *101 Things You Can Do for Our Children's Future.*

A Game a Day
www.agameaday.com
Puzzles, word games, and brain teasers that encourage creative thinking and build problem-solving skills.

The Giraffe Project
www.giraffe.org
The Giraffe Project works to inspire K–12 students to be courageous, active citizens. Their site includes helpful resources and extraordinary stories about heroes of all ages who are willing to stick their necks out to help others.

GoodCharacter.com
www.goodcharacter.com
Discussion questions, learning activities, writing assignments, and other useful resources for educators. Recommended by the Parents' Choice Foundation.

Learning Peace

www.learningpeace.com

This site for teachers, parents, and administrators will help you create more peace in your schools, homes, and communities. By teaching and modeling conflict resolution, anger management, anti-bullying, and character building, you can create more peaceful interactions among the kids you know.

National Education Partnership—Help for Parents

www.nea.org/parents

When parents are involved in their children's education, kids do better in school. Here's advice from experts on how to help your child achieve and succeed. Includes guides for parents on understanding testing; helping your child with reading, math, and science; and getting involved in your child's school.

National Mentoring Partnership

www.mentoring.org

A wealth of information about becoming and finding a mentor, this organization provides connections, training, resources, and advice to introduce and support mentoring partnerships.

Search Institute

www.search-institute.org

Through dynamic research and analysis, this independent nonprofit organization works to promote healthy, active, and content youth and communities.

INdex

About the Authors

Ann Redpath, Ed.D., earned her doctorate from Columbia University Teachers College. She is an education curriculum developer, author, award-winning editor, and former publisher. She is now directing the development of a leadership curriculum for Girl Scouts of the USA. Both **Pamela Espeland** and **Elizabeth Verdick** have written many books for children and teens. Pamela's books include *What Kids Need to Succeed* and *What Teens Need to Succeed*. Elizabeth's books include *Germs Are Not for Sharing, How to Take the GRRRR Out of Anger*, and other titles in Free Spirit's Best Behavior™ and Laugh & Learn™ series.

Other Great Books from Free Spirit

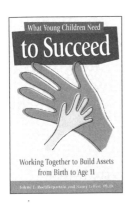

What Young Children Need to Succeed
Working Together to Build Assets from Birth to Age 11
by Jolene L. Roehlkepartain and Nancy Leffert, Ph.D.
Based on groundbreaking research, this book helps adults create a firm foundation for children from day one. You'll find hundreds of practical, concrete ways to build 40 assets in four different age groups. Comprehensive, friendly, and easy-to-use, this book will make anyone an asset builder and a positive influence in children's lives. For parents, teachers, all other caring adults, and children.
$11.95; 320 pp.; softcover; illust.; 5¼" x 8"

Leader's Guide
by Jolene L. Roehlkepartain and Nancy Leffert, Ph.D.
Ready-to-use workshops for parents, educators, and other adults who work with children from birth through grade 6.
$19.95; 152 pp.; softcover; 8½" x 10⅞"

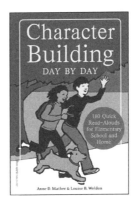

Character Building Day by Day
180 Quick Read-Alouds for Elementary School and Home
by Anne D. Mather and Louise B. Weldon
In elementary schools across the country, teachers are expected to provide at least five minutes of character education each day. This book makes it easy to meet that requirement in a meaningful way. It includes 180 character vignettes—five for each of the 36 weeks in the school year—grouped by trait. Each is short enough to be read aloud; all can be used as starting points for discussion, to support an existing character education program, or as the basis for an independent program. For educators and parents of kids in grades 3–6.
$14.95; 208 pp.; softcover; B&W illust.; 6" x 9"

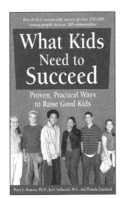

What Kids Need to Succeed
Proven, Practical Ways to Raise Good Kids
Revised, Expanded, and Updated Edition
by Peter L. Benson, Ph.D., Judy Galbraith, M.A., and Pamela Espeland
Our proven best-seller identifies 40 Developmental Assets kids need to lead healthy, productive, positive lives, then gives them more than 900 suggestions for building their own assets wherever they are. Parents' Choice approved. For parents, teachers, community and youth leaders, and teens.
$6.95; 256 pp.; softcover; 4⅛" x 6⅞"

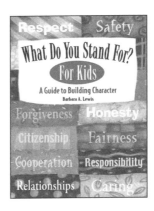

What Do You Stand For? For Kids
A Guide to Building Character
by Barbara A. Lewis
True stories, inspiring quotations, thought-provoking dilemmas, and activities help elementary school children build positive character traits including caring, fairness, respect, and responsibility. From the best-selling author of *What Do You Stand For? For Teens.* Includes updated resources. For ages 7–12.
$14.95; 176 pp.; softcover; B&W photos and illust.; 7¼" x 9"

The Adding Assets Series for Kids

Each book: 80–100 pp., 2-color illust., S/C, 5⅛" x 7". Ages 8–12. $9.95

People Who Care About You
Kids build the six Support Assets: Family Support, Positive Family Communication, Other Adult Relationships, Caring Neighborhood, Caring School Climate, and Parent Involvement in Schooling.

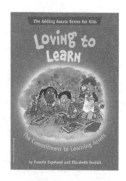

Loving to Learn
Kids build the five Commitment to Learning Assets: Achievement Motivation, Learning Engagement, Homework, Bonding to Adults at School, and Reading for Pleasure.

Helping Out and Staying Safe
Kids build the four Empowerment Assets: Community Values Children, Children as Resources, Service to Others, and Safety.

Knowing and Doing What's Right
Kids build the six Positive Values Assets: Caring, Equality and Social Justice, Integrity, Honesty, Responsibility, and Healthy Lifestyle.

Doing and Being Your Best
Kids build the six Boundaries and Expectations Assets: Family Boundaries, School Boundaries, Neighborhood Boundaries, Adult Role Models, Positive Peer Influence, and High Expectations.

Making Choices and Making Friends
Kids build the five Social Competencies Assets: Planning and Decision Making, Interpersonal Competence, Cultural Competence, Resistance Skills, and Peaceful Conflict Resolution.

Smart Ways to Spend Your Time
Kids build the four Constructive Use of Time Assets: Creative Activities, Child Programs, Religious Community, and Time at Home.

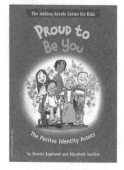

Proud to Be You
Kids build the four Positive Identity Assets: Personal Power, Self-Esteem, Sense of Purpose, and Positive View of Personal Future.

*To place an order or to request a free catalog of SELF-HELP FOR KIDS®
and SELF-HELP FOR TEENS® materials, please write, call, email, or visit our Web site:*

Free Spirit Publishing Inc.
217 Fifth Avenue North • Suite 200 • Minneapolis, MN 55401-1299
toll-free 800.735.7323 • local 612.338.2068 • fax 612.337.5050
help4kids@freespirit.com • www.freespirit.com